THE NEW JOB SECURITY

THE NEW JOB SECURITY

REVISED

THE 5 BEST STRATEGIES FOR TAKING CONTROL OF YOUR CAREER

PAM LASSITER

TEN SPEED PRESS
Berkeley

To Allison and Teel, my shooting stars, burning ever more brightly

To Bic, my strength, one day at a time

All rights reserved. Published in the United States by Ten Speed Press, an imprint of the Crown Publishing Group, a division of Random House, Inc., New York.
www.crownpublishing.com
www.tenspeed.com

Ten Speed Press and the Ten Speed Press colophon are registered trademarks of Random House, Inc.

Grateful acknowledgment is made to the following for permission to reprint previously published material:

Two cartoons, Rhymes with Orange (3/9/1999), © 1999 by Hilary B. Price, and Rhymes with Orange (10/24/2004), © 2004 by Hilary B. Price. King Features Syndicate. Reprinted by Permission.

Lyrics from "Facets of the Jewel" by Noel Paul Stookey, copyright © 1996 by Noel Paul Stookey. Published by Neworld Music Publishers. Performed at Northfield Mount Hermon School in September 2001. Reprinted by permission of the author.

Library of Congress Cataloging-in-Publication Data

Lassiter, Pam.
  The new job security : the 5 best strategies for taking control of your career / Pam Lassiter. —
1st rev. ed.
      p. cm.
  Rev. ed. of: The new job security : five strategies to take control of your career. c2002.
Includes index.
  1. Career development. 2. Success in business. 3. Job satisfaction. 4. Job security. I. Title.
HF5381.L342 2010
650.1—dc22
                        2010023444
ISBN: 978-1-58008-377-5

Printed in Canada

10 9 8 7 6 5 4 3 2 1

First Revised Edition

CONTENTS

ACKNOWLEDGMENTS

This edition of *The New Job Security* takes a different approach than the last. The former one established five core strategies that allow you to master your career for the long term (okay, you can say "forever" if it doesn't feel too long), whether you're employed or in transition. The strategies haven't changed since then (except for some fresher wording), but the tactics have, and stay in touch—they'll continue to change. I interviewed more than twenty experts for this edition, asking them, "How has career management changed in the past five years?" Boy, did they have ideas! You'll see them here, integrated into an overall plan of creating satisfying work. I interviewed people from many different groups that will affect your future: human resource professionals, executive search firms and recruiters, experts in social networking, executives at AARP (for retirement trends) and the American Library Association, directors of university career centers, networking mavens, and compensation and legal gurus. Thank you to Ann Anderson, Ellen Mahoney, Fred Foulkes, Deb Cohen, George Davis, Stuart Sadick, Bruce Walton, Susan Hand, Jeff Moore, Jennifer Scott, Robin Talbert, Cathy Ventura-Merkel, Deborah Russell, Kathleen Christensen, Jim Rettig, Kate Brooks, Stacey Rudnick, Chris Sullivan, Virginia Steinmetz, Lauryn Franzoni, Robyn Greenspan, Randy Stevens, Tom Wilson, Philip Gordon, and Jim Hartley. It is because of their openness and sharing that I've been able to create a template for the future for you. The ultimate thank-you, however, goes to you, the amazing professionals with whom I have worked that are moving up or moving on, who have allowed me to share your journeys and stories. Thank you for your trust.

My supporters for more than twenty years, Dave Opton and Warren Radtke, offer strength in both book writing and life. Dave, your wisdom and research appear throughout this book. Warren, you're always there to keep me grounded and laughing. Who would have guessed that Monty Python is in career counseling? Ken Hablow, you've produced wonderful graphics that magically appear with no notice from me and no moans from you. This book wouldn't have gotten off the ground without all three of you.

Ten Speed Press, you understate the number of gears that you have; you run on at least twenty. Aaron Wehner, publisher, and Julie Bennett, editorial director, you make biking uphill look easy. Not only have you managed an operation well during complex times, but you both recognize the core significance that satisfying work has in our lives. Bravo. Lisa Regul, managing editor at Ten Speed, you're absolutely The Best. Your macrovision, your objectivity, and your ability to put together puzzle pieces transcend anything that I could have done on my own. As the editor for this book, you created a smoother, better oiled machine. Well done. Odds are that without Kara Van de Water and Patricia Kelly, you, the reader, and I wouldn't be meeting right now. Thank you to all.

The final thank-you goes to the world's best supporting family, Allison, Teel, Jack and Susan, Nancy, and Bic, with hugs and love. Your stars are being hung in the sky right now.

INTRODUCTION
Career Whiplash

Any changes in your work life lately? You might be laughing right now, saying, "Where do I begin?" Whether you've been let go from your company, chosen to leave, are looking for something new, want to grow within your current company, or just want to hold onto what you have, the dynamics of the job economy have changed dramatically in recent years. Career whiplash is now a preexisting condition for most of us.

Despite this new job economy, with its sharp transitions, intense competition, and high churn rate, too many of us are using old career management skills. Regardless of your age, it's easy to have picked up old expectations, old habits, and old mind-sets. If people around us are looking for work, we assume that how they're approaching it is correct, right? Bad habits are contagious. Ask yourself:

- Do I look primarily for approved job openings, typically through the Internet?

- Do I keep my head down at work, doing my job without tracking marketplace trends and developing skills I'll need to be in demand in the future?

- Do I strategically stay in touch with those in my network and help them even when I don't need anything in return?

- Do I negotiate win-win situations to get the money and working conditions I want?

If you answered "yes" to the first two and "no" to the second two, you have old job skills with the attendant career risk. In the new job economy, learning the 5 best strategies will put you out in front, making sure you're in charge rather than unemployed or stagnating. Out in front is where you want to be.

This book is your guide to the new rules for career management. Using current research and information gathered from more than thirty years of experience as a national career management consultant, I have identified and integrated results-driven approaches for people who want to develop their own New Job Security. Contrary to popular opinion, there is job security out there; its location has just moved. The New Job Security is centered in *you*, not in a company. It's portable.

CREATING YOUR NECK BRACE FOR CAREER WHIPLASH

It's a good thing that job security is portable, because we're moving a lot! The statistics in ExecuNet's *Executive Job Market Intelligence Report* (2009) bring home our dramatic lack of stability. Executives expect to hold a job for 5.6 years and end up doing so for only 2.3 years. We think that we'll work for the same company for 6.6 years, but we remain employed by that company for 2.8 years. What we plan for and what happens are two different things. The call for our own independent plan for job (or career) security is clear. Is the idea that you're in charge new? No. What's new are the ways that people find jobs, whether they are looking for a new position within the same company or trying to break into a company from the outside. What's new is the economy, in which you're a hot commodity one year and yesterday's newspaper the next. What's new are the demographics: boomers are finding themselves searching for jobs at middle age, and Gen Xers are discovering that the start-ups have stopped. What's new is the idea that not only are you responsible for your own career, but that you actually have a significant degree of control over it. You have the ability to make your own career neck brace that will allow you to observe the rapid changes in the job market but not be subject to their collateral damage.

The experience of working with professionals like you—incredibly accomplished people who take the risk of trying new career management strategies to accomplish their professional goals and succeeding—is what drove me to write this book. Unfortunately, nobody teaches us career management strategies before we join the workforce and realize we need them to develop our careers. Even if you were lucky enough to pick up some basic strategies in college, those strategies have changed. Mailing your résumé directly to companies you'd like to work for and responding to published job openings, which used to be considered best practices, now often result in low yields and a high level of frustration. The good news is that you can change as well, and *The New Job Security* will give you the tools you need to manage your career effectively, not just for a single job hunt, but for your lifetime.

Learning to predict and direct most of the forces that affect your work requires taking a step back to see the big picture. First, see if you recognize yourself in the following scenarios. They represent forces that affect all of us. Then we'll get into exactly what the New Job Security is, and how you can get it . . . quickly.

"What do you mean, a pink slip? Termination? Me? There's been a mistake." Gordon had been working for his employer for more than twenty years, had been promoted regularly, had received good performance evaluations, and was doing the organic chemistry work that he loved. This pink slip, which wasn't even pink, had to be an error.

Sure, he'd seen his shares of stock in his publicly held company erode in value as earnings had slipped, but his chemical research was at the heart of the company's products. They couldn't keep the money coming in without the core products that Gordon's research helped produce. The idea of his job being vulnerable to some of the changes he'd seen in other parts of the company was so foreign to him that he had ignored the tremors going through his own division.

"Why me? This doesn't make sense!" But to his company, cutting Gordon made perfect sense.

Professionally, Gordon was in a holding pattern. He'd done most of his intellectual development in college, more than twenty-five years ago. He'd gone to work for his current employer shortly after finishing his bachelor's degree in biology. He'd taken some workshops that his employer had offered, but not many, and only those on topics he believed would directly benefit his current work.

Staying in touch with professional trends outside the company had been difficult for Gordon. He occasionally read articles in professional journals, and he had taken some graduate courses in chemistry twenty years ago. He found professional association meetings painful, so he avoided them. "Too many people are standing around, and there is too much chitchat," he said.

Socially, Gordon was a private person. He did his job and kept in touch with a small group of friends. At work, he wasn't terribly interested in life in the other divisions, corporate politics, or company finances. He was only interested in his research, saying, "I thought if I just kept my head down and did my work I'd be safe." That approach proved to be fatal.

If Gordon had taken the time to look up from his work, he would have seen two warning flags waving wildly in front of him:

- Most of the people who worked with Gordon had advanced degrees, a master's or doctorate, while he had only a bachelor's.

- His colleagues had degrees in chemistry, the department's main focus; Gordon's degree was in the less directly related field of biology.

Gordon had assumed that his increasing experience would offset his professional weaknesses, but his colleagues were becoming increasingly experienced at the same time, so when his company hit an economic speed bump, he was vulnerable.

Could Gordon have changed his direction?

Barbara was brilliant but had sharp edges. She worked for an organization that wasn't planning to let her go because she could deliver hard messages that other people couldn't about performance, compensation, and terminations; they also valued the diversity that she brought to her division and her twenty years of experience. Barbara, however, wasn't convinced of her permanence when she called me in for coaching. She was shocked and angry that she had received a negative 360-degree evaluation and word-of-mouth feedback. The consensus was that she wasn't a good team player and she wasn't acting as professionally as she should for her level in the organization. Her lack of political savviness was proving to be her undoing, and her reputation was on the slide.

Head of human resources for a large division of her company, Barbara was used to reacting quickly. Fires on her desk were self-igniting; she could stamp out one and more would appear. Attending meetings with groups outside her division was required but not welcomed. More fires would ignite in the meantime. What Barbara couldn't see was that:

- She was keeping her head down dealing with problems as they came up rather than prioritizing her time.

- She wasn't delegating some of the more routine jobs to her staff as her work grew, and therefore she was not setting aside time to do the planning and strategy that was critical at her senior level.

- Her staff wasn't helping her reputation. Between irritating people outside the division and not following through on certain tasks, several staff members were affecting Barbara's reputation without her knowledge.
- She wasn't widely known in her company and had no profile at all in her profession outside her company.

Barbara had become so comfortable in her job and organization that she had stopped thinking about staying awake to the outside world, continually developing her skills, or being conscious of how she was building support within her division and organization.

Could Barbara change her patterns?

Michael is twenty-six years old and, by all measures, he should be a hot commodity in the job market. After finishing his undergraduate degree in finance at a major university, he headed for an investment banking firm to get some firsthand experience. He followed through on his master plan to get three years of work experience before enrolling at a well-known business school for a master's in business administration (MBA) degree that would make him eligible for some of the most prestigious and well-paying jobs available.

As the source of our economic wealth continues to shift from manufacturing to information and services, the "knowledge worker" continues to rule. Graduates of well-regarded MBA programs comprise a pool of knowledge workers that the world's best companies target for bright, motivated hires. Michael put himself on the path that leads to these high-level jobs by enrolling in a world-class MBA program. When he started classes, however, he discovered that he had become a little fish in a big pond. He's now in classes with people who are as smart as or smarter than he is. His first job successes have paled as the bar has moved higher. Having completed the first year of his program, he's now competing for coveted summer internships at companies that could catapult him to long-term career success.

I met Michael in a networking seminar I presented to MBA students. He was clear about his own goals. "I want to be a consultant with a professional services consulting firm. I want to design strategy for Fortune 500 companies, become a partner, and reap the rewards." What *he* wanted, he could articulate, but when I asked him, "Why should a company hire *you?*" there were five seconds of dead air. That's a long time for an aspiring consultant. He hadn't thought about *the company's* needs. Most of his fellow students are targeting the same consulting firms, investment banks, well-funded start-ups, and a select group of other companies.

How is Michael going to get their attention and differentiate himself from the rest of the pack?

As you can see, controlling your career isn't about age, experience, when and where you got your degree, or what your plans are for the future. It's about attitude. It's an orientation to the outside world. It's learnable.

 To evaluate your level of risk in your career stability, go to www.thenewjobsecurity.com and complete "Work Risk/Old Dog Analysis."

WHAT IS THE NEW JOB SECURITY?

The New Job Security is a work agreement that you make with yourself. You consciously decide to take the initiative in your work life, to set your own course for your current employment and future alternatives. No, this doesn't mean that you're going to tell your boss what to do and tell everybody else to get out of the way. It does mean that you will have your own professional goals and fallback plan. You decide how you're going to play to win, and you tweak your strategy according to the cards you are dealt. As you transfer the control of job security to yourself, you'll develop an overall strategy to help you get what you want from your work. You'll learn how to develop a demand for your services, either at your current company or a new one, so you will always have choices. You'll identify goals and the skills that you'll need to reach them. You'll develop backup plans to help you conquer the challenges that will inevitably appear. Anticipating change and being ahead of the game, positioned where you want to be before shifts in the economy or company occur, will keep you vital. Watch out world: you're taking control and you're going to make a difference.

Once you've created your New Job Security, you can:

- Move successfully within a company
- Move externally, with little trauma, to interesting alternative jobs
- Create multiple income streams, if you choose

- Shape your job so that it reflects your values and goals as well as your expertise
- Plan for your career transitions (including your eventual retirement) so they're under your control rather than someone else's

To achieve the New Job Security, you just need to become comfortable with the 5 best strategies that I teach in my practice, which thousands of people are now using successfully. Without these skills you are at a significant disadvantage, both while you're employed and while you're in transition. *With* them, it's like being the only person to have discovered SAT prep courses when the exam is coming up. Who's going to do better?

THE 5 BEST STRATEGIES

The order in which I've presented the 5 best strategies is not random. I begin by laying a strong internal foundation, move into more external concerns, and end with steps for negotiating the conditions of your new (or revised) job. If you jump straight to the money (Strategy #5: Negotiate in Round Rooms), you won't typically have the base built yet that allows other to say "yes," so take your time and work your way through them. Once you master these five strategies, you'll continue to use them throughout your career to achieve the type of work life you want. (They'll even work with your kids or partner, but I'm not going there in this book.)

Send Clear Signals

Sending the right message determines your results. Of course, you need a plan before you know what your message is, right? If you're reading this book, you're going to have both. You will no longer say, "There are no job openings," "I don't have the right qualifications," "I'm too old or young," or "I can't move up in my company," because you'll be sending out the more positive signal that you're a catch. You have a lot more options than you realize.

Market for Mutual Benefit

If you lead with the business needs of your "target markets" rather than your own needs (focusing, for example, on ways to increase their profitability rather than your interest in a promotion or employment), you will get their attention and differentiate yourself from the crowd. Using their vocabulary shows that you already understand their business at their level.

Stop Looking for Jobs

The number of approved job openings is finite. The number of problems to be solved is infinite. Which category would you rather go after?

Build Sustainable Networks

Developing networks wisely has taken some hits and changed a lot in recent years. Social networking sites have added to the noise and the pressure to nurture everyone in your network simultaneously. The goal is to feed and sustain a network that you select from the noise so that the members of your network are motivated to help you over the long term.

Negotiate in Round Rooms

Negotiating strategies are simple and often require only that you use the right vocabulary at the right time. You can put them to work quickly, and you can use them for more powerful results for the long term. These alone will pay not only for this book, but for some nice vacations as well.

What's the bottom line? The New Job Security comes from *you*. It is within your control, not your company's. Does all this sound like a tall order? Actually, it isn't. All 5 of the new strategies, which are illustrated in Jim's story below, are learnable. And if you practice them until they come naturally, you'll be prepared for change. You may even create it.

Jim leveled out the career roller coaster with impressive speed and skill. In his early fifties he left his position as a senior administrator at one of the world's most prestigious hospital systems because his division had been restructured and it became clear that his work style wasn't going to fit in with his new boss's. He had always done a little consulting on the side to improve operational efficiencies for healthcare product manufacturers, so now was his chance to develop that business. He knew how to do it, so he did. Promoting a consulting business over several years came easily, but it didn't bring the job satisfaction that Jim desired. He wanted to be part of a team, and he wanted a more predictable income, even though his current one had increased substantially.

Getting into a larger, for-profit company when you're an independent practitioner with not-for-profit experience is a major challenge. He started out by doing a direct mail campaign, sending unsolicited letters to potential employers, and he got no results. Old dog tactics. Jim began to feel discouraged and trapped in the job he had created but didn't want any longer. As he started learning and practicing new career management skills that oriented him toward marketplace needs, his results changed. He targeted where he wanted to be and what he needed to do to get there. He repackaged himself in both his verbal and written communications. He networked deliberately, not randomly. Within months, he had accomplished his goal: a job in the for-profit world, developing business in the new healthcare practice of one of the world's fastest-growing information storage companies.

The story doesn't end there, however. Within fourteen months, Jim was laid off. When a company's cycles clash with an economy's cycles, something is bound to give, and the most recent hires are usually the first to go. But Jim's attitude was entirely different this time around. When he was given his termination notice, Jim had the presence of mind to be complimentary about his experience with the company that laid him off. He told the senior-level executive who eliminated his job, "On a scale of one to ten, this job was a twelve. Thank you for the opportunity to have been part of this team. I really enjoyed it." The executive immediately started scrambling to find a way to save Jim from the list of those cut. Jim didn't want to be saved if the rest of his department was gone, but he left with great references.

The layoff didn't catch him off guard. Jim was tracking business, industry, and company trends long before the announcement was made. He had interviews lined up. He was much more competitive than before he took the job because he had created a strong network; developed new, highly marketable skills; and could clearly articulate how he would be an important part of his next employer's success. Jim wasn't going around to companies asking them what jobs they had open. He had a specific plan about how he wanted to combine his skills with targeted companies' market opportunities and how he wanted to set them up to capitalize on emerging business. Companies were drooling over his ideas. By the way, the company that laid him off offered him a different job one month later. He was now in a position to negotiate his conditions. What would you do?

Let's take a look at the 5 strategies that Jim used. His positive, externally oriented mind-set (Strategy #1: Send Clear Signals) kept him in touch with his markets both inside and outside his company, even when he didn't need them. The ideas that he presented to companies as he was developing new relationships were based entirely on identifying and meeting *their* needs, not his (Strategy #2: Market for Mutual Benefit). Not waiting until there were official job openings but finding ways for companies to be more successful meant that people were eager to hear his ideas and create work for him (Strategy #3: Stop Looking for Jobs). He already knew the people and the companies that he wanted to approach before the cutbacks came at his company (Strategy #4: Build Sustainable Networks). He did not discuss compensation until a job offer was imminent, when he would have maximum leverage to negotiate for his personal and financial goals (Strategy #5: Negotiate in Round Rooms). Practicing these 5 strategies made Jim highly desirable. You can be, too.

When he learned new career management strategies, Jim's results changed. Using his five new strategies he stopped projecting anxiety about work, he started planning and networking strategically, he identified work he loved doing and who was having problems getting that type of work done, and he discontinued his old pattern of sending out direct mail. As his information base and confidence grew, people sought him out. And he made sure that the skills he needed within his profession remained sharp. Whether it was new product knowledge or relationships with potential clients, Jim stayed in front of where he saw the growth coming. By the way, since the last edition of this book, companies are now chasing Jim. He's a hot commodity. It worked.

What does the future hold for your career? People are looking for their next jobs and planning their careers in a whole new way. The five new strategies in this book are more subtle and persuasive than any interviewing tips or how-to-write-your-résumé ideas that you learned years ago, if you were fortunate enough to get any career training at all. The five new strategies go far beyond the concepts taught in outplacement seminars, alumni groups, and self-study programs. They will teach you how to develop yourself not only when you need a job, but also while you're on the job and into an active retirement. Career management is no longer just a between-jobs task. It's something you'll want to adopt for the long term, and it is within your control. Welcome to the New Job Security.

SEND CLEAR SIGNALS

"Ninety percent of the game is half mental."
—YOGI BERRA

"I've never had to look for a job before. They've always come to me. My company has always offered me something or recruiters have called. This is not what I had in mind at midcareer." This is the lament of the professional. I hear it frequently, and you may have experienced similar emotions yourself. The lament expresses a loss of dignity and a loss of control, but that's about to change.

PINBALL VERSUS PLANNED CAREERS

In order to develop your own portable job security, you'll create a master plan during the course of this book that you can use as your career GPS. In this chapter we're going to capture your goals, values, and experience into a working plan, and then shape how to articulate it to the outside world so you can successfully execute your plan. By the end of the book you'll have built the framework that will allow you take control of your career for the long term. Good news: it's doable!

Before you start contacting people you know for career conversations, let's talk. Getting the right message out to the right people is going to make a big difference in your results. To get the working plan behind generating clear signals, we'll need to be on the same page in defining how a job is different from "work" or "a career" so you can distinguish between them. As Richard N. Bolles said in his seminal book *What Color Is Your Parachute?* (Ten Speed Press, current edition),

"A career is technically your total life in the world of work. . . . A job is a particular kind of work in a particular field or occupation, where you set your hand to particular tasks using particular skills."

In other words, a job has well-defined parameters, and typically a job description. When you started reading this book you were probably focusing on your next job. That's important, and it needs to be done. The best jobs, however, come when you're not thinking about them one at a time, not grabbing at a job just to have one, but thinking about future jobs in a sequence. "How does this job set me up for where I want to go?" is a question that you'll want to be able to answer.

HOMEWORK

Looking Two Jobs Ahead to Plan Today

Think about a couple of jobs that you would consider having *two* jobs from now. They could be logical extensions of your current work or fantasy jobs that you've been contemplating. Sources of inspiration can be your current organizational chart, interesting-sounding jobs that friends have, titles in higher-level job listings, or titles that you run across in business publications you're reading.

- List at least three jobs that sound interesting two jobs from now.

  _____

  _____

  _____

- What characteristics do these jobs have that make them sound interesting?

  _____

  _____

  _____

- What kinds of skills does this work require? (If they aren't listed in a help wanted ad, ask people who might know.)

  _____

  _____

  _____

- What could I be doing in my current (or next) job that would serve as a springboard for the job after that?

  _____

  _____

  _____

You'll want your next job to help build the management and technical skills, the connections, and the industry knowledge that will set you up for your subsequent job. Use the requirements of your second job from now (even if it's what you want to do in retirement!) as a test for whether you need to begin shifting some of the content of your current one or, if you're in transition, whether the job you're considering fits with your future plans.

Thinking about your future—about where you want to be heading, even if it's just two jobs away in the same company—starts putting you in control. If you're employed, your boss may tell you what the company has in mind for you. They may want you to replace someone, to move to a different location, or to expand or consolidate your division. In some ways, isn't it a relief that someone else is doing the hard work of deciding the best place to apply your skills? But stop and think before you answer your boss. Is that new position heading you in the direction you have in mind for your future?

If you're in job transition, a job might fall into your lap early in your campaign. Uncle Frank is happy to put your inventory management skills to work in his warehouse, even though his wire and cable aren't your first-choice products. The good news is that the job is available now, it pays you a decent wage, and it ends the job campaign. But stop and think before you answer your uncle. Is the job heading you in the right direction?

The problem with both of these situations is that they're examples of "pinballing." They lack a plan and are reactive. Whole working lives can be based upon a series of reactive decisions, thus becoming pinball careers that are determined by what they bounce off of. A career might bounce off a boss who wants you to do something for the company, a convenient job offer, the relative who wants to help, or the recruiter who calls. They're not bad options; they're just accidental. Saying "yes" without comparing the opportunities to your goals can lead to a random series of jobs that doesn't build a set of compelling skills. A random series of jobs with a random series of skills doesn't build up the reputation that you'll need to take control of your career.

Taking control of choices about where you work and what you do will come more easily as word gets out that you're a star. A pinball career doesn't give you the time necessary to build industry knowledge and professional relationships. If you jump around from industry to industry and from function to function, you will spend more energy on learning curves than on mastery. This doesn't mean not to jump if you aren't happy, but it does mean that you should do research up front so you can limit the number of major changes to your career. If you can, stick to one main direction for a good stretch of time. A straight path allows you to get some traction in your area of expertise and industry; you'll light up your professional scoreboard and the recruiters' iPhones. You're a pinball wizard.

> If you jump around from industry to industry and from function to function, you will spend more energy on learning curves than on mastery.

YOUR FIRST SIGNALS

Underneath the shock, anger, and resentment (if you've been terminated by a company), or the apprehension, frustration, and feeling that you're trapped (if you're currently employed), comes an element of fear. "What if the right company doesn't come along? How will I handle rejection? How will I maintain my lifestyle and my plans for my family? Will I be able to land something that is at least as good as my old job?" Or, "What if I want to apply for a job outside my division and my boss decides that I'm being disloyal? Will people become suspicious if I start trying to build relationships in another department? What if I apply for a position and don't get it?"

The pain is real, the fear is real, and the stress of transition is real. I often recommend Elisabeth Kübler-Ross's book *On Death and Dying* (Simon & Schuster, 1997) as reading for executives going through difficult career transitions. Dr. Kübler-Ross outlines seven stages that we go through when facing death or loss. People ending a job, especially if they've been with the company for a long time, experience a similar series of emotions. You can't force yourself through the stages, nor can you will yourself into the final stage of resolution until your mind is ready. However, I'm going to ask you to put most of your painful feelings in a box that you access only when you're at a safe time and in a safe place with a small group of trusted people. Although addressing these feelings is critical to healing, sharing the pain with a broad group of people can actually stretch out a process that you'd like to end quickly. You want to generate positive action and referrals in your network, not an "ain't life miserable?" type of sympathy. The signals you send out make a difference from the beginning.

Sending clear signals, the first strategy, means disseminating to your world the information that will motivate others to act on your behalf and, as you'll see in the next strategy, learning how you can help them in return. If you've been laid off but can demonstrate to your professional community that you haven't been leveled by your former company's decision, that you can even understand why they needed to make some tough calls, and that you now have a chance to focus on new, interesting work, how do you think you'll come across? *Strength attracts strength.* Let that sink in. To attract the right opportunities, you'll want to come across as the winner that you are. You'll send clear signals of strength by seeing both sides of the story and moving on to the future. You'll be easier to talk to if you keep your emotions on the positive side, and you want to be easy to talk to right now.

The more you appear forward-thinking and the less you air your dirty laundry, the more you can engage your colleagues and friends in discussions about where the growth is in your industry and the economy and the faster you will move into your future job. When you are in that new job and engaged in interesting and challenging work, your pain will truly disappear. "My old company actually did me a favor by terminating me" is a reaction that I frequently hear a year after the event. It's amazing what time, sending clear signals, and an action plan can do.

If you see yourself in the executive's lament at the beginning of this chapter and you feel inexperienced when it comes to job hunting, try looking at things from a different perspective. This is your opportunity to plan what you want to do for work rather than simply react to what the marketplace throws in your lap. Congratulations. If you're midcareer and this is the first time that you've looked for a job, you're going to learn a process that will serve you well for the rest of your life. You're going to be in control, maybe for the first time. What may have been a pinball career up until now—beginning with an offer from a recruiter in your senior year at college, then bouncing off various unplanned events—is about to become a planned career that meets your own as well as a company's needs.

Jeffrey Katzenberg, CEO of DreamWorks Animation (think *Shrek, Kung Fu Panda,* etc.), recently said, "One of the most difficult and painful and ultimately most valuable lessons came from being fired [as studio chairman of The Walt Disney Company]. It really just opened all kinds of doors for me that I never really would have pursued. DreamWorks Animation . . . would not exist were it not for getting fired from Disney. I was kicked out the door, and everything . . . that was bad at the time was ultimately invaluable. That's what fueled me to get on and understand that, if anything, I had been held back" (*New York Times*, November 8, 2009). You don't have to go through trauma like Katzenberg's to realize that you have control over how you react to events and that things will be better on the other side.

CLEAR SIGNALS FOR
TWO TOUGH QUESTIONS

Start sending clear signals by giving yourself a way to answer hard questions that others will inevitably ask when you're least prepared for it. The first question that will pop out of their mouths, usually right after you've left a company, is *"What happened?"* This is your most vulnerable time, because you might be in pain if you've been terminated or you're feeling somewhat at loose ends if you have chosen to leave. People will hit you with "Why are you leaving?" and then *"What do you want to do?"* right away because they want to be helpful as soon as they hear your news. You run the risk of losing their attention and referrals if you're not prepared to answer, but who's thinking rationally at a time like this? After completing the assignment below, you will be.

Work through this exercise now if you're anticipating leaving your job for any reason. Even if you're currently employed and talking to people outside of work to gather information, they'll inevitably ask, "Why do you want to leave?" Having an answer will give you more control during times of change so you don't miss the support or ideas of a single person who is interested in helping. Try drafting several versions of your answers until you arrive at something that is both honest and positive.

HOMEWORK

What Happened? Why Are You Leaving?

 A blank, printable form for this exercise can be found at www.thenewjobsecurity.com.

The questions "What happened?" and "Why are you leaving?" are perennial favorites. Turning these questions to your advantage and directing the conversation toward the future are your two objectives. You may have one shot at some people who are asking, so work out the kinks to your answers so you can give clear signals from the start.

1. Answer the question "Why are you leaving?" in the most positive way possible, without airing any dirty laundry. Use no more than two or three sentences, covering just the high points and, ideally, the company's point of view as well. "Well, it's bad news and it's good news. The company made a decision to consolidate two departments into one for cost savings. That's the bad news, but they did what they needed to do. The good news, however, is . . . "

2. Describe the opportunity. Explain why the parting will actually be an opportunity for you. Reflect a positive attitude. You're in control, sig-naling strength. "This will actually be an opportunity for me because it will allow me to concentrate on . . ."

3. Envision the future. How will the company that you're considering benefit from your transition and from your unique set of skills? "As a result, I am looking for a company that . . ."

4. Ask a *business* question. It gets the other person talking and moves the conversation toward future possibilities. You are *not* asking, "Where are there job openings?" or any question using the word "opportunities" (the code word for "jobs"), because they probably won't know. You *are* asking a business question they'll have an opinion about, such as, "What companies should be thinking about cleaning up their emissions before anything is mandated by the government?" You can take it from there.

If you're talking to a company representative, change the question to ask about the organization itself, such as, "Am I correct in assuming that you . . . (have plans to introduce Product X, want to convert to a new type of system, or so on)?"

If you're talking to a friend or colleague, you can use the business question by itself. "Are you aware of any companies that want to . . . (grow their inter-national sales, turn around their operations, or so on)?" I call it the "cocktail party" question because you can use it with anyone, anywhere. Try a couple of different questions to see which ones get you the best information.

See what you just did? You just did what every good politician does intui-tively . . . changed the topic. You're now talking about the future and business needs rather than your past—a much more useful place to be. People don't want to hear all the details about why you're leaving a company. Don't waste valuable time with good lead sources by focusing too long on history. You now have a structure for coming across strongly, positively, and quickly to someone who is expressing concern. Practice saying your spiel before you hit prime time. You're already gaining control over your presentation and sending out clearer signals to others.

KNOW YOUR VALUE

Let's define "value." I'm using the word in two senses. The first sense is an intrinsic one: you value yourself as a competent, intelligent human being, independent of any associations with your work or your employer. It may seem obvious to be telling you, a professional, that you're of value. You wouldn't be where you are today if you weren't. I'm continually saddened, however, to see the number of highly competent people who start doubting themselves personally when their affiliation with a company has ended. "I've not only lost my job, I've lost my identity," one senior-level professional confided in tears, describing why he was having trouble projecting a positive image when meeting people. He had lost touch with why he was, and is, of value. Tapping into your sense of self-worth will make a dramatic difference in your success in the marketplace. If you're not projecting confidence now, fake it for a while. Send signals that suggest you feel stronger than you actually do. It's amazing how faking success, knowing that you're going through a temporary blip, can actually reestablish your personal sense of value.

The second sense of your value is your uniqueness and worth in the job market. This will show on your résumé, and you need to continue to develop your value if you want to stay competitive. It doesn't matter whether you are currently employed or in transition. Having hot skills is what it's all about. The great people at a major high-tech manufacturing company that I outplaced, whom I trained to set up and run their job campaigns, didn't have a clue that their skills were obsolete until they were laid off. With an average tenure of twenty years, they were still drafting mechanical prototypes on drafting tables with pencil and paper. They were not computer-proficient, and they weren't aware that AutoCAD had taken over their industry. They had stopped learning and had lost touch with the outside world. They were becoming obsolete and increasingly unemployable, but they didn't recognize it.

Here are the warning signs of obsolescence. Do you see any of these things happening in your career?

- **Not Knowing Your Strengths**
  Why does (or did) a company value you? Why should the marketplace value you? How have you grown recently? Can you communicate

your value clearly? This does not mean bragging, by the way. It means getting results. (You'll be thinking through your own values in the following homework.) When I ask highly talented professionals to identify their strengths, they often struggle to list only four or five points. They've lost touch with their unique personal value. If you can't identify your strengths, how can you communicate them to others? Expanding your awareness of your skills not only makes you feel good, but it's also a basic part of product knowledge. Having the right vocabulary to express your talents to your audience will increase their "consumption" of you as a desirable commodity. Send clear signals.

- **Complacency**
  Losing touch with your sense of value starts with feeling complacent in your current job. You've mastered it and people trust you, so you keep doing what you've learned to do over the years. You never think "Will I still have this job next year?" or "What can I do to improve?" because you are comfortable. Habit and repetition become the norm rather than pushing the envelope. You stop learning new skills to do your job better, like you did when you were first hired, and instead you just do the same things you did last year. You're in a long-term relationship, and you start taking it for granted.

- **Isolation from Outside Networks**
  As you become engrossed in a new job and build professional and personal relationships with your colleagues, your relationships with people outside your job may diminish. You may not notice this isolation because you're still socially active, but you're still increasing your risk. This is the onset of the inverse security monster. The more you feel secure because you have been at a company a long time, and the more you neglect your connections with the outside world, the less secure you actually are. You might not be looking for a job, but the monster preys on those who become complacent. You're cutting off your access to other companies, to external information, and to your competitive edge.

  > The more you feel secure because you have been at a company for a long time, and the more you neglect your connections with the outside world, the less secure you actually are.

- **Losing Confidence**
  Even though you may read the three warning signs above and decide, "No problem, I have those under control," the confidence that you

project will determine your ability to send clear signals in the above areas. A lack of confidence may seep through in your tone and your choice of words, such as, "Thank you *so* much for taking my call. I know how busy you are, and I'm grateful for your time." Hey, you're busy, too! They're lucky to hear from you! A lack of confidence could also be communicated through your body language. For example, your shoulders might not be square, your handshake could be less firm than usual, and you may talk about yourself a lot instead of drawing out your audience. If you've stopped exercising and getting good haircuts, these ragged edges can send the wrong signal about your confidence level. Remember, *strength attracts strength*.

Knowing and Presenting Your Value

If you're dubious about either your personal or professional value at this point, or what you have to offer, how are you going to come across to potential employers or to your boss during performance appraisals? Do your homework. Practice on some lower-level luminaries. Wait to approach your first-choice employers until you are ready to make a good first impression. "Playing it off-Broadway," so to speak, rehearsing your Elevator Story and job creation ideas, will lead to sell-out audiences when you're ready to hit the big time.

The president of a company received a telephone call from someone who had spent a long time networking to get access to him. "This guy found four handshakes that eventually led him to me. He worked hard setting up relationships with people who would tell me to take his call."

"When it was time for the telephone appointment, he started the conversation by giving me a five-minute overview of his career, then saying, 'John [a mutual friend] promised that you'd be a good guy to talk to, that you were bound to have some ideas for a guy like me.' Then there was dead silence while he waited for me to come up with ideas for him. I had been prepared to help him with some referrals, but when I heard his total lack of focus and confidence, I lost interest. He wanted me to figure out his life for him. I don't know what a 'guy like me' is, and I'm not sure he did either. I wouldn't bother my friends by referring him unless I thought he was bringing them something of value."

The moral of this story is never say "like me"! This all-too-common error combines the sin of not knowing or being able to express your personal and professional value with the sin of asking the listener to do all the work for you. You end up irritating the listener and blowing a good lead. Lack of clarity about his own value and expectations from the phone call caused this professional to lose an interesting connection. How much better it would have been if the job seeker had asked the president about trends in the industry, how he would respond to certain challenges in his field, what the most important skills would be for someone in financial management, or to identify the two greatest challenges in his company (see more about this in Strategy #2: Market for Mutual Benefit). *Anything* would have been better than asking for "ideas for a guy like me."

The homework below will help you identify your strengths and value, then will clarify your focus and direction. You will be able to present yourself well, and "like me" will be history.

HOMEWORK

Know and Communicate Your Value

Here are three ways to start capturing your value, strengths, and skills. Start with your professional attributes, and then add the personal ones. Go for volume first, and refine the list later. Your goal for this exercise is to develop a clear list of your top five to seven strengths, a concise way to communicate them, and an alternate way of describing them for those listeners who may need to hear things from a different angle to understand your message.

1. **Inventory Your Skills**
   Jot down your skills, strengths, and assets. You won't think of all of them at once, so keep adding to the list. Synonyms count. Give yourself a reward if you list more than twenty skills.

   Examples of skills might include having in-depth expertise in your discipline, building strong teams, meeting deadlines consistently, and developing products that sell well.

2. **Ask Friends**
   Isn't it ironic that our friends and colleagues typically know more about our strengths (and weaknesses) than we do? Ask people who will be honest with you about their perceptions of your main talents. Tell them ahead of time that you're doing some "product research" and will be happy to return the favor; they may come up with more thoughtful responses. They may introduce ideas that you never would have thought of on your own.

3. Create a PAR Story

The Problem–Action–Result (PAR) format has been around for years, and it still works. A PAR story succinctly describes an accomplishment that you're proud of. It's a way to discuss your accomplishments without bragging because you're just telling a story. PAR stories are also very flexible; one story can describe multiple skills. Here's how you can put together your own PAR story.

- Describe a Problem. ("Sales were going downhill and we couldn't get our new products out of R&D . . .")

- Describe specific Actions you took to resolve the problem. Speak in bullet points, very simply and clearly. Use "I" rather than "we." ("The first thing I did was to call the team together . . .")

- Describe the Results of your actions. Quantify them whenever possible. ("As a result of the new systems and revised products that I introduced, within two quarters we were able to increase . . .")

- What additional strengths, skills, and assets does this story demonstrate?

 Once you've written one PAR story, write four more stories about four of your skills that will interest employers using the PAR form found on www.thenewjobsecurity.com. If you select strengths that the marketplace values, you'll be well prepared for the main content of any interview or performance appraisal.

You have strengths. You're a valuable commodity. Write out your stories so you can see your accomplishments and then refine those stories and practice telling them. Build up the answers to the last question about the additional strengths that your skills demonstrate and you'll be prepared to adapt your stories to different listeners with different needs. Your stories are multifaceted diamonds. Turn the diamond around and show the listener the appropriate facets. One employer might want to hear about your leadership skills. Great. Tell them a story. Another employer may be interested in your technical expertise. Fine. Tell them the same story with a different statement of the problem and relevant action steps. The results—how your company came out ahead—might actually be the same. You don't need a hundred stories to prepare for job interviews. You need five that you're comfortable telling, along with the additional strengths these stories demonstrate. You're being honest, you're being brief (two minutes, max), and you're being interesting and entertaining because you're just swapping stories.

REINVESTING IN YOURSELF: YOUR CLEAR SIGNALS FOR THE FUTURE

Okay, so you're sending (tasteful) signals that you're accomplished, and you're on top of the hot skills of the moment, but how are you going to maintain that reputation into the future? "Continual improvement," as the manufacturing mantra goes, will work for you as well. We don't have the luxury of assuming that what we know and do today will be of value tomorrow. "How do I have a clue what my skills should be tomorrow?" you ask. Good question. As you'll see when we talk about résumé development, you have market research right in front of you in the form of help wanted ads, job descriptions, and business trends. Get the skills that your markets ask for in them and stay current. Anticipating skills that companies *will* need and getting them early earns you bonus points. Skills, by definition, are all learnable. Given the right information, the right approaches, and the right vocabulary, you can network effectively, develop hot skills that you enjoy using, know how you're profitable, and understand what your options are at any given moment.

Learning which skills are essential for your success and then acquiring them shouldn't be put off until you're unemployed. It is much easier to learn new skills when you work for a company that supports your ongoing development because it is in their best interest to have competitive employees. Companies can supply you with new equipment, colleagues who can answer questions, tuition remission, opportunities to attend conferences on new approaches, and the ability to test them out and demonstrate results in a lower-stakes environment than a new company's. Gordon could have made himself an attractive job candidate—and possibly avoided the "hit list" to start off with—if he had developed his skills with his current employer.

Regardless of whether you are in transition or currently employed, your concern might be the same: "Where will I find the time to develop new skills? I'm barely keeping my head above water as it is." In Stephen Covey's book *The 7 Habits of Highly Effective People* (Simon & Schuster, 1990), he tells a story about an exhausted woodsman who had been sawing down a tree for five hours. When asked why he didn't stop to sharpen the saw so the process would go much faster, the woodsman replied that he didn't have time. Developing your skills on a continual basis is like sharpening your saw. If you're not expanding your professional repertoire, you're at risk of becoming obsolete. According to Covey, "This is the single most powerful investment we can ever make in life—investment in ourselves, in the only instrument we have with which to deal with life and contribute." You won't be developing skills randomly, however. You first have to identify which skills will be important in your field and that are interesting to you, and then go out and get them. If an employer doesn't provide the time or funding for your education, invest in yourself. You're worth it.

"But my company doesn't pay the tuition for the skill upgrade I'm going to need." Or, "I'm out of work so I can't go to the professional association meeting." Sorry. No whining; get creative. Prioritize what is most important to keep competitive and go after it. Period. If you need a course on C++ and it's important for your future plans, you'll find a way. If you can't afford to pay tuition and your company won't cover it, apply for a scholarship, take the course over the Internet, or trade skills with a friend who uses it in her work. If you're self-conscious about attending a professional meeting because you aren't affiliated with a company, see if you can trade registration fees for working for the group running the conference; this will give you an identity and get you inside. If you're creative and work the bottom side of the circle (see The Marketing Circle: What Goes Around, Comes Around, page 55) trading needs with those of other people, miracles happen.

"I'M THE BOSS. ADIOS, MUSHINESS!"

Maybe you've already accepted, or perhaps even welcomed, the fact that you're the boss of your own career. Being responsible for setting, maintaining, and adapting your overall career direction, though, can feel pretty daunting. You can achieve this, however, if you can do two things: describe what type of work you want to do (function) and where you want to do it (industry). These two pillars are the essential infrastructure for your career direction.

Being Mushy Backfires

Do you agree with the old adage "You can't be all things to all people"? If so, look at your résumé and listen to how you describe what type of work you'd like to be doing. Are you keeping yourself open to any possibility? "I want to run an operation and use my management and team leadership skills."

Did you just distinguish yourself from the pack? I see many professionals who are too broad in their approach to the market in an effort not to lose any potential jobs. They fear that if they commit to a specific type of work or to working within a specific industry, they'll be pigeonholed. If you're too specific about your desires, you'll miss out on other jobs that a company has open that might be a fit. Right? Wrong. The paradox is that *the more you try to increase your choices within the job market by generalizing about what you can do for people, the less other people can be of help.* Can you imagine an athlete trying to keep the sport in which she has specialized a secret? The more clearly you can describe your skills, eliminating any mushiness, the more employers will respond to you.

Allen entered the office greatly discouraged and left even more so. He had been referred to an international executive search firm and expected help in positioning himself. He'd been given a courtesy meeting with this firm because he had hired them to conduct senior-level searches on multiple occasions. Having sold off several of the companies that he had been running for a worldwide security products manufacturing holding company, he was ready to make his own transition. He'd been traveling constantly for his international job, but holding the world record for frequent flyer miles was not his objective.

Much to Allen's surprise, the search firm didn't offer the type of help he was expecting. Allen thought that he would walk away with his choice of the searches that matched his skills. He didn't. Not only do search firms not work that way, but this one didn't believe that he was focused enough to present him to clients.

Allen had received a rude shock from the search firm. Puzzled that his excellent track record hadn't been an immediate hit and embarrassed by being in the position of needing help rather than giving it, he couldn't understand why the search firm wasn't being helpful. "I really can do anything. I've run several companies and would be happy to do that again if I didn't have to travel so much. I'm excellent at motivating people and turning around operations. The company or industry I go to doesn't matter. These strengths will work anywhere."

Is Allen right? Yes. Does it matter to the employer? No.

Companies, boards, and especially search firms want specific, relevant experience. They want people who have done the same type of work in the same industry as theirs, ideally with their competition. This matching of industry and function between the position and the candidate is what I call the "round hole–round peg" phenomenon. Is it fair? Maybe not. But it's the norm, so you might as well take advantage of its predictability and strategize to make it work for you.

This doesn't mean that you can't change fields or industries. People do it all the time. It does, however, mean that your chances of getting what you want at the level and salary that you want will improve if your presentation clearly signals why your background adds value in your new field. Your audience is not interested in figuring out new ways your skills might fit with their company. They're busy. Do the figuring for them.

The most common place for mushiness to show itself is in résumé design. Many people are leery of placing an employment objective in the first section of their résumé. But to avoid stating an objective out of fear of losing opportunities is like being a shy boy at a school dance who never approaches the group of girls. He *could* get a lot of attention, but he doesn't because he's not direct.

Many head hunters and human resource professionals have told me, "If job seekers can't figure out what they want to do and tell me in their résumé, I'm not going to do it for them. I'm going fast. I'm skimming. I don't have time to analyze their wishes if they don't look focused."

Meet the employers' needs. Supply an objective. This will also help you focus the rest of your résumé and hone your skill in communicating your strengths. "I want to increase sales for an instrumentation manufacturer, preferably one that would like to grow its international markets" is what you might tell someone verbally. Your objective would be "senior sales management for instrumentation company," with supporting bullets about sales successes in the body of the résumé and an international or management bullet thrown in for flavor.

Allen developed one résumé with one set of examples and vocabulary for industrial manufacturing firms, then a separate résumé that used many of the same examples but different vocabulary designed to meet the expectations of electronics firms. Remember how your accomplishments and strengths are like diamonds that you can rotate to show different facets to different people? That's just what Allen did. He ended up looking equally attractive to both groups of companies because he did the thinking for them. If you keep your message simple and clear, using the industry's vocabulary and referring to their needs and profitability, you'll do well. For more about this, see Strategy #2: Market for Mutual Benefit.

A Sense of Direction

As noted above in "I'm the Boss. Adios, Mushiness!" there are two main points you'll want to communicate to others.

- Function: What do you want to do?

- Industry: Where do you want to do it?

Let's see how this plays out. After some brainstorming, Allen came up with the following list.

FUNCTION: What Do You Want to Do?	INDUSTRY: Where Do You Want to Do It?
Jobs that might be a fit	***Categories of companies with which I have (or want) experience***
CEO, president	Electronics manufacturing
General manager, division president of several companies	Holding company
	Companies going through transactions: acquisitions, mergers, divestitures
Consultant	
Running U.S. operations for an international company	Security manufacturing
	International technical companies with plans to expand into the U.S. market

Read the list vertically rather than horizontally. Allen first thought about the function category, adding titles he had already held or might consider holding. His industry list worked the same way. Including items in each category that he had actual experience with was important. They'll eventually be his "round peg" category in a job search, or the part of his job search that will move the fastest since search firms and companies prefer candidates who are currently in the same function and industry as their opening. Including some new items of interest was helpful, too. Allen could follow up and research a new function or industry to see whether or not they truly offered greener pastures. Beware of changing industry *and* function at the same time. There will be definite salary and learning curve implications if you're a rookie in both categories.

Take a look at Allen's two columns. Do the left and right columns mix and match? Might Allen be CEO or president of a company in the right column? Might he become a consultant to several of them? Your list could give you multiple options as well.

Clarifying your own industry and function goals is the next step. At this stage, you're just brainstorming so there are no wrong answers. If you have a dream that you'd like to think through, write it down. In addition to round-hole–round-peg (same function, same industry) target markets, you might want to consider the "circus clown" opportunities. Not that you would want to be a circus clown (would you?), but there may be a fantasy job you have been thinking about for years. Why not check it out now? I hate to see someone kicking himself or herself five years after a major job change saying, "Why didn't I just check out that other idea when I had a chance?" There will always be bad days at even the most perfect job, and you want to feel reassured on those days that you made the right call, sort of like dating multiple people before you get married. Have you always wanted to start your own company, turn your hobby into a vocation, do something socially relevant? Test-drive some creative ideas now, along with the more traditional ones. You will learn if one fits with your goals, values, and strengths in comparison to your other alternatives.

HOMEWORK

Communicating Your Direction

 A blank, printable Function/Industry form for this exercise can be found at www.thenewjobsecurity.com.

Work on your lists vertically. Then sit back and take a look at them across the columns when you're done.

- Function. Be inclusive. List all the job titles that intrigue you as well as ones that you've had and enjoyed. What titles are now being used for the work you love? You can get ideas from job listings, the Internet, *The Occupational Outlook Handbook,* or titles your friends have or that you read in the media. Forget about where particular jobs might be located; just start doing some market research. Look at the titles only; we'll come back to the rest of the ads in Strategy #3: Stop Looking for Jobs.

- Industry. List any industry in which you have experience at this point, even if you don't love it. (Okay, you can leave it off if the memory of it makes you ill.) You will be of greater value when you have knowledge of an industry, and you don't want to eliminate any just yet. By industry, I mean the category of work that your employers are or were in: Ford is in the automotive manufacturing industry. AT&T could be broken down into different parts of the telecom industry, such as broadband, wireless, or residential services. Warning: High tech doesn't count as an industry. It's too broad. Break it down into the type of work the company does.

Next, include any new industries that sound attractive to you. Moving to a new industry takes a little more work, increasing your need to network and to educate yourself, but it can be done.

In each column, check off your top two to four favorites.

You're developing clear signals now about which industries interest you. Identifying your favorites will set you up for the target marketing described in Strategy #2: Market for Mutual Benefit.

The next step is to start assessing the viability of the industries you've checked off. You'll be spending a good deal of time, maybe a lifetime, with some of these industries, so it's time to be painfully analytical. Do you still want to own that Blockbuster franchise? You have a lot at stake in deciding where your industry is headed, so you want to collect data on its health during your market research phase. "Why did you stay in the textile (or automotive, or tool and die, or whatever) industry so long?" interviewees will be asked when they decide to make a change. It's the old slide rule problem. You could be the best slide rule maker in the world and produce a perfect product, but if no one is going to buy your product, how much time do you want to waste developing those skills? I'll give you ways to respond to the interviewer's question later in this book, but it's easier to take your industry's pulse on an ongoing basis and make the transition to an interesting alternative industry earlier rather than later.

As you progress in succinctly describing what you want to do and where you want to do it, you're taking control of your career's direction, decreasing your susceptibility to a pinball career, and increasing your potential for job satisfaction. Being the boss feels good.

Getting the Word Out So People Actually Respond

You're about to hit prime time, so you want to look like you have your act together, which, of course, you do. Two of the clear signals that you'll want to send most frequently throughout your career are your Elevator Story (a brief description of your work and goals) and your résumé. Your Elevator Story and your résumé are verbal and visual proof that you know where you're heading. The act of thinking through both of them, of structuring how you want to describe yourself to others, is an end in itself. Even if you're happily employed, having both of these at your disposal is part of career control. You can use your Elevator Story socially when someone asks, "What sort of work do you do?" If you're employed, you can use your résumé as a bio if you publish some research or an article, speak to a group, or do some approved consulting on the side. Updating them is much easier than starting them from scratch, so spend some time on them now, regardless of whether you're settled or in transition, and you can build on them over the years.

An Elevator Story with a Penthouse If you were asked "What do you want to do?" while on an elevator ride, you'd need a concise and brief answer, wouldn't you? Voilà, an Elevator Story is born. You're going to be explaining both to current acquaintances and to new people what type of work you're interested in, so you'll want to do two things: clearly describe your goals and motivate people to help you. Although some people will simply suggest that you tell people about yourself in two minutes in order to tell an Elevator Story, the more specific suggestions I provide will yield greater outcomes. Adding some results and asking a thought-provoking question will set you apart from those who relate a generic Elevator Story, and then let silence fall. You want to engage people in a conversation that not only intrigues them with your skills and entertains them with some humor, but also asks them to interact by soliciting their opinions about business trends—a much less aggressive tactic than hitting on people for names and job openings. You've just gone straight to the top with your Elevator Story, to the penthouse level where the successful, confident people hang around.

Let's walk through the format, and then you can get started writing your own story.

- Introduction. The first sentence is an umbrella statement. "I have more than _____ years experience in _____." "More than twenty years" is as large as the number needs to get. You might start sounding a little too geriatric otherwise. If the number of years is small, simply say that you have "in-depth" or "extensive" experience.

- Three skills. Keep it simple and conversational. "What I particularly enjoy doing is _____." Look at the list of skills you came up with in your homework earlier in this chapter and pick out three strengths that you are certain will be of interest to potential employers. Express each in a brief sentence or two. "What I particularly enjoy doing is getting teams that have never worked together before to surprise themselves with their own success. I also like to untangle a customer's technical problems so they're thanking me a year later. And I enjoy selling against stiff competition. I must thrive on abuse." Not only did you introduce humor, an important element to keep people listening, but you also implied as many as ten additional strengths, such as leadership, happy customers, and strong sales results, without bragging. Once you have one Elevator Story comfortably taped in your brain, you can switch your three skills to fit your listener's interests. Stay away from boring expressions such as "I like exceeding customer's expectations." Eyes will glaze over.

- Two results. "As a result, I have been able to _____." This is the part that is really going to sell you. Listeners remember the results more clearly than the rest of the story and can resell you to their colleagues on this alone. Look back at the PAR stories that you wrote earlier. Pick from the bottom line, literally. If you can get some numbers or profitability into your results, so much the better.

- Question. "Are you aware of any _____?" This is an important conversational tactic. Most people don't think to continue their Elevator Stories by lobbing the ball back into the listener's court for some useful information. You're smarter. "Are you aware of any professional service firms that might be interested in new business by introducing some ancillary services?" Note that you *didn't* ask for job openings. That's a dead end. You did something much more difficult and much more effective: you did the thinking by defining the type of company that might have an emerging need that would fit with your background, then asked a question that they can't say "no" to. (You'll get more details on this approach in Strategy #3: Stop Looking for Jobs.) Good questions do not come easily. They take tweaking and refining until you receive answers that give you information that enables you to progress. Weren't you wise to capture the opinions of a person who was interested in you when you had the chance?

Now for your own Elevator Story.

HOMEWORK

Creating Your Own Elevator Story

Additional blank, printable copies of this exercise can be found at www.thenewjobsecurity.com.

- **Introduction**
  "I have more than _____ years of experience in _____."

- **Three Skills**
  "What I particularly enjoy doing is _____."

- **Two Results**
  "As a result, I have been able to _____."

- **Question**
  "Are you aware of any _____?" Remember that this is a business question and not a query about opportunities that are available. For example, you might ask about "companies that need to review their compliance with the new regulations," but don't inquire specifically about job openings.

Once you have sketched out an Elevator Story that you like, try it out with a friend, at a social gathering, or at a networking meeting. The more you become comfortable with it, the less you'll have to think about what you're saying and the more you can concentrate on your audience. You're getting the word out to your network, plus now you have an answer to the dreaded interview question, "Tell me about yourself." Just change your last question to, "Is that the type of background you're looking for?" It will be.

Passing the Five-Second Résumé Test The tangible tool that describes your work is your résumé. Boy, are you about to get a whole new perspective on résumé writing than you've had before. I'll pass along the secrets to creating a résumé that will be pulled out of the stack and consistently receive compliments. You can take it from there with the actual writing. The key is *product marketing*. It seems so obvious, but no one else is doing it. You're in luck because you're getting insider information. Here's the three-step drill:

1. Define your main target market. (Use your industry listings, or the categories within them, for this.)

2. Define the needs of this target.

3. Present your product (you) in terms of its needs.

Sounds pretty simple, doesn't it? But most people follow the opposite approach when they're writing their résumés. Most people will throw everything in their career history on the wall and let their potential employer decide what sticks. This approach makes one giant fallacious assumption: that the recipients of the résumé are actually going to read it. They aren't. They may skim it. But they're not going to spend time reading every word or figuring out what you really want to do and which are the best places for you in their company. They're not mean or insensitive; they're just busy. If you've been on the other side of the desk, you know that the rate at which potential employers blow through this information is *five seconds per résumé*. They're going fast, and they're not really paying attention. Can you show someone how you're going to make their company more profitable in five seconds? If you can, then *that* will slow them down. Now that you know the rules, you can design your résumé with the five-second skim in mind. Not only will you send clearer signals, but you'll get more results.

Let's assume that you have already completed the first step. You've identified industries of interest in your earlier homework, and you know your target markets or groups of companies with similar characteristics. In the following example a senior-level engineer is targeting telecommunications companies.

The second step, defining the needs of these targets, involves some homework. You'll want to discover the hot buttons of the companies to which you'll be applying. There are two ways to learn about these needs:

1. Ask senior-level professionals in and around your targeted industry.

2. Analyze job listings from the Internet or search firms.

When asking senior-level professionals about market needs, talk to those whom you will *not* be approaching for work. You're in the market research phase now, and you should not contact potential employers until you are fully armed. "What do you guys do around here?" does not play well with a potential boss: it gives crossed signals. People such as friends, former employers, colleagues who have moved into other companies, or professional association members would be appropriate. In the process of exploring the job market, you're going to be talking with a lot of sources. Strategy #3: Stop Looking for Jobs and Strategy #4: Build Sustainable Networks will delve into this further. One question you can ask is, "What are the four most important skills you'd be looking for if you were hiring a training director?" Ask them, "Where is this industry going to be in three years?" and similar questions. Listen to what they have to say. Take notes. After you've asked three or four people the same questions, some themes will emerge. *These* are market needs. *These* will be captured in your résumé. Not only do the answers determine the viability of your function, combined with an analysis of job listings, you'll have a résumé that they can't resist.

HOMEWORK

Who Has the Information You Need?

- Whose opinions would you value about the type of work you want to do? (Ideally, these are people who won't be hiring you.)

- Who knows about what's happening in your target markets, the type of industry you're in or want to be in?

Set up some time to talk with your sources either in person or over the phone. Email is a distant third choice. Strategy #4: Build Sustainable Networks will teach you how to make the most of an informational meeting.

You don't need to talk to people before you look at job listings, nor is the reverse necessary. You can work on the two approaches simultaneously or in whichever order makes sense to you.

The next way to pinpoint market needs, analyzing job listings, will be your secret weapon. Here's what to do, but keep the secret to yourself so you can always outshine the competition. I developed this approach years ago, and my clients started getting attention that others weren't. That's the point. Find ten to fifteen job listings that sound really appealing. It doesn't matter what part of the country they're in or even if they're a year old. Some of the places you can find them are in professional or association journals, on company websites, on job boards, through Google, or on LinkedIn. Newspaper listings are slipping as a source, aren't they? If you're at a more senior level, www.ExecuNet.com, www.6figurejobs.com, or www.TheLadders.com will work. (After having worked with ExecuNet for twelve years, I'm a fan, as you'll see. There's more about them in Strategy #4.) If you're at the highest levels, analyzing executive search firm job descriptions will work well combined with talking to colleagues you're *not* targeting. Include jobs you've been recruited for or responded to in the past year as well.

Now, start taking apart the fine print. I take notes when I'm doing this. Jot down the qualifications, the requirements, and the main functions of each job. Look for the recurring patterns and words in ten to fifteen ads. By the time you finish, you'll be able to name the top five points that you need to prove in your résumé. Eureka! The words that show up in a cross-section of companies within your target market are needs that are of interest to all of the rest of the companies in this group, too, and they belong on your résumé. Back these up with your experience in these areas and they become your Sharp Skills which you can hold up like a mirror to reflect back to the companies just what they want to see, plus you can convey your competitiveness and differentiate yourself from others in language that they can understand. The Sharp Skills are your golden nuggets that are the merger of your strengths and market expectations. You can demo these in your résumé, your Elevator Story, and your PAR stories during interviews. Heather added "mobile" to "marketing" and discovered that the responses to her conversations about "mobile marketing" were dramatically better than her conversations about "marketing," where there's a lot of competition and few differentiators. You'll get attention because you're focusing on your *market's* needs, not your own.

Let's see how another professional, a senior-level engineer, could determine the market needs and the Sharp Skills he needs with a little research. He is already clear on his function and industry:

- Function: Senior engineering management (VP, director)

- Industry: Telecom, wireless, networking

To track down market needs, our engineer might consider a variety of sources, including the Internet and professional associations. The newspaper had no ads at this level, once again confirming that newspapers are not the best source for higher-level openings.

Just skim the boldface text in these ads (emphases added), and you'll see what the engineer has to consider.

VP of Engineering in Telecom

Reports to CTO. **Lead development effort** for a second-stage software provider developing bandwidth management tools for broadband market. Responsible for **design, planning, and development** of one or more components of product applications. **Lead development teams** and senior developers in development and implementation of product components required by specifications developed and provided by product management and other sources. **Develop budget and project schedules** for all projects, monitor progress, and report status to senior management. **Hire, motivate, and appraise development team.** Ensure projects are completed **on time and to quality standards.** Facilitate **communications** upward and across project team, including project status, justifications for variances, and technical information. Serve as **focal point for other departments** on project status and other project information. Organize project through development of project plans. Ensure projects are completed according to product specifications and are properly documented. Ensure product **architecture and implementation is maintainable** and extendible. Ensure that documentation gets appropriate level of **technical review** support, **QA test** plans meet project requirements, and appropriate development procedures are followed. Must have degree or equivalent experience; graduate degree preferred. 15+ years in **software development,** with 7+ years in leadership roles. Experience in **C/C++ OOA&D** development environment. Ability to lead and motivate teams of developers. Experience with a variety of **development tools** (e.g., JDBC, Enterprise Java Beans). Proven experience in leading **software product development** projects. **Organization and planning skills. Outstanding communications skills, both oral and written.** Experience in a **startup** environment preferred. Experience in cable or communications industry preferred; reference ExecuNet in response.

VP of Engineering
Wireless Communications Company

Lead design and analysis team of 35 mechanical, structural, and electrical engineers and technicians in **new product development and modification** of existing product lines ranging from 1.2 meter through 34 meter in size. Must be able to provide **innovative design solutions. Management** experience a must. Assure all **project schedules and budgets are met; schedule and allocate design workload as well as develop and implement engineering standards** for all disciplines in an environment where designs are often modified and tailored to customer requirements. Must have **experience as VP,** director, or manager of engineering in $25M+ company. Ideal candidate has **supervised the engineering department that designs large structures.** Must have 10 years engineering experience. Must have BS engineering in structural/mechanical engineering. Must have strong management/technical leadership. Demonstrated success in standardizing designs as well as developing and implementing engineering standards for all disciplines within an engineering department. Must be **hands-on, high-energy shop floor person, who will ensure quality, on-time design project completion.** Ability to **prioritize and organize resources** is essential, as is the ability to **work under pressure and handle multiple tasks. Ability to communicate** and work effectively with all departments and at all levels within the company. Possess excellent business judgment, problem-solving abilities, and management skills; reference ExecuNet in response; paid relocation.

Director of Engineering
Networking Company

The qualified candidate will be a critical **leader** in a fast-growing IP services and routing protocol organization. This company is seeking a senior individual with a strong background in the **networking** industry with a minimum of 8–10 years of experience with at least 6 years of management experience in software to direct a software routing protocol organization. Qualified candidates should have experience with **OSPF, BGP, IP, MPLS traffic engineering and/or RSVP signaling.** This individual requires in-depth understanding of **routing architectures and routing industry standards.** In addition, qualified candidates must have a proven track record of delivering a router to market. Additional responsibilities include developing **project schedules, recruiting, hiring, motivating, evaluating, and retaining software engineers.** This position interacts with a skilled **team** of hardware, software and test engineers as well as customers, marketing, and industry leaders. Effective **communication skills**, flexibility, a strong **teamwork** approach, and the desire to work in a fast-paced startup environment are necessary for success. This role will report to the Vice President of Engineering and requires an MSCS/EE or equivalent. IEEE Job Site

Here's the exciting part. Even without knowing a thing about electrical engineering, I can tell you what Sharp Skills a senior-level engineering manager's résumé should include and can write an appropriate Elevator Story just by analyzing the trends in the ads. You can do it, too. Combine the recurring themes from the ads in your industry and function with the feedback you have from talking to senior-level professionals, and you'll have killer communication materials and approaches.

Here are some themes that emerged in the senior engineer's ads.

- Demonstrates technical development leadership skills
- Manages projects so schedules and budgets are consistently met
- Creates and implements innovative design solutions
- Motivates teams to work well under pressure with strong communication skills
- Ensures that quality standards are met or exceeded in all projects

There they are: the market needs, trends, and your Sharp Skills that are the core points that you'll want to embed in your résumé. The following sample résumé format I developed adapts easily to multiple functions and industries, and both employers and search firms love it. "You did my job!" and "You're just what we're looking for" are comments my clients have received. Why not? You're just reflecting back your market's own vocabulary tied to *your* own skills. Remember as well that someone will probably spend only five seconds skimming the first page of your resume. If you don't use boldface type to hook them on the points of greatest importance in five seconds, they may move along to the next résumé in the stack. Do you read every word of other people's résumés? Lead with your profitability and the readers will quickly see that they cannot afford *not* to hire you.

See how this market-based approach plays out in the format below. This résumé is for people who are *moving upward* in their careers.

THOMAS A. SMITH

123 Main Street
City, State Zip

876.543.2100
tsmith@gmail.com

OBJECTIVE

Senior-executive position in biotechnology/health care industry

SUMMARY

Experienced health care executive with proven expertise in creating new business, directing complex operations, managing finances and P&L, and developing results-oriented strategic plans. Strong record of increasing revenues and controlling costs in multiple-site operations. Recognized for leadership abilities, strong communication skills, and improving corporate profitability.

PROFESSIONAL EXPERIENCE

Biotech, Inc., Newton, MA, 2004–Present

Senior Vice President of Operations

Responsible for field sales and operations of outpatient treatment centers and multisite GMP laboratories. Directed corporate departments of medical affairs, nursing, laboratory operations, and quality assurance and quality control for a start-up biotechnology company providing novel cellular immunotherapy for cancer. Performed corporate strategic planning, coordinated sales and marketing efforts, and assured optimal patient care. Implemented corporate-wide Quality Assurance Program.

- *Developed and implemented successful strategic plans,* including financial and operational analyses, for refining operations of pilot site. Operational changes resulted in a 12% savings.

- *Opened multiple-site treatment centers* by establishing policies and procedures, hiring and training personnel, controlling costs, and managing sales staff in developing referrals and new patients, generating new revenue streams.

- *Focused marketing strategy* for introduction of new technology, resulting in 74% increase in sales within a year.

- *Managed Materials and Process Review Board,* a multidepartmental senior management committee that reviewed and approved all operational issues, including process development validations and policies and procedures, to ensure total quality management.

- *Developed new multisite cGMP-compliant laboratories* (current Good Manufacturing Practices) by combining expertise in FDA regulations with practical knowledge of protocol validations and sterility procedures.

- *Reduced cell-processing breakeven costs by 35%* by increasing protocol efficiency of internal operations and lowering staffing utilization while meeting cGMP regulations and maintaining quality of product and patient care.

HPI Health Care Services, Atlanta, GA, 1989–2004

Senior Vice President of Operations, 2001–2004

Directed all national operations, including fiscal responsibility, for $60 million company providing management of hospital pharmacies, materials management, home infusion therapy, medical equipment, and nursing services. Developed new business ventures. Supervised 6 vice presidents and 1,100 employees in 106 sites nationwide.

- *Initiated capitated/cost guarantee contract resulting in sales of $27 million* by analyzing client's cost history, forecasting cost savings, and performing trend and financial analyses.

- *Negotiated management agreements to improve profitability,* including 6 contracts that yielded $3 million net profit on an annualized basis.

- *Improved financial performance* by instituting strict budgetary controls and by implementing operational efficiencies, resulting in exceeding budgeted profits every year.

Vice President of Operations, 1999–2001

Responsibilities similar to Senior Vice President of Operations. Initiated computerization of billing areas, cutting billing time in half.

- *Created individualized marketing plans* for each account that resulted in a 20% increase in client retention.

- *Streamlined staffing patterns,* eliminating level of field management that resulted in savings of $500,000 annually while increasing revenue growth and client contact.

Regional Vice President, 1997–1999

Planned, implemented, and directed health-care administrative services for Eastern Region. Translated corporate objectives into regional operational plans and goals. Assured quality care and optimal services. Controlled costs and maximized profits.

- *Achieved 27% increase in profitability* by tightening billing procedures and strengthening purchasing controls.

Regional Director of Operations, 1994–1997

Marketed and managed company's health care services across four-state area. Hired, trained, and supervised 77 health care professionals.

- *Surpassed sales targets,* increasing annual volume from $6 to $8 million and doubling profits within first year.

- *Introduced successful new services* with first national nursing home contract and new Home Health Care Services that generated $1 million in first year.

Eastern Regional Director–Material Management, 1992–1994

Promoted from Unit Manager (1989–1990) to Area Director (1990–1992) to Eastern Regional Director with responsibility for marketing and coordinating all equipment and material production, distribution, and logistics functions for new service line. Directed staff of 40 employees.

- *Developed and introduced new business* by identifying customer needs, then introducing new services that met expectations. Increased sales by $4.5 million annually.

EDUCATION

Master of Business Administration (MBA)
Xavier University, Cincinnati, OH, 1992

Bachelor of Science
St. Louis College of Pharmacy, St. Louis, MO, 1985

MARY H. LAMB

74 Pasture Lane, Watertown, MA 02188   mlamb@gmail.com   508.321.6789

OBJECTIVE

Marketing/sales management position in food or hospitality industry

SUMMARY OF QUALIFICATIONS

- *Marketing experience with food and hospitality,* from designing strategic plans that clearly identified target markets, goals, and how to get there to developing products and services that anticipated market trends. Introduced and promoted new product lines for companies that dramatically increased revenues.

- *Strong sales and negotiating track record* that includes training and managing successful sales teams and negotiating contracts and prices to corporate advantage. Developed strategies that increased overall sales sixfold.

- *Ability to penetrate key accounts with industry relationships* developed over twenty years of experience. Credibility with professional associations as a guest speaker and lecturer, as the subject of feature articles in media, and from industry board memberships (AIWF) that create a strong referral base and access.

- *Product knowledge,* from expertise in planning and implementing major events to teaching college courses that emphasize product development and marketing.

- *Recognized presentation and communication skills* from unprecedented sales generated after product demonstrations and by consistent commendations from audience.

- *Create and direct promotional events.* Arranged cooking demonstrations by Julia Child and Jacques Pepin; the first food and wine festival at St. Andrews in Scotland for the hotel and travel industry; multiple trade shows and corporate functions; and all aspects of international tours. Increased visibility and sales.

PROFESSIONAL EXPERIENCE

Principal, Senior Marketing Director

MBF Consulting–Atlas Fabrics Store, Inc., Worcester, MA, 1998–Present
Responsible for planning and operating a successful business primarily focused on management of special events, corporate and annual meetings, fund-raisers, promotionals, and trade shows. Designed and implemented marketing strategy, advertising and promotional campaigns, media coverage, and representation of the company to the public.

Director of Public Relations, Consultant

Kitchen, Etc., Dedham, MA, and North Hampton, NH, 2008
Developed and produced promotional activities for business and new products, including special events, product demonstrations, and favorable, free publicity in the media. Consistently increased sales over projections and improved company name recognition.

International Tour Director

Trafalgar Tours, London, England, 2003–2005
Primary responsibility for media relations, tours, and special event management for international celebrities. Produced a promotional video for new business development. Knowledgeable about values, culture, norms, and expectations of other countries.

EDUCATION

M.Ed., Suffolk University, Boston, MA, 2003

B.S. in Speech, Emerson College, Boston, MA, 2001

Graduate coursework in **Business Management** and **Special Event Management,**
Bentley College, Waltham, MA

When you're changing fields or have recently graduated from school, you don't typically have a lot of relevant experience from an employer's perspective. The beauty of this format is that it allows you to gather your hooks, or relevant selling points tied to results, from throughout your work and volunteer experience, and then present them up front in one solid block. This looks much more impressive than the more traditional format if you don't have the right titles or companies to lead with. You're leading with their needs and how you can address them instead. You just got their attention.

Read Strategy #2: Market for Mutual Benefit and Strategy #3: Stop Looking for Jobs before finishing your résumé. You'll get some additional ideas that will make your presentation even more powerful.

HOMEWORK

Identify Job Themes

1. Find ten to fifteen help wanted ads that are of interest to you, preferably in a fairly narrow range of functions and industries.

2. What words and themes keep reappearing?

3. How could you state these themes succinctly? And how can you show your results in these areas?

These market needs will be the base for developing your résumé. Show that you are profitable any time you can work it in.

With these themes, you have just defined the Sharp Skills that the employers in your markets want you to have. Show them that you have these Sharp Skills every chance you get—in phone conversations, on your résumé, and in interviews. Keep testing them against marketplace needs every six months or so, even when you're settled in a job. This is solid career management data that you'll want to keep refreshing so that you don't become obsolete. Whether or not your company wants to keep you at the cutting edge of these skills is up to you and them. They shouldn't train you in things that are not relevant to their best interests. *You* shouldn't stay with a company for the long term that doesn't want to keep you—and, as a result, themselves—competitive. If certain Sharp Skills are important to you and your company isn't going to support their acquisition, you must find a way to get them anyway. Creativity counts as a Sharp Skill.

JOB SEARCH FOR FUN AND PLEASURE

The capstone to sending clear signals about your career strength and direction comes with wrapping everything together with an upbeat attitude. Combine your sense of value and your ability to manage your career with having fun, and things start happening. Fun is not what you feel like you're having right now, though, is it? The ability to enjoy the journey as you're making changes is easier said than done. Fun is not a casual, superficial point, however. If you can get your head to the point of truly being curious about what you're learning, of wondering how you can help other people, of watching the marketplace and predicting its direction, of exercising so you look and feel good, you might actually start enjoying it. If you look like you're having fun—if you are upbeat and positive—people will be attracted to you. As you learn more about the overall marketplace, and not just your specific job, you'll be of more value to more people. Guess what starts happening to your number of leads, referrals, and points of recommendation as people start realizing that you can help *them*? They'll grow like the lines waiting for the newest Apple product. Your reputation is spreading. Having fun improves your results.

The Chemistry Factor

We're getting into an area that I seldom see discussed, but which has a major impact on the results of any job campaign you might be contemplating: *what you are like to be with*. In fact, how people feel about being with you is typically the primary driver in what opportunities become available to you as you progress in your career. Can you think of job openings, either internal promotions or external hires, that did not go to the most qualified applicant? Enough said. Chemistry can often trump credentials. Use it to your advantage.

How you use the chemistry factor to your advantage gets back to having fun, relaxing, and what you'll learn in Strategy #2: Market for Mutual Benefit. If you can be enjoyable, comfortable, and fun for others to be around when you're in transition, you will increase your odds of reaching your goals. Here's the challenge: If you are truly unhappy with your work and want to move quickly, you will be feeling anxious. Feeling anxious releases some sort of molecules into the atmosphere that scare off other people. Yes, your good friends will stick with you, but they're not typically the ones with job alternatives for you. If they were, you'd have a new job already. You can build more connections if you relax.

Robert was two months away from being married. He had started up a company, and as CEO and founder he had managed what had become a good-sized operation. He sold it, making $40 million from the sale, but then lost much of the money in various investments and paying alimony for an earlier marriage. He was now financially strapped. In addition to needing income, he needed something to do. Intelligent and highly accomplished, being unemployed was not his idea of a good time. He was starting to get desperate about finding work. Pursuing listings on job boards and help wanted ads, he waited, passively, for openings to be posted, then mailed back responses with his résumé. A direct mailing had yielded nothing. His desperation increased.

Robert decided to postpone his wedding until he could find work. All he could think or talk about was where he might get a job. According to Maslow's hierarchy of needs—a pyramid that shows that we have to meet our most basic needs at the bottom of the pyramid before we can rise to self-actualization—Robert was at the bottom level, in the survival mode. He was targeting lower-level jobs just to find something, anything. The harder he tried, the more elusive the opportunities became. It wasn't working.

Why wasn't Robert landing the interviews that he so painfully wanted and for which he was so very qualified? If you were on the other side of the desk and someone approached you who seemed truly desperate for work, how would you react? Like a swimmer trying to grab a ball in the water, Robert was actually repelling his target by creating too many waves. Robert had another major challenge; he was using the two lowest-yield activities—responding to job listings and sending out direct mail—to generate the activity for his campaign. We'll get to alternative campaign strategies in the later chapters. For the moment, let's focus on chemistry.

Socially, you'd much rather be around people who are relaxed, who have common interests, who can listen well, and who have a sense of humor, right? In other words, they're fun. Being fun doesn't mean you have to have slap-on-the-back camaraderie. It doesn't mean that you need to be a raging extrovert or the life of the party. It means that you're comfortable with yourself and enjoy conversations with others.

Professionally, it is no different. A relaxed, collegial relationship *as an equal*, regardless of the difference in the levels of your titles, is not only more fun, but will also end up selling you better. *This is a level playing field.* The CEO is not going to talk to you simply because he has nothing better to do. If the CEO accepts a meeting with you, you already have something that makes you worth talking to. It could be networking connections, your expertise, your knowledge of a company that the CEO would like as a customer, or simply that he is desperate to fill an unadvertised job opening. Regardless, you have a lot more to offer than you realize, and figuring out what that is is *your* job. If you realize that your opinions and reactions to interviewers are just as valuable (or more so) than their reactions to you, you'll come across well. A confident mind-set that draws out the employer builds the chemistry that leads to job offers.

In case your mind and body aren't in agreement yet, try the cocktail party mind-set. Think of meeting with someone at a company as an invitation to a cocktail party. (Note that I didn't use the word "interview." That just raises the bar for everyone.) At a cocktail party, you are open, curious, willing to meet new people, and have the freedom to walk away. The stakes are low; there is no such thing as failure. If you don't like someone, you simply talk with someone else. You approach the party thinking, "Maybe I'll meet some interesting people or some new friends." If you don't, it isn't the end of the world.

A meeting at a company is nothing more than a very small cocktail party. If you think of these people you're meeting as potentially interesting people or new friends, it puts you in control. You can evaluate them also. You'll talk about things you have in common that interest both of you, as you would at a cocktail party, and if you don't feel *your* interest building, it might not be a good fit. During the meeting, let your sense of humor emerge. Relax and your body language will be at ease, too. You won't sit waiting for the next question, like you're on a firing line. You'll be asking questions and interacting as you would with a potential new friend. Guess what happens to the other person's interest in you when you are relaxed, are genuinely curious, draw *them* out, and have some insights into what her company is doing?

Being a Contrarian

I see many professionals show their support and enthusiasm for a company by becoming more of a yes-man (regardless of gender) during a meeting than is normally their style. Being supportive of all of a company's actions won't differentiate you, especially when you're interested in a higher-level position. Be a little bit of a contrarian by demonstrating your insights about improved performance and competitive pressures. Challenging some of the decision maker's assertions, as long as it's done in a professional and humorous way, will make him or her slow down and think about what you've just said. This should not be an in-your-face challenge, but rather a suggestion, such as:

- "I may have some ideas for you. Have you thought about doing . . . ?" (Insert a *brief* strategy that you think would work better than their current one and listen to their reaction.) This is the lead-with-a-question-but-get-the-cannon-pointed-at-the-right-target-before-you-fire approach.

- "I've had a great deal of success using a slightly different approach. Want to hear about it?" Wow them with a brief PAR story that ends with the same results that they want.

- Reframe the problem. "It sounds like you have an open-system problem but you may not be getting the results you want because you're using closed-system approaches." You could even move to the whiteboard at this point and illustrate your point. This is a consultative approach that you can use to show you bring a fresh perspective.

Remember, however, that with any of these three methods for demonstrating your leadership and initiative you don't want to give them all of the answers. You're selling too hard if you give them all your ideas early on, and you also risk losing them if they don't like your approach or they feel they can take your ideas and address their needs without you. Why buy the cow when the milk is so cheap? You want to draw out the other person in a meeting or interview so you can learn about their needs, then show your leadership qualities when they are relevant and in relation to those needs. You're enjoying the intellectual stimulation and the conversation along the way so you're still having fun, right?

It is your job to create this initial friendship if you want the relationship to continue. It starts at the beginning, with the first contact. You never want to create the image of being desperate, even if you feel that way.

THE BOTTOM LINE

When you combine the feeling of confidence that you offer something of value with the sense that you control your own direction in the marketplace and the idea that managing your career may actually be enjoyable, what happens? You've broken some patterns and you're mastering the first strategy by developing the thinking and the behaviors that send clear signals. You now can set your career direction, communicate your function and industry clearly, and gather feedback that moves you forward. In addition, you can test your career decisions—such as "Which job should I take?" or "Do I really need an MBA?"—against expectations for your profession and avoid a pinball career. You know how to design your résumé, your Elevator Story, and other communications to meet market needs. People with ideas and connections will be attracted to you and want to help because you project a relaxed confidence, are thinking of *them,* and are having fun. You *are* "The Boss," sort of like Bruce Springsteen.

MARKET FOR MUTUAL BENEFIT

"If you are not thinking customer, you are not thinking."
—PHILIP KOTLER

While giving the marketing section of my seminars, I've learned that the subject of marketing has a bad reputation in some quarters. Just like a couple of the kids you knew in high school, its reputation has been sullied because of who it is hanging around with and what people think it is. Marketing has been hanging around with sales, and to many, sales is synonymous with high pressure, like telemarketing calls on Sundays. Being fast, manipulative, or slick are some of the connotations that professionals come up with when I ask them their impressions of marketing. If you share these negative associations, let me ask you to suspend your preconceptions for a while. Not only is marketing a fascinating discipline, but it also has direct implications for your career management.

In *Kotler on Marketing: How to Create, Win, and Dominate Markets* (The Free Press, 1999), Philip Kotler describes classical product marketing as "discovering unmet needs and preparing satisfying solutions." This idea has parallels that can make a dramatic difference in your overall work success. It's the conceptual base that I use for my career management practice (and it doesn't hurt when applied to life in general, either) that results in setting you, a professional managing your career, apart from the crowds. Can you think of yourself as a product in the marketplace? If you can objectify yourself this way, clear a lot of your emotions out of the way, and understand that you're looking for the right consumer (employer), you'll unleash a torrent of successful practices and approaches that you can use to your advantage. After an outplacement workshop I gave for a biotech firm, an accomplished Ph.D. came up to me and said, "One of the most striking things I remember from today is your saying that I'm a box of Tide on the shelf and asking why someone should pick me. I'd never thought of myself this way, but it actually makes what I'm going through easier." Let's see how it works for you.

MARKETING: THE FOUR P'S PAY OFF

Marketing is the planning strategy that transcends the selling process. Peter Drucker, an internationally renowned business strategist, once said, "The aim of marketing is to make selling superfluous." Although this may seem a trifle optimistic, it demonstrates the power that discovering unmet needs and creating relevant solutions can generate to pull people toward you versus the more painful "push" practices of cold calling, selling yourself during meetings, and direct mailing. Why not use these ideas to build a demand for your services? The four P's of product marketing will convince people to track you down instead of the other way around.

The four P's—product, placement, promotion, and pricing—describe the optimum methods for driving product (you) consumption by various markets (your favorite industries). Take a look at how the four P's help you start on your own marketing plan in the homework below.

──────┤ HOMEWORK ├──────

The Four P's Pay Off

The Four P's of Product Marketing	Consumer Product Example	Professional Career Example	Your Strategy
Product: Item or service to be consumed with specific features and benefits. Covers product research and development, including how new products are created or current products can be improved.	Coca-Cola	Your strengths and assets that can be consumed (hired) and will benefit the consumer. You can do your own product upgrades, such as acquiring training and building new skills.	Features (your skills): Benefits (how you differentiate yourself, your value):

The Four P's of Product Marketing	Consumer Product Example	Professional Career Example	Your Strategy
Placement: Distribution methods. The channels through which the product reaches the marketplace.	Vending machines, grocery stores, fast-food chains	Networking, search firms, job boards, professional associations. May include your geographic preferences.	Preferred ways to reach your market:
Promotion: Methods to develop awareness and consumption of a brand name (Coca-Cola) and specific products (Diet Coke and Classic Coke).	Media advertising, sponsorship of sporting events, placement in movies	Résumé, word of mouth, speaking engagements, writing for professional publications and blogs (see the Develop Your Reputation graphic on page 204).	Preferred ways to build your reputation and brand in front of the right markets:
Pricing: Amount to charge for a product or service depending on production costs, margins, geography, competition, desired image, and what the market will bear.	Retails at approximately $2 per serving	Compensation and benefits package, bonuses, partnership, etc. (See Strategy #5: Negotiate in Round Rooms.)	Different paths to arrive at the right price ("cheap" is not an allowable word):

Isn't this cool? You can use this process to develop a marketing plan for yourself that cuts down on *reacting* and initiates *planning* and *strategy*. Warning: You're not going to have all the answers for the column about your strategy yet. You'll want to modify them as you continue reading this book and do some market research.

To get started, you need to define yourself as a product. This can be challenging even for a vice president of marketing because this time, the product or service is *you*. Refer to the strengths and skills that you identified above and build on them. Your strengths are no minor point, because you will use them to develop product differentiators. In other words, how are you, a software engineer, unique from other software engineers in the marketplace? What are your Sharp Skills and your differentiators?

During economic downturns, when companies begin to disappear, the presidents of those companies frequently call me. Each conversation starts, "I'm sure that I'm different from most of the people that you talk to. I've been president of a small company that doesn't exist any longer, and now I want to run a more stable company." The problem, however, is that they don't *sound different* when they present themselves to prospective employers. Everyone presents himself or herself in the same way, even though each individual is highly competent and unique. They are the boxes of Tide on the shelf that we talked about earlier. Here's where product development comes in. How do your experience and accomplishments, the features of the "product," benefit your market and differentiate you? *You need to do the thinking for other people. They aren't going to exert the energy.* The more you've analyzed yourself in relationship to market needs, and the more that you use the language that your *future* employers rather than your past ones use, the faster that new, improved box of Tide will be plucked off of the shelf and taken home.

How are your markets going to find out about you? What distribution channels or placement (the second "P") are you going to use to let people know that you're out there? I strongly suggest networking as your dominant method, but you'll want to consider search firms and relevant websites as well. These channels, however, are primarily for approved job openings. Why wait? Be conscious of where your markets hang around now so you can build relationships early. The best channels may well turn out to be the golf course, chamber of commerce meetings, or the board of a nonprofit. Do your homework about where your interests and your markets overlap before you decide the best "placements" for you so you don't waste your valuable time.

Promotion, the third "P," sticks in the craw of most professionals. "Promote myself? That's not me. That's so sleazy." I agree. I don't "promote" myself either. The word has "carnival barker" written all over it. I *will*, however, help other people, be active on several nonprofit boards, speak at conferences, participate in professional associations, have an attractive website, and write. These are all activities that I believe in and would support regardless, but they have additional benefits (see also Develop your Reputation on page 204). Being visible in your profession is now easier than ever to achieve given the ongoing need for content on websites and the constant demand for someone to step forward and solve business problems. A résumé is the most obvious vehicle for promoting yourself, but often it is not the most critical one if you follow the strategies in this book of building relationships and leveraging market needs first. If you substitute "What are the best ways to build my brand and reputation?" for "How do I best promote myself?" you'll get the results that you want with none of that carnival barker feel.

The final "P," pricing, is a topic that you don't want to blindside you. What are you worth in the marketplace? Start becoming aware of how your type of work is valued in the marketplace now, and then we'll combine your information with some killer negotiating tactics when we get to Strategy #5: Negotiate in Round Rooms.

YOU CAN'T HIT THE BULL'S-EYE IF YOU DON'T AIM FOR THE TARGET

Prior to delving into your marketing plan, go back to the industries you chose in Strategy #1: Send Clear Signals, and choose three or four target markets. Target markets are groups of companies with similar characteristics. Biotech, chemical manufacturers, insurance, commercial real estate, and telecommunications companies, for example, are markets that have their own separate problems, vocabularies, and needs. At least two of your choices should have some connection with your background. *The greater leap you take from your roots, the harder the search and any salary transferability become.* This doesn't mean not to take a leap. By all means, now is the time to test any dreams, but combine your drive to become a brain surgeon at fifty-three with exploring options within your "safety net," jobs that are a target or two closer to your current experience. If you multi-task for a while, you'll actually have an outcome and income stream after you've finished your market research, analysis, and campaign. Allen, in Strategy #1: Send Clear Signals, is a great example of someone who identified target markets. The list of industries in which he had experience became his list of target markets, as long as they were within his geographic constraints and preferred sales parameters. He enjoyed the industries he had worked in previously and was willing to continue searching those industries locally.

Allen also listed some industry categories that were not exactly what he had been doing but were close enough that the companies in these markets should be interested in his background (holding companies doing multiple transactions and international companies opening domestic operations that weren't in his specific area of expertise). That's a great idea for you, too. Choosing some related-but-different target markets can open up your search. Ask yourself, "Who would be interested in my set of skills?" Your Referral Triangle (see opposite) for each company you've been in will give you some clues.

Your Referral Triangle: They Love You Already

One way to generate ideas about groups that are related but different is to look at your Referral Triangle. Analyze the three categories of business that surround the companies in which you have worked: vendors, competitors, and customers. Where would your skills fit in these categories?

You probably don't want to work for all three of these groups, and your skills probably won't fit with all three. People in the retail industry, for example, aren't typically able to turn to customers for information, networking, or employment. People in business-to-business sales, however, may discover that they can change

Your Referral Triangle

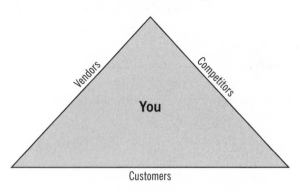

to another industry because they have the same customers in common. You can "sell" your "book," that is, the relationships that you're currently protecting but that you can bring to the table for the right employer. (Don't laugh. Attorneys, investment managers, and consultants do this all the time.) Look at the categories that are of interest and see whether any target markets make sense for you. A physician is surrounded by equipment, medications, software, and services that are targeted to improving her performance. One of these vendors may be interested in hiring a physician who knows the vendor's customers, has immediate credibility, and can suggest how the company might improve its products. Leaving private practice to work with medical instrumentation, pharmaceutical, humanitarian, or insurance firms is not unusual for doctors any longer. You may have people out there just waiting for your skills with a little repackaging.

Two other points about the Referral Triangle: First, even though you may not want to work for any of the vendors' companies in your Referral Triangle, they may be great sources of information. Sales reps who come to your company probably aren't going to be the ones to hire you, but they know what's going on with their customers and their own company. The smart ones are usually willing to help you get into another company. You might consider them as a possible vendor in the future.

Second, if you're in transition, have a noncompete agreement, and are concerned about even mentioning the names of the competition out loud, don't worry about it too much yet. As a rule, time will take care of this. Your current firm is a source of references, experience, friends, and a lot of memories. Even if you consider working for the competition at some point, you would never breathe a word of competitive information to your new company, even without a noncompete, right? Your reputation is everything. You can talk with companies as long as you aren't flying in the face of some legal or ethical agreement. I've seen plenty of people in job searches take long enough with the interviewing and selection process that the noncompete was a moot point by the time the job offer was made, negotiated, and accepted.

When you start building your network in Strategy #4: Build Sustainable Networks, you'll discover that you can revisit the Referral Triangle and apply it to each company for which you've worked to give you additional ideas for leads and connections. They just may be waiting for you.

A Hit List of Your Target Markets

What's the point of developing work in several target markets simultaneously? Speed, choices, and control. If you explore one target market at a time—a sequential search—you might decide at the end of six months that you don't really want to work at an advertising firm, or maybe the economy has wiped out that sector. If you only then begin to check out your second choice, you've already lost a lot of time. You're also missing out on a lot of opportunities if you pursue only one target market at a time. Within a geographic area—the San Francisco area, for example—no target market can generate as many job offers as several markets combined. The number of companies that you'd want to work for within a given category that also happen to need you at the same time is finite. The more people that you have pursuing you, the better. It ain't over until it's over, as Yogi Berra must have said about job searches, so you need the volume of choices that several target markets can generate. If you don't have enough companies going into the job "pipeline" at the beginning of the search, you're not going to have any choices coming out. Choices lead to *control*. Working with multiple target markets lets you search faster, increases your choices about where to go, and thus gives you greater control over the immediate outcome as well as your ongoing work satisfaction.

Speaking of control, you're now going to hear about one of the most important tools you can use if you'd like to change your job or explore other companies. Regardless of whether you're currently employed and benchmarking best practices, in transition, or identifying corporate boards where you might belong, making a "Companies of Interest" list will delight those in your network and give you direction and a daily to-do list. Between you and me, we can call it your "Hit List," but when you're sharing it with others, you won't sound as predatory with the "Companies of Interest" title.

Take a look at the example on the following page. *You* create this. *You* take control rather than waiting for other people to make referrals—a reactive, random, slow process. By exerting the energy to come up with some companies within your target markets that might be of interest to you, not only do you learn a boatload about the marketplace that you'll need to know to sound competitive, but you'll also make it easy for your network to help you.

Companies of Interest

Ben Rogers
ben@gmail.com • 765.987.6543
International Marketing

Optical Instrumentation	*Medical Diagnostic Equipment*
Cynosure Inc., Westford, MA Stephanie Allison, COB	Analogic Corp., Peabody, MA John Teel, President
GSI Group Inc., Billerica, MA Charles Taylor, President, CEO Richard Filip, COB Robert Blair, VP, CFO	Boston Scientific, Natick, MA Peter Bowyer, COB James Christopher, President Lawrence Keith, Exec VP, CFO
Evergreen Solar Inc., Marlborough, MA Richard Mayfield, COB, CEO Terry McCleskey, Sr VP Marketing	Cybex International, Medway, MA Walter James, President, CEO Roland Nicholas, VP Marketing
Osram Sylvania, Danvers, MA Charles Goldston, President, CEO Wilfried Hastings, Exec VP, CFO Mike Abbott, VP Brand Mgmt	Hologic Inc., Bedford, MA John Stevens, COB, CEO Glen Crowder, Exec VP, CFO
Palomar Medical, Burlington, MA Alex Dunlap, COB Joseph George, President, CEO Joan Filipone, VP Marketing Walter Ohlmstead, VP Bus Dev	Inverness Medical Inc., Waltham, MA Ron Abbott, COB, CEO Lydia Jacob, VP Gordon Carter, VP Marketing
Parker Hannifin Corp., Woburn, MA Jack Thomas, President, CEO Anne Lindsay, VP Marketing	Accellent Inc., Wilmington, MA, Robert Kohl, CEO Elizabeth Ray, Sales and Marketing Jude Stevens, CFO
Smith Nephew Inc., Andover, MA Susan Kwok, COB Scott Joslin, President Tiger Eckstein, Finance	Nova Biomedical, Waltham, MA John Schniewind, VP Sales Frank Williams, President Virginia Wallace, CFO
Tech Etch Inc., Plymouth, MA Bickley Gollinger, President Daniel Miller, President, CEO Jon Whitney, VP, CFO	Thermo Fisher Scientific, Weston, MA Barrie Blythe, President, CEO Jack Denis, President James Adrien, Sr VP

(Names have been changed to protect the innocent.)

This is a sample of an actual target list that a client developed and used very effectively to generate conversations. These weren't conversations asking "where are there job openings?" but rather, "These are the types of companies that I'm thinking about that look like they should be growing their international markets. What do you think? Who should be on the list that isn't? Who shouldn't be on the list?" You learn a lot and get a lot more information with open-ended questions.

HOMEWORK

Your Hit List (a.k.a. Companies of Interest)

 A blank, printable form for this exercise can be found at www.thenewjobsecurity.com.

1. Choose two target markets that may hold some potential for you. "High tech," "business," or "financial services" won't work because they're too broad, unless you're in a small town that doesn't have many choices within each field. "Biotech," "consumer packaged goods manufacturing," and "commercial banking" are target markets that consist of groups of similar companies.

2. Set up a two-column table and put the name of a target market at the top of each.

3. Start populating the list with potential companies of interest and three to four people within each company who might be above or at the level where you would be.

   - "Wait! I don't know who the companies are, much less the names of their decision makers!" True. They change all of the time, anyway, so it's impossible to be totally up-to-date. You have a giant resource at your disposal: *your local public library.* You may have resources at your alma mater's libraries that you can access online as well.

   - "I can get everything I need on my own computer." Yes and no, Jim Rettig, president of the American Library Association, reports. You *can* get a tremendous amount, but you can't be as efficient or exhaustive as the librarian in the business section of your library can be, or teach you to be. They'll have memberships or licenses to use some giant databases and research materials to which you wouldn't have access, plus they can show you how to overlay your geographic preferences with your industry choices to get companies that might be of interest. Use of libraries across the country is going up, Rettig reports; they're green, they're free, and they have Internet access. What's not to like? If you prefer having research done for you privately, ask a librarian if he can do hourly work on the side.

- Information will come from at least three other sources: word of mouth, your own brain, and the media (newspapers, business publications, television, and the Internet). Use them all. You're an equal opportunity lister.

Warning: all information is incorrect somewhere; you just don't know where. Databases with company info submitted a year or so ago are particularly vulnerable. I tell my clients that they're lucky if 30 percent of a database is helpful, so screen accordingly. Databases are a good way to discover companies you didn't know about and executive names, so just make sure that Johnny is still the VP of a target company before you spend a lot of time doing research on him.

We'll get into more details about when and how best to use your Companies of Interest list (a.k.a. Hit List) in Strategy #4: Build Sustainable Networks, but in the short term, start capturing your ideas of interesting companies in one place. If you can group them into separate buckets, or target markets, as you're going, that's a bonus. If you have more than two target markets, start a separate table to avoid looking like you're going in too many different directions and confusing your network. You're building a focused tool that will generate conversations and many more leads.

THE MARKETING CIRCLE: WHAT GOES AROUND, COMES AROUND

Listen up. Here comes *the* most critical graphic and one of the *most* critical concepts in your career management, the Marketing Circle. It is such a powerful driver of building relationships that your career will grow using this strategy alone. Put it together with the other four career strategies in this book and you're going places.

It all starts with a simple circle, with you on one side, and a potential employer on the other.

The Marketing Circle

 A blank, printable Marketing Circle is available at www.thenewjobsecurity.com.

Your Needs

On the top half of the circle, start jotting down things that *you* want from an *employer*. This goes for your current employer if you'd like to move up within your company. You might start off with income, for example. How about challenging work? Try to define that one a little more precisely. Flexibility, recognition—keep the ideas coming. Write these things down so you can see your expectations in front of you. Take a break and then come back to your list. Any new entries? Did you first think of things that you feel are missing from your current employer? That's natural. Now what about things your employer provides that you value but may take for granted, such as benefits, visibility in a hot growth area, or work that you really enjoy doing?

Two areas that people often miss when they're developing their employment goals (yes, that's what you're doing) are the type of physical environment they like to work in and the type of people they want to work with. As to your physical environment, do you like a structured, formal downtown office, a converted warehouse with arcade games, or bunny slippers in a home office? Don't eliminate your second- or third-choice environments from your search yet, while you're still learning about the marketplace, but being comfortable with the environment you finally select is important. Surroundings can reflect culture and values, and you'll want yours to fit with your company's. What type of environment is important to you?

What type of people do you like to work with? Do you prefer to be on your own, do you want to lead a company of highly technical workers, do you want to be on an interdependent team with people having different skill sets with abilities equal to yours? If you clearly define your preference of colleagues and environment—having listed everything from the type of corporate culture you'd like to the type of boss you'd like—your odds have just gone up for finding the right future employer.

The Marketing Circle: Your Needs

Now, before you've gotten too far into your job search, is the best time to define your preferences for your next employer. You have just developed a template. You can use this template as a measuring stick for potential offers, with one caveat. Is any company perfect? Just like a spouse, there are few perfect choices. Making conscious trade-offs instead of letting them creep up and surprise you six months into the job is the point.

The advantages of clarity in what you're looking for from an employer are subtle but powerful:

- Lower error rate. If someone offers you a job, what's your first reaction? Do you enjoy looking for a job? The job seeker will subconsciously skew what he is looking for to fit the offer. Who likes to stay on the job market just for the thrill of the hunt? Accepting a job without honestly comparing it to your needs often results in your not lasting in the job for too long, or being unhappy with what you're doing.

- You project more confidence, hence attract more response. You have expectations that are important and need to be valued. They level the playing field. You won't lead with your list of expectations, but you're going to talk about them before things are over. The employer isn't the only one with some power.

- You know your trade-offs for negotiation later. If one of your goals is flexibility, for example, after they extend an offer you might ask, "I see some models of telecommuting in your company. They sound like they're saving you overhead on real estate and attracting some talent that you wouldn't be able to recruit otherwise. What if we try one day a week telecommuting for this job and evaluate it at the end of three months to see if it's working for both of us?" The way you ask the question and when you ask the question are important. We'll come back to this after we fill in the other side of the circle.

- You know what topics to avoid for the earlier stages of any interview. Your needs are a hidden agenda for the short-term and medium-term. Sorry. Employers aren't terribly attracted by your need to leave early to go to your daughter's soccer game. Emphasizing it during an interview can be lethal. "Not fair!" you're saying. "If most of my needs aren't met, I'm not going to want the job." If you don't meet most of *their* needs *first*, you're not going to have a job offer to reject. Stay with me while we look at the other side of the circle, and then we'll come back to this point.

An Employer's Needs

First, the critical question: What does an *employer* want of *you*? Professionals in my seminars typically respond: skills, cultural fit, loyalty, and problem solving. These are all good answers and correct. There's something more important, however. What's a one-word definition of a successful company? Think about it.

Inevitably, the right answer comes back: profitability. Profitability is the bottom line, in all senses of the word. If you can demonstrate that you're a profitable employee, you will stand out from the masses. Even if you want to work for a nonprofit, the managers will be sophisticated enough to know that they have to compete for market share (percentage of potential business) and bring in profits; it's how they spend their revenues and how they account for them that differs. Profitability, for better or worse, rules. Use it. If you can demonstrate that you're profitable, do you think that an employer will be more attracted to you?

The Marketing Circle: An Employer's Needs

You   **Employer**

Problem solver
Marketplace knowledge   Dependability   Client relationships   Skill set
Leadership ability   Cultural fit
                Supervision skills   Technical expertise

Profitability

Proving Your Profitability

The flashing neon-light message from the Marketing Circle is that you have to show your profitability to attract the attention of a potential employer. "But," you say, "how I am I supposed to show profitability when my expertise is in researching molecular oncology? My job is to focus on scientific breakthroughs, not profits."

Ah, the seeds of the answer are in the mission. Breakthroughs create profits. Profitability comes in many different forms, and it is *your* job to think this through and present it with confidence. You'll get more attention and better results if you take the initiative to translate your work into profitability for an employer because they won't spend time on it.

> Showing your profitability will attract the attention of a potential employer.

How have you been profitable in your work experience? You have benefited your company(s) in more ways than you realize. Let's look at the two most obvious ways that you've been profitable.

1. Making Money. How do you make money for a company? This goes for nonprofits, too. The following list is certainly not inclusive, but it will start you thinking. Check off any items that may be relevant, and jot down any specific events that come to mind.

They may turn into stories (PARs) or hooks for résumés and conversations:

- You've increased your company's visibility in the marketplace (this includes speaking engagements, participation in professional meetings, writing for publications, and being interviewed).

- You've set up strategies, plans, and structures that enabled your company to reach its goals.

- You've closed a sale.

- You've built relationships with customers.

- You've initiated relationships with people or companies that might become customers.

- You've trained customers to use your product or service correctly, to their satisfaction.

- You've turned around a problem with a customer.

- You've developed products or services, sometimes with breakthrough thinking, that have responded to customer or market needs.

- You've researched data, technology, or information that has enabled you to improve the quality of a product or service.

- You've benchmarked the product against the competition and have set standards to differentiate your product or services.

- You've recruited, hired, and retained top talent.

- You've ensured that employees at all levels stay well trained and competitive.

- You've developed a structure that encourages employees to perform at their highest levels.

- You've set up a structure to access capital when it is needed.

- You've built relationships with financial markets.

- You've improved the reporting of information for better decision making.

- You've acquired, divested, merged, or spun off companies for your company.

- You've delivered a product or service internally or externally on time and under budget.

- You've done something for your company that others couldn't or haven't.
- Others?

Odds are that you're increasing profitability for your company all of the time and aren't thinking of it in these terms. It's time to change. Company results will reflect the difference in your thinking, as will your pocketbook.

2. Saving Money. The flip side of making money is not spending it! That also creates profitability. You save money in multiple ways all of the time for your company. Check off any of the following items that apply and add more. Once again, jot down any specific incidents that the examples trigger so you can refer to them when you're developing your résumé and thinking through responses:

- You've done more with less, including fewer people and limited time. (You're bound to have several examples in this large category.)
- You've integrated businesses, consolidated operations, or reduced overhead or operating expenses (another giant category).
- You've improved quality.
- You've streamlined manufacturing processes.
- You've reduced inventory, reduced scrap or waste, or reduced "bugs."
- You've improved field installation and/or service so fewer things go wrong.
- You've reduced purchasing costs by buying or budgeting wisely.
- You've re-engineered processes, streamlined the supply chain, and reduced inventories.
- You've converted information systems so accurate information can be accessed quickly and easily.
- You've outsourced operations.
- You've increased energy efficiency.
- You've managed reductions in force.
- You've structured compensation systems so they're competitive, but don't overcommit the company when revenues are low.

- You've thought of ways to do things faster, better, or cheaper (without lowering quality) that other people haven't.

- Others?

You're pretty good, aren't you? Keeping track of how you are profitable isn't something you should wait to do. If you wait until you're between jobs to figure out why you're good, not only have you forgotten half of the things that other people would really value (and you've taken for granted), but you've buried any numbers or metrics that would quantify your impressive results. Track numbers whenever you can. Otherwise, track results and outcomes. A college administrator said that she "increased parent satisfaction, commitment to the institution, and word of mouth referral" by running loyalty-building parents' programs. You don't see any dollars listed, but you can visualize them flying out of the parents' wallets into the bursar's office.

So What?

If you aren't sure that the items you've checked off above really get across your point about what a difference you've made, you haven't been specific enough yet. Saying that you've outsourced operations, for example, really doesn't describe the results. To get closer to an example of profitability, ask yourself "So what?" after each statement.

I outsourced the payroll operation.

So what?

So we didn't have to do it in-house any more.

So what?

So I was able to eliminate two positions and transfer a third person to an open requisition that I would have had to fill anyway. She preferred the new assignment, too.

So what?

So we saved nearly $100,000 in the first year alone, even deducting the cost of the payroll service. I freed up some space that another department could use, and we decreased our own headaches substantially. The employees don't really care about where their checks are coming from, as long as they come.

Bingo.

You just created a hook. A "hook" is a selling point that you can communicate quickly and clearly and that emphasizes results. The hook in the above example could be, "I analyzed and implemented an outsourcing program for the company that resulted in providing superior services to our employees at 40 percent of what we had been spending. What has been your experience with outsourcing programs?" Not only did you state your hook, you strategically followed up with an open-ended question on that topic to link its applicability to your target company. The conversation keeps going in the right direction.

By the way, hooks can come in other flavors, to mix a metaphor. Alex decided that he would use his current expertise (in resolving corporate SAP challenges) and create a new one from his international IT consulting skills (strategy for competing against outsourced, offshore IT firms that are gobbling up business) to differentiate himself from others. He created a leap-into-the-future hook that is more than a Sharp Skill. This is "skating to where the puck is going to be," as Wayne Gretzky would say. His hook for any professional IT consulting firm is, "I'm working on bringing IT consulting back to the U.S. from India/Ireland/Israel, etc. Should we talk?" Companies can't afford *not* to talk to him because he'll be creating a profit center for a company and himself. Oh, another flavor of hook is, "I know your mother." Works every time.

What are your hooks? Develop two showstoppers that you can drop into conversations, LinkedIn profiles, résumés, and Elevator Stories that will have your audience asking for more. Jack of all trades, master of two.

What Ifs

In case you're still tempted to downplay your own profitability, saying, "But it wasn't just me . . ."

- **What if I wasn't responsible for the final outcome?**
  Many people are responsible for a final outcome; few claim it. Can a company turn out a successful product or service without numerous people behind it? Own your part. It will emerge as, "I developed the prototype that went on to result in more than $5 million in new sales for the company in its first year." You're not claiming credit for the entire process, but you claim your part and share in the glory of the outcome.

- **What if the project was cancelled, and all of my work was lost?**
  This happens. It can be crushingly disappointing, but even in the best companies, avenues of research, product development, analysis, and investment are sometimes dropped. Describe what you did accomplish, and then stop the story at its peak. Though possibly incom-

plete, your hook is still valid. "I developed a new process for coating the boards that addressed some of the failures we were seeing in the field. It was the first time that anyone had been able to do that, and the VP of engineering was thrilled." You didn't mention that your division was sold before your idea was integrated into the product, but you tell them, of course, if they asked what happened. In the meantime, you've proven your competency.

- **What if I hate to brag?**
  That's the nice thing about telling a PAR story (see Strategy #1: Send Clear Signals or download the PAR form at www.thenewjobsecurity. com). You aren't bragging. You're telling a story. People typically talk in stories. Listen at your next social gathering and you'll hear them. People enjoy listening to stories. You're not talking about you. You're talking about results.

- **What if I'm not in job transition, but am currently employed?**
  So much the better. You can start building your arsenal of amazing accomplishments now. Guess when it pays off? At your next performance appraisal. If you don't normally get appraisals, ask for one. Track your results all year and you can set the agenda for the meeting. You're going to know things about your results that your boss doesn't have a clue about.

HOMEWORK

Track Your Results

Start a file on your computer or in a notebook, preferably one that is at your home. Record your results in it. Don't wait until you've achieved some major, earth-shattering feats or you won't have many entries. Sometimes surviving a day is quite an accomplishment. Stop taking things for granted; other people will value what you're ignoring.

Collect your accomplishments first, and then quantify them as much as you're able. A PAR story is an easy way to get started. If you're part of a large project, track the results of the whole project. Ask yourself "So what?" until your part is as close to the money as possible. The last sentence with the results is your hook.

List at least five ways that you have been profitable for companies in your career. End each example with a hook. Now you can fine-tune the results portions of your PAR stories so the hooks land the big fish.

THE "MUTUAL BENEFIT" PART OF MARKETING

After a lot of preparation, you're now ready for the mutual benefit part of marketing. This is where it gets fun.

It's About *Them*: Talking So Others Can Hear You

Okay, now that you have completed the whole circle, here comes what I promised you earlier in the chapter, one of the *most* critical concepts in your career management execution: *When you're talking with people, especially potential employers, where are your conversations focused? On the top side of the circle, or the bottom?*

This is product marketing at its best and makes a huge difference in your response rate. *You've identified the needs of your target market (the bottom side) and present the product (you) in terms of those needs, not yours.* Presenting yourself in terms of your market's needs may sound easy, but it's trickier than it looks. You have to do the thinking for your potential employers about what's in it for them to

> All your communications with potential employers should focus on *their* needs, on the bottom side of the circle.

make decisions in your favor. They're busy and aren't paying 100% attention. They may care that you aren't being paid fairly or that you've just been laid off from your last job or that you have a bad boss, but that isn't going to motivate them to hire you (or promote you, or give you a raise, or help you get a job in a different department). On the top of their minds is how they can put out the fires on their desk, be profitable this quarter, and meet their deadlines. Only by staying attuned to *their* needs will you motivate them.

In my seminars, when I discuss the critical nature of concentrating on the employers' needs, everybody agrees with me. However, our own needs still sneak back into our communications. Disciplining yourself to think and communicate on the bottom side takes practice, but you'll see results.

A Marketing Circle Quiz

Test yourself with the following four examples. Can you see how some of the following strategies emphasize the needs on the top side of the Marketing Circle (your needs), while the more successful ones focus on the bottom side (the employer's needs)?

- In a résumé, the objective reads: Challenging position in a growth-oriented company.
  Better objective: Senior executive position building global business through organic growth and acquisitions.

- During an interview, in response to "Tell me about yourself," you respond, "Well, I graduated from college in 1972, and I'll give you a summary of my work experience since then . . ."
  Better response: An Elevator Story (see page 31). Select the strengths that best coincide with the needs you believe they have and respond in two minutes, max.
  Best response: "I have more than fifteen years of experience doing (whatever it is they need that you do). So I don't bore you with my entire life history, would you like to tell me a little more about what

you're looking for in this position, and I'll tell you where we overlap?" You're getting them to talk first . . . a power tactic.

- During an interview with a biotech company, you're asked, "What sort of work have you been doing?" You respond, "I've been helping to develop the LR2000 for some time. As you may know, that, along with the Q2X work I've been doing, is going to be a big breakthrough in fiber optic technology." (The company you're talking with isn't in fiber optics.)
  Better response: "The work I've been doing sounds like it's very similar to some of the development work you're doing around the topical applications of XYZ. Am I correct in understanding that the compound's absorption is one of your main areas of interest? I can tell you about my work in that area." Forget the product names that are used in your old company and any vocabulary that your target market doesn't need (such as fiber optic, if that isn't their field). Use their vocabulary as much as possible. Emphasize sameness, not difference.

- When you're asked "What's your salary?" you respond "I've been making a hundred thousand a year, so need to stay there or higher."
  Better response: "I'm sure you pay competitively. What did you have in mind?" (See Strategy #5: Negotiate in Round Rooms for more info on negotiating.)

See the difference? The first example in each situation was from the top side of the circle, but the better and best responses moved them to the bottom side. By focusing on the bottom side of the circle, the better responses motivate your listener. There are few of us who aren't motivated by our own and our family's best interests. Those of us who aren't are already in religious orders. The secret, however, is that by meeting someone else's needs, you meet your own as well. This is marketing for mutual benefit: you end up getting what you're looking for by helping others reach their goals. The benefit is mutual . . . and done sincerely. (There's more on this in Strategy #4: Build Sustainable Networks.)

When someone does a favor for you, what do you want to do in return? It works both ways. As you build your relationships by demonstrating thoughtfulness, you're putting deposits in a bank for future withdrawal. You're accruing interest in the meantime, in all senses of the word. The help you offer now may have nothing to do with a job opening that you want. It may mean sending someone an article recommending a place to go fly-fishing since you've discovered that you share this interest. But you're building a relationship and helping someone else. You can meet people's needs directly or indirectly. Either way works.

- *A direct bottom side:* A potential employer is rolling out a new product in a month, but her director of media relations was just recruited away by another company. Given your background in advertising, you ask whether they'd like some help pulling together their promotional efforts in the interim. Note that you didn't ask for a commitment, you just offered to help. (See Strategy #3: Stop Looking for Jobs.) She's listening. She is in a corner and has to deliver.

    This same approach is golden at your current company. You can build relationships and your reputation anywhere in a company, including with your own boss, if you identify needs and respond to them. Be careful, though! You don't have much spare time, so be very strategic about where and whom you offer to help.

    In direct bottom sides, as well as with your résumé and all conversations with potential employers, it's safe to assume that profitability, or the path to it, is your underlying theme. Emphasizing ways to make an employer successful will have the ripple effect you want.

- *An indirect bottom side:* You and a potential employer discover that you both have seventeen-year-old daughters who are going through the college-selection process. After hearing about his daughter's interests, you discover that you went to one of her first-choice schools. You say, "No guarantees, but I'll see if I can help." You'll want to meet the kid first so you aren't recommending her blindly, losing credibility yourself and setting her up for potential failure if she isn't a fit. This gesture is a quadruple win: the employer, his daughter, your alma mater (because you only recommend kids that you honestly think will benefit them), and you, the Nice Person. Deposits in the bank. No strings or expectations attached.

- *An out-of-office bottom side:* I can't resist giving you an example of how to Market for Mutual Benefit in your personal relationships, too. Your spouse doesn't want to do something that you want to do, such as go to the theater. You know that your spouse loves to get together with another couple, however, so you see whether they are interested in joining you if you can get tickets and if your spouse agrees. You learn that tickets are available, then you ask your spouse whether he would like to go to the theater with the other couple before you buy or commit to anything. This is how you Market for Mutual Benefit. You defined the needs of the target market (your husband who likes to socialize with friends), and then presented the product (a night out) in terms of your spouse's needs. This works with teenagers, too.

How Do I Know What Their Needs Are?

Good question. It's hard to talk from the bottom side of the circle if you don't know what an employer's needs are. As President Bush (both of them) said, "Espionage is a dirty business." You won't actually be doing anything clandestine, but it's in your best interest to gather information about your target markets from multiple sources. If you depend on a company's annual report or their website, you're reading only what the company wants you to see. One of my clients discovered that the defense contractor that was aggressively courting him was being indicted for fraud. They'd never brought it up in the interviews, obviously, so if he hadn't done his homework, he might not have known to avoid them until it was too late.

How do you determine a company's needs? By reading and talking. On the reading side, you already know to use the Internet and your library. Sometimes a company's problems are spread all over the media or can be predicted by reading between the lines. Rapid growth rate or recent venture funding means that hiring will soon follow. In a recession or downturn, new regulations or stimulus programs from the government will need to be interpreted by the companies they affect, enforced by regulatory bodies, and then monitored for compliance and results. Hiring for these positions will occur at all levels. Sarbanes-Oxley created multiple jobs, as do government programs on both the public and private sides. Should you prefer hiring someone to dig up information for you, the professional association of researchers, the Association of Independent Information Professionals, is a resource. Doing research on your target's *competition* gets you extra M&Ms.

On the talking side, ask your friends and colleagues what they know about the companies that interest you. We'll get into this more with Strategy #3: Stop Looking for Jobs, but finding contacts in and around potential target companies is the best way to check out the reputations of the management team and the board, two groups that will determine your long-term well-being. You can research their backgrounds as well. This will help you establish what you have in common, such as going to the same undergraduate school or liking golf, which will come in handy for future conversations.

As you're doing your research, keep a list of the questions that occur to you about what's happening at the company. Their needs are not far behind. Why did the earnings slip for two quarters in a row? Will the product they're developing have a lot of competition? By doing your homework, you'll have a good idea about what their needs are, the bottom side of the Marketing Circle, before you ever talk to them.

A warning: When talking to an employer, don't state what you've learned in your research as a carved-in-stone fact. If you read that a mutual fund the financial services company you're targeting runs is doing poorly in the marketplace, address your concern in a question instead. "How are you thinking of responding to the anxiety in the marketplace about high-growth funds?" This typically works better than, "Wow! You really got trashed in the market last week." You won't trigger any defensiveness, you'll show that you know that everything you read isn't necessarily accurate (except for some career books), and you'll gain information from them. Well done.

This Is for Real, Folks

The satisfying thing about marketing for mutual benefit is that you start off wondering, "Is this some sort of game?" and end up realizing that you're truly helping others and helping yourself at the same time. Sounds corny, but it's habit forming. This is not a game, nor should you start helping others within your professional network if it feels fake or insincere. You should help others because you want to or you'll be frustrated when a favor isn't noticed or isn't repaid according to your timetable. Your motivation must come from inside. The need to help others doesn't quit when you land a job, either. This book is about career *management*, not just finding your next job.

"Where do I find the time?" you might ask. Good question. The answer is to look back at your Companies of Interest list. You can concentrate on helping a finite group of people with whom you want to develop relationships and then refer others to different resources. You're just not going to have the time to help everyone, but you can at least give them some alternatives. You'll get some ideas about how to do this, including Sixty-Second Networking, in Strategy #4: Build Sustainable Networks. It's doable. You Market for Mutual Benefit as you continue in your day-to-day work. As you supervise others, you motivate them by meeting their needs (the bottom side of their circles), such as letting them manage their schedules so they can do things like go to their kids' soccer games. They'll love you. When you leave a company, avoiding a meltdown will provide you with greater options in the future: references, networks, or even being rehired or consulting with your former employer. It happens all the time. Those are your benefits, or the top side of your circle. Their benefit is a peaceful transition, among other things. If you're recruited and need to turn down a company or search firm, try to give them the name of someone else who might work out and notify the other person that you did so. How many friends did you make with that transaction?

THE BOTTOM LINE

A satisfying and strategic by-product of marketing for mutual benefit is the way your reputation grows. When you make suggestions about how you can enhance someone else's profitability or help someone on a personal level, you'll gain much more than potential interest in you as a job applicant or promotable employee. You'll gain respect and recognition. You'll build trust because you took a risk on someone else's behalf. You've given something of yourself without expecting anything in return.

Of course, your kindnesses will be repaid in many ways. Not only will your short-term responses grow, but people you have helped will tell other people about you as well. A good reputation builds repeat business and promotions. The moral of this story is to *start now*. "Pay it forward" now. Start building the relationships and connections that will support you throughout your career now. Answer the needs of selected people within your target markets. You are no longer asking people to help you to fix your problem; you have regained your creativity and your dignity and taken control of your career. You're putting your safety net into place. That's essential to your New Job Security.

STRATEGY #3

STOP LOOKING FOR JOBS

"To try to make the future is highly risky. It is less risky, however, than not to try to make it."
—PETER DRUCKER

When professionals describe the pain they feel after having been rejected or, worse yet, ignored by multiple companies, their discouragement is palpable. "I was a perfect fit for their opening and I didn't even hear back from them." Or, "After the initial screening by the search firm, they wouldn't even return my calls." Or, "I applied for a promotion in another part of my company, didn't get it, and now my boss has cut me out of the information loop."

There's an easy solution to feeling like roadkill. Stop looking for jobs.

People are always taken aback when I say this. "How can I? Job openings are real, and they're currently available. That's where the income, security, and opportunities are." Like Willie Sutton, who chose to rob banks because "that's where they keep the money," professionals know that a company is where the jobs are kept, and so job listings or search firms must be the best way in. This is true sometimes, but not always. Posted job openings, regardless of whether they're listed on a company's website, on a job board, internally, or with a search firm, are just a fraction of what's happening. The same goes for search firms. Not all companies can afford or choose to pay others to do their searches for them. You can have it all. You can have relationships with search firms, know how to draw *them* to *you*, respond to the few ads that are worth your time, and then use the majority of your time to hang around "where they keep the money," addressing company problems that are just waiting for you to solve them.

SELF-ABUSE: JOB POSTINGS AND SEARCH FIRMS

When you're in transition, there's a natural tendency to go to the Internet to comb for openings on job boards and ask search firms for help first. They're obvious sources of approved, funded opportunities where you can shortcut this job search and get to work quickly, right? Not necessarily. They're actually forms of self-abuse. If you can see the openings, everyone else can, too. If you can respond quickly, everyone else can, too. If you're mass mailing search firms, everyone else is, too. They're the most competitive sources for job openings that you can find and, bluntly said, neither channel to the job market is geared to help you. Their goal is to help the employer. Follow the money. They can be a source of abuse or disappointment for you. Once you understand the motivations of search firms and the employers behind the apparent job openings and realize that they aren't responding to *any* candidate (okay, a slight exaggeration) and that it's nothing personal, it gets easier.

Before we talk about how to stop looking for jobs, however, we still need to talk about the best way to approach job listings and search firms, because they *are* distribution channels to the overall category of "work to be done." (Remember the "P" for placement in the four P's of marketing?) They advertise only a fraction of the available jobs, however. You don't want to totally ignore these visible jobs, but you will want to spend your time where the work is likely to be: in the networks

How (a prestigious university's) Alumni Get Jobs

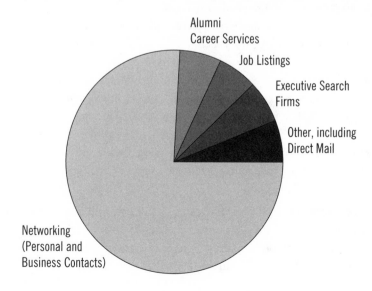

Alumni
Career Services

Job Listings

Executive Search
Firms

Other, including
Direct Mail

Networking
(Personal and
Business Contacts)

> Job listings may get 3 percent of your time, search firms, 10 to 15 percent.

that lead to job creation. The best campaigns use a combination of approaches or distribution channels, varying the amount of energy spent on each according to the odds of it paying off. Job listings may get 3 percent of your time, search firms, 10 to 15 percent. You'll know the right percentages for you as your campaign progresses, but the chart on the previous page gives you some guidelines. After looking at these traditional distribution channels, is sitting in front of the computer all day responding to openings and cold calling search firms the best use of your limited time? You don't have to ignore them, but do it in your off hours. There are more creative approaches with less competition and higher yields.

Job Postings: Recruiters Are A-Twitter

Now that you're forewarned, let's look at how to leverage the time you *do* spend responding to job openings. Boy, talk about career whiplash. How jobs are advertised has changed dramatically since the last edition of this book. Remember sitting with the Sunday morning paper and a cup of coffee going over the "help wanted" section? You're showing your age if you do. There are still help wanted ads in newspapers, but not many, and they don't accurately represent openings that are available to the public any longer. The distribution methods have changed completely in the past five years. Job openings may be listed on job boards, on a company's website, in various publications, through aggregators or professional associations, or elsewhere. They're scattered all over. Use that to your advantage.

Aggregators How do you use chaos to your advantage? Use aggregators. If you're using them and other people aren't, you're making better use of your time than your competition is. Aggregators search millions of jobs from thousands of job boards, help wanted ads, newspapers, websites, and publications within seconds to find the key words you're looking for. Blair Heavey, a senior executive of multiple successful Internet companies, including Open Market and Be Free, reports that the two most helpful job aggregators on the Web are www.simplyhire.com and www.indeed.com. Susan Leahy, a PR guru, says that they don't capture 100 percent of the jobs all of the time, but they make the best use of the time that you're willing to spend on publicly listed openings.

Job Boards, Including Craigslist Be selective. Aggregators will take care of many of these listings for you. Although Monster.com is still the largest job search engine in the world, competition is coming in from the side. Social networks (see following) are offering free alternatives to company recruiters, and they're growing all the time. According to www.wallstreetjournal.com on October 20, 2009, "Relying solely on job-board listings, which have been shrinking, isn't enough these days. There were roughly 3.3 million jobs advertised online in September of 2009, compared with 4.4 million in September 2008 and 4.7 million in September 2007 according to the Conference Board." Craigslist is luring away entry- to mid-level listings from higher-priced boards as well, but as traffic to their site increases, so does your competition for their openings.

There's another dark side to search engines in addition to their corporate clients drifting to cheaper alternatives. How do you want companies to perceive you? In other words, what is your brand? If your résumé is posted on all of the search engines and boards and is easy for people to find, not only will every bottom-feeder try to sell you something, but search firms with mid- to executive-level job openings won't be too intrigued. If you're easy to find, why did their client need to pay them thousands of dollars for you? The middle ground is closed networks such as ExecuNet, where members pay to belong, or LinkedIn, when you set up your profile and include industry "hot buttons," but don't talk about looking for a job, so passive recruiters can find you . . . or both.

Social Networks The action is moving over to social networks, such as LinkedIn, Facebook, and Twitter in the United States; Xing in Germany; and Viadeo in France. This isn't going to be a primer on social websites; that's another book. We *will*, however, talk about the implications for finding jobs on them in this chapter, and then discuss how you might use them to build your reputation and relationships later in Strategy #4: Build Sustainable Networks.

All recruiters see social networks as great sources of "passive candidates," that is, people who aren't looking for jobs, as well as a way to spread the word about less confidential openings quickly and economically. A recruiter in Washington, D.C., needed five licensed social workers in Puerto Rico, according to a June 2009 article published by the Society for Human Resource Management (SHRM). "Using #jobangels and #jobs on Twitter, she tweeted the opportunity which was retweeted by her 1000 followers. In 48 hours, she had filled three of the jobs." Things move fast.

Advertising by companies doing hiring and job openings pop up frequently, either overtly or covertly, on LinkedIn and Twitter, and increasingly on Facebook. An example of an overt listing would be a direct posting or advertisement by a recruiter in an interest group on LinkedIn; an example of a covert job opening would be trolling by all levels of search firms for the passive candidates who work in companies of interest ("Let's mine this site for everyone who works at Genzyme"). Ellen Mahoney, vice president of human resources at Harvard Business School, reports that they're now successfully using passive recruiting on social networking sites for senior-level jobs. "What your interests are, what groups you're in, the leadership you demonstrate in your profile all speak to your qualities as a candidate," she says. Heads up. You've just gotten The Message from the employer's perspective. You'll need an impressive professional profile on LinkedIn with key words embedded regardless of your job status since you're always on view. Facebook is more casual, but take off the pictures that you don't want your boss/recruiters/mother to see. You'd be amazed at the negative decisions and rescinded employment offers that have happened because of unthinking comments, criticisms, and photos that people post on their Facebook profiles. The top three peeves described by SHRM about postings on social networking sites are 1) indications of illegal drug use, 2) negative discussions of former or current employers, and 3) info in your profile that contradicts your résumé. You have been duly warned.

"Social networks aren't for anyone over fifty," you might be saying. "Executives at my level don't use them." Au contraire. Do Bill Gates, Vinod Khosla, or John McCain count? How about the companies that use social networking sites? SHRM reports that 27 percent of the searches companies do on these sites are at the executive level. How about LinkedIn's partner in France, Apec, finding an additional partner because they wanted access to employees at a lower level than your average LinkedIn member? And the average age of the users is increasing on all of these sites every day. Knowing how to use the technology and following or linking with some other respected executives who are already on them show that you're savvy and technologically current . . . two points that offset the "he/she's too old for this work" stereotype. Being visible allows firms to find you for senior-level and board positions and allows you to help others before you need help in return. If you are so famous that you want no one to get through, put up your privacy settings. Hey, it used to be so easy to get through to Barack Obama.

Corporate Websites Debra Cohen, Ph.D., chief knowledge officer at SHRM and the source of a lot of the information in this section, reports that many companies only accept applications online now. "They want to capture data in a single location to automate the hiring process as much as possible, even with senior-level employees. You can talk to whomever you'd like in a company, but you're not a candidate until you talk to HR" due to compliance and reporting requirements. A new trend is for companies to have a ".jobs" extension after their company names online so you can go directly to the career section of their websites (www.coke.jobs, www.ibm.jobs, www.microsoft.jobs). Aggregators will save you some of the preliminary research, but you'll want to check out the company website as you're drawing up keywords to put in your résumé and zooming in on specific companies.

If you're responding to job postings, regardless of the source, just be aware of a couple of inconvenient truths. First, just because you see a job opening doesn't mean that it's for real. What may look like a straightforward request for skills could actually be a cover for other objectives. A company might want to demonstrate to the federal government department responsible for immigration services that they need a green card for a current, highly skilled employee by showing that no one else in an applicant pool is as well qualified. A company might have a highly desirable internal applicant for an opening and place an ad as a confirmation that they have the right person. They may be trying to build their database and collection of résumés in case of turnover. A blind ad (that is, one with no company name listed) could even be placed by a consulting company hired to find out what their client would need to pay if they recruited for the job described in the posting; in other words, they're conducting a salary survey. You've probably seen "salary history must be included to be considered" as you've skimmed through the ads.

> The most important part of responding to a job opening is putting your network into action if you're really interested in the position.

There isn't a salary survey behind every request, obviously, but you don't have to play a company's game by answering the salary question. (See Strategy #5: Negotiate in Round Rooms for more information.)

Second, given the overwhelming volume of responses to publicly posted jobs, the most qualified people may not be asked to interview not because they're not worthy, but because the human resources screener fell asleep before she finished reading all the résumés or performing the key word searches (ah, human frailty enters into the selection process more than we want to know). You're better off if you assume that people are not going to get back to you and build it in as a move in a chess game rather than taking it personally.

The rule of thumb is to go ahead and respond, always to a specific name that you can track down if it isn't listed, but don't put your heart in the envelope or the email. Usually you can track down either the person who would be making the hiring decision from the company's website, a search engine, a directory or database in the library, or LinkedIn. Having a generic response for ads in your computer that you can pull up when needed and modify slightly, if the opening is worth the effort, will save you time and limit your emotional investment. Just promise me that you won't become discouraged if you don't hear back, even though you're perfect for the opening. Keeping yourself motivated is the key, and odds are high that the lack of a response has nothing to do with you. Just do end runs, limit the time you spend on responses, or develop strategies that draw *them* to *you* (see Strategy #4: Build Sustainable Networks).

If you're really, really serious about an opening, use my "pincers" approach. It takes more time and uses up some "chits" with your network, so don't pull it out for every little ad that flits across your screen. The pincers approach is a two-tiered response: responding as instructed to the posting so your résumé is in the "good do-bee" pile, and networking into the company at the same time. (LinkedIn could be helpful here.) This shows that you follow the rules, but it also keeps you from getting lost in a stack on a desk in human resources. If you can contact someone inside the company, ask, "What is it like to work there? Who is handling the search? What's the management team like? What do you think of the products?" This could start building an internal champion. You haven't asked her to put in a good word for you yet, but see how the conversation goes. She might volunteer to do so, in which case you can graciously accept, assuming that her name and reputation is one that you'd like to have representing you within the company. If she doesn't volunteer and you're comfortable asking, say, "Can I get you to put in a good word for me with [the hiring manager]?" She'll typically be happy to do so.

Finding the Right Recruiters If you're in a mid-level or entry-level position, you may want to include contingency or contract recruiters as part of your overall marketing plan. Remember, they're *not* working for you, nor are the executive search firms, so they're not there to help you find the right job for *you*. As noted above, contingency recruiters work with higher volumes and payment upon filling vacancies, so they're incentivized to move quickly. Deciding if their opening is the best fit is *your* job.

Do your due diligence and find a handful of recruiters that you trust, and then use all of the approaches we'll go over here to build relationships and help them. How do you find them? Ask colleagues, check out Peter Weddle's multiple helpful online guides to recruiters, and start following some recruiter blogs. Jeff Moore, a recruiter at Google, says, "The advantage of following blogs before participating is that you get to know the protocols and norms, so you will start off with the right impression. Now's a good time to begin." Susan Hand, a savvy recruiter in the technology space, recommends the professional associations of ERE (www.ere.net) and the Association of Employment Professionals (AOEP; www.aoep.com) as places to find her colleagues. She says, "They are groups with progressive recruiters that offer free time to the industry . . . I prefer AOEP for its more personalized approach and smaller membership, but ERE is great as well." Her tip about going to a recruiter's own profile and checking out recommendations they've received from hiring managers and candidates so you can identify the good ones is golden.

Search Firms: Being Known Before You're Needed

I have heard literally hundreds of professionals say, "I've let the search firms know that I'm out here. They have openings at the level that I want, and they carry real, ready-to-be-filled jobs. I'll see what happens." Search firms sound like they're out there to help you, to match your skills with jobs that they have in their inventory. They're not. If you're thinking that search firms will help shorten your search, you're going to be disappointed.

Follow the money (what's on the bottom side of their Marketing Circle). Who pays the search firms? Companies filling openings pay search firms to find *exactly* what they are looking for. That means that search firms are working for the *companies*, not the job seeker. The search firm considers the company that hired them a client; you're the candidate. Retained firms operate at the higher ends of the salary scale and are paid regardless of a search's outcome. Contingency firms work at the lower end of the salary scale and are paid only if the position is filled. Some firms may do both, in different divisions. Know which category any search firm that you might work with is in, as well as its reputation, because they are motivated differently and behave differently. Your response to them should be different, too. There are books, such as John Lucht's *Rites of Passage at $100,000 to $1 Million+* (Viceroy Press, 2000), that describe the categories in more detail. Just don't bother with the direct mailing to the search firms that some of these books recommend unless you have nothing better to do. You'd rather differentiate yourself by networking in rather than by being a cold call that comes in a mail bag (or email) along with the junk mail and thousands of your competitors. Retained firms will do whatever they can to meet client expectations, and to meet them quickly. If you're not an exact match with a position's specifications, a major search firm typically will not consider you. They're not being discriminatory or unfair or mean; they just don't get paid for going "out of spec," or presenting candidates (you) who don't exactly match the client's

> If you are changing functions or industries, a search firm will have a hard time presenting you to a company.

specifications. If the client asks for a yellow duck with an orange bill, and you are a white duck with an orange bill, you may still make the right noises and have webbed feet, but their client won't be happy.

Stuart Sadick, partner and global sector lead of Consulting and Advisory Services at Heidrick & Struggles, reports that presenting all of the "round pegs and round holes" is their first priority and this sometimes eliminates going outside of the client's industry. Looking for work through your network is a better bet than using a search firm if you're not a "round-round." Rather than wasting energy bemoaning the unfairness of search firms not helping you with your functional or industry change, understand for whom they are working. They're anticipating and meeting customer needs as quickly as possible, which explains why they don't get back to you a lot of the time.

Including search firms as part of your strategy is fine. Since 10 to 15 percent of professionals find their jobs through search firms, you don't want to ignore them. But you also don't want to spend 60 to 70 percent of your time on them. Job seekers think that they're making progress on their search when they send off résumés to search firms, not realizing that the odds of a "hit" on *any* direct mail are around 1 percent, according to Dave Opton of ExecuNet, source of ongoing marketplace research, and during a slow time it could be lower than that. Boom times are a little easier, but it's always important to *be known before you're needed*. Stay tuned for how to *help* search firms and get them to pay attention to you rather than asking them to help *you* in direct mailings . . . not a good use of your time.

The Big Five search firms, the five executive-level and international search firms that handle some of the most senior-level searches in the world, are:

- Heidrick & Struggles, www.heidrick.com
- Korn/Ferry International, www.kornferry.com
- Russell Reynolds Associates, www.russellreynolds.com
- SpencerStuart, www.spencerstuart.com
- Egon Zehnder International, www.ezi.com

These top firms typically manage searches for jobs with a compensation of $250,000 or more. As you can imagine, these firms are the hardest to penetrate on a cold-call basis because their openings are highly sought after and the process is typically confidential. I've had partners from all five firms speak at the executive networking sessions that I ran for ExecuNet (a great resource described in Strategy #4: Build Sustainable Networks). All the partners emphasize the importance of building relationships with them. They are not a quick phone call you make when you want a job. If the goal is being known before you're needed, what's going to make them put you in their BlackBerries? Building your reputation is the best answer (see the last chapter, Conclusion: You Don't Have One), but being helpful to them by 1) acting as a source, and 2) referring them to companies that might need to conduct a search will get you points as well.

There are two ways to find the search firms that are the best fit with your "vertical" (that is, your industry) and your experience: word of mouth and lists. Finding out about search firms through word-of-mouth referrals from their corporate clients who retain them to conduct searches trumps all other methods. Since search firms don't want to bite the hands that feed them, they will typically talk to "friends and family" of their clients, regardless of how busy they are, so find the handshakes that lead you to the right people. Try out this conversation next time you're chatting informally with friends or colleagues:

"Have you worked with any search firms that you've found particularly helpful?"

If they answer "Yes," say, "They sound like they did a good job for you. Was there someone that you worked with in the firm whom you would recommend?"

If they volunteer a name, say, "What I'd like to do is call that person, use your name, then ask if we can talk. They may be conducting some other searches that would be a fit. Would that be okay?"

If you get the green light, say, "Thanks. I'll see whether I can help them with referrals for some of their other searches." (Better yet, "The company I used to be with is looking for a marketing VP, and I may be able to make an introduction." Or, "I was just talking to a company that is looking for a COO. I'll tell them about it.") "I'll let you know what happens."

See how you just accomplished multiple goals at the same time? You:

- Moved from cold calling a search firm to networking into it.

- Got a referral from a client of the search firm. This makes a huge difference in how much attention the search firm will pay when you call.

- Took the pressure off your networking contact. By offering to help the search firm with referrals or market information, you gave your friend a selling point to use if he's talking with the search firm about you. You're actually doing the firm a favor, using the bottom side of the Marketing Circle to level the playing field, so your friend feels good about putting you two together.

- Maintained control. You asked to use your friend's name and make the connection yourself. Now you can move at your own pace. You give up control when someone else makes the call for you. (They may mean well but never get around to it.)

You can see that getting a response either to a job posting that you're serious about or from a search firm often comes back to networking. Handshakes will move you from the "B" or "C" pile into the "A" group, and maybe—just maybe— into that BlackBerry.

What Search Firms Want George Davis is a global managing partner on the Executive Committee of Egon Zehnder International, one of the five prestigious firms mentioned above, and co-leader of the Board/CEO Practice. In other words, listen up. You're about to get the truth from the source. In a presentation he gave to one of my ExecuNet meetings, George outlined exactly how senior-level job seekers should approach search firms. He recommended the following (the parenthetical statements are mine):

1. Don't depend on recruiters. They are only one channel to the job market.

2. Do your homework on search firms:

   • Is the company contingency or retained? (Does the company get paid to put someone in the slot, or does the long-term relationship matter?)

   • Is the company a boutique, large, or a single shingle? (A boutique is a small firm that typically specializes in a particular industry or function. A large firm will have multiple offices, often international, and cover various industries and functions. A single shingle is a sole practitioner. Some in each category are very good, and some aren't. Check them out.)

   • Which partner and office should you contact? (Contact the one that handles your specific industry in your geographic area of interest.)

3. In your communications to recruiters:

   • Give them some context. Be precise. (Tell them what companies you've worked for. They need to know the scale of your responsibilities up front. Tell them your title and major responsibilities. Quantitative results are appreciated. Don't ramble or you'll lose them. Your Elevator Story will work well here.)

   • Don't be creative. Fact-based, chronological résumés are easier to digest.

   • Sending résumés by email is preferred now.

   • Provide proof of your skills and relevant industry experience.

- Don't expect an invitation to a meeting after the first date. (They typically will meet with you only when they are screening you as a candidate for a current search.)

- Remember the golden rule: How can you help them? Be proactive. Do you have referrals for them? (Do you know other candidates that might fit their searches or other companies that might benefit by using a search firm?)

- Relationships take time. Touch base.

- Don't use a cutesy opening paragraph to stand out from the crowd. "I delete immediately," Davis says. (You *do* stand out from the crowd—by showing poor business judgment.)

- *Get a personal referral if you want your résumé to be read.* (The emphasis is all his and underlines just what I've said above. Search firms are like any other part of your network, only more harried, especially during a recession. Make cold calls at your own peril.)

He's right. And these expectations apply to all of the major search firms. You now have insider information.

You've Been Digitized   Over the past several years technology has profoundly changed how search firms work, and it would be hard not to notice. When was the last time you sent someone a paper résumé? Don't bother. "We never throw away paper résumés," Stuart Sadick jokes. "We recycle them all." Electronic ones are much more efficient when employers or recruiters want to perform key word searches, so hear that as reinforcement of the way that I propose you design your résumé in Strategy #1: Send Clear Signals. You have to do the research to determine what competencies your markets want to see and give them back their key words in boldface in your résumé. Both the search firms and the actual employers will be visually or electronically skimming your resume for these words.

What about the cover letter that you're emailing with your résumé? Dave Opton of ExecuNet knows the answer cold from his employer and search firm research: keep it short and focused. Period. Anything that smacks of a form letter or that requires scrolling down (or even paying attention) to read is history.

A consistent theme that emerged in a lot of the interviews I did is *control*. Neither the companies nor the senior-level recruiters want there to be broad-based knowledge of most of their openings. Once the information gets out to the public, they are overwhelmed with responses, and it becomes more difficult for them to find the quality candidates that they could find more easily through word of mouth, their BlackBerries, highly targeted or blind ads, database research (sign up for the ones that the Big Five executive search firms often have on their websites if you're qualified), or passive recruiting on LinkedIn and, to a lesser extent, Facebook. Yes, this is a trend enabled by technology and its unlimited boundaries, but it's also the age-old habit of networking. Didn't Eve tell Adam what the serpent wanted?

Let's get started on some action steps and homework for job postings and search firms, and then we'll see how *not* looking for publicly posted jobs will dramatically broaden your options.

HOMEWORK

Job Postings and Search Firms

1. Job Postings: If you've responded to job openings in the past several months, regardless of their source, pull them out and add the companies to your Companies of Interest list if they are still of interest to you. You may want to network into some non–decision makers in these companies to gather information. (We'll discuss this more in Strategy #4: Build Sustainable Networks.) The job you applied for may still be open, the company may have additional needs, or the new hire may know of some other jobs that she ended up turning down.

2. Search Firms: Pick out five to seven search firms or recruiters that look interesting and relevant to your search. Identify each firm's specialist in your industry and then try to network into that person. How can you help him or her?

THE BIRTH OF A JOB

To give you more options than waiting for job postings, recruiters, or search firms to surface—in other words, *reacting* to the marketplace—let's look at how jobs are created. This is truly the main course: how to find meaningful work not by looking for jobs but by *creating* them. A job's boundaries are artificial; they change all the time. How a company divides work in order to produce its products and services must evolve continually because market needs, technology, and economic conditions can shift overnight, changing the demands on the company. Have you looked at the job description for your current job lately? What you're doing has changed from what you signed on for. You can take advantage of these changes to create the type of work that you'd like to do by tapping into the job formation process earlier and not waiting for approved, funded, highly competitive job openings to appear.

Let's look at how jobs are created to see why getting involved earlier can give you more interesting choices. Jobs don't just "exist" when a company is started; they are born when there are problems or opportunities. How many employees did Hewlett-Packard have when it was started? Sears, Roebuck and Co.? Harley-Davidson? Your company has just won a new contract; you have a deadline and aren't sure whether you can make it; you're not getting accurate, timely information for decision making; you don't have enough business. There are millions of problems every day in every operation, and good times can create them as well as bad times. These pressures may not lead to someone thinking, "I need to get some more help here" so much as "How in the world am I going to handle all of this?" Can you tell where I'm headed?

Traditionally, internal pressure mounts to the point where it becomes clear that additional help is needed. Then a manager, or a smart administrative assistant who plants the seed, realizes that it's time to get serious and start the formal hiring process. This is not something they embrace joyfully; they have other things to do, but there's no choice. More help has become essential. In order to actually hire someone, many steps are needed. Someone needs to take responsibility for shepherding the job through the system. Job descriptions, consensus with other employees, budgeting, approvals, and timing all need to be worked out. Once a job becomes official, it's often posted internally first. Then, and only in a small portion of cases, is it advertised publicly on a job board or trade magazine or through a search firm. If you worked in human resources, would you really want to post a job publicly? It costs a lot, brings in a lot of garbage, and gets people mad at you for not responding to them. Posting a large, expensive want ad is closer to an act of desperation than a standard operating procedure.

If a company does place an ad, someone's in-box will now be overwhelmed. The company will call some people in to interview, but often those who looked good on the screen won't be as impressive in person. Back to the database and the key word scanner. Eventually the company will find a candidate, check references, and make an offer. The offer will be negotiated and finally accepted. You've probably been on the company's side of the table before. Does the process normally work in this smooth, linear fashion? No; it's messy and it's slow, primarily because it must be worked into someone's already full schedule. To the job seeker, the process and the response time seems even slower.

A timeline of the hiring process would fall into a bell-shaped curve. See how an approved job opening is visible to the world outside the company for just a small portion of time, if at all? Look at the slopes on either side of the curve: one leads up to the job's approval, funding, and advertisement, and the other side leads down to the final selection. *You can approach a job from either side of the bell curve.*

The Birth of a Job

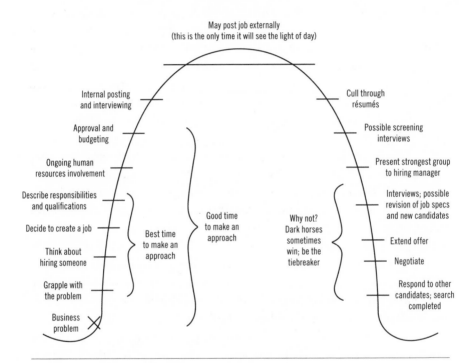

May post job externally
(this is the only time it will see the light of day)

Internal posting
and interviewing

Approval and
budgeting

Ongoing human
resources involvement

Describe responsibilities
and qualifications

Decide to create a job

Think about
hiring someone

Grapple with
the problem

Business
problem

Best time
to make an
approach

Good time
to make an
approach

Why not?
Dark horses
sometimes
win; be the
tiebreaker

Cull through
résumés

Possible screening
interviews

Present strongest group
to hiring manager

Interviews; possible
revision of job specs
and new candidates

Extend offer

Negotiate

Respond to other
candidates; search
completed

The right side of the slope leading to a candidate's selection is fairly straightforward. A company will be heavy into the interviewing mode after having collected as many reasonable applications as possible, both internally and externally. If you approach a decision maker at this stage, you might hear, "I'm sorry we didn't meet sooner. We're just in the process of selecting our finalists." Or, "We're not accepting any more applicants now." If you know they haven't hired anyone yet, you don't have to quit trying entirely, however. Ever seen a house purchase fall through at the end? You might be the white knight that can break a deadlock or put the deal back together. You might rescue a company after another candidate's references didn't check out, after a candidate accepted another offer, or after a candidate's spouse couldn't relocate. The company really doesn't want to reread all those résumés again. I've conducted job searches and dreaded going back through the electronic or paper piles. You may have had to face the black hole of more résumé screening, too. Now, as a job seeker, you can provide a solution by helping them get back to solving the problems that were creating the job in the first place.

UNCOVER THEIR NEEDS

The left side of the slope leading from the birth of a job to the internal posting is fertile ground for creating meaningful work. Whether you want to grow within your current company or move to a new venue, this is the slope on which jobs are created. The point is to stop looking for a job and start looking for problems to be solved, and then become the solution.

Jobs are finite. Problems are infinite. Why not go after the infinite pool? If you can identify where the pressure points are in a company and position yourself as someone with solutions, you've just created a new job for yourself. What's particularly fun is that you're choosing a problem that you find interesting, then shaping your response to it in concert with a potential boss. You may be able to influence the responsibilities and level of a job rather than fit yourself into an already established pigeonhole. I've had clients not only write their own job descriptions but also create their own compensation plans at major companies. How thoughtful of the client to save the busy boss so much time. You could be coming close to creating your ideal working conditions, or as ideal as they can get.

In addition to shaping a job to your satisfaction, do you know what else this strategy does? *It eliminates the competition.* That's a big deal. Since this isn't a formal, posted job opening, the company hasn't developed a profile of the ideal candidate. They haven't pulled in hundreds of résumés from people who can walk on water. They aren't thinking that you're a square peg trying to fit into their round hole because they haven't even bored the hole yet. You're solving their problems without wasting their time and money on an extensive (or expensive) search. Good for you. Maybe some portion of what you saved them will show up in your pocket, especially if you bring this up during negotiations.

> Stop looking for jobs.
> Start looking for problems
> to be solved.

Isn't this great? You're not sitting around any more waiting for some semi-relevant jobs to be posted. You're taking the initiative, targeting companies and industries that are of interest, identifying their problems, and then packaging yourself as a solution. This strategy gives you much more control over your career. Carol used this approach of looking for problems rather than job openings to test out three different companies before she selected the one she wanted.

Carol was a very successful product manager for a large, nationwide insurance firm when she was "restructured." Although angry about her fate, she didn't lose much time looking back. After identifying four target markets for potential employment that would fit with her experience, interests, and goals, she started researching the marketplace to determine its needs.

After doing her due diligence and learning which firms were growing, who still needed help, which decision makers she should meet, and what the potential was in her various markets, she narrowed the field. Two of her original four markets had the profile she wanted.

Using her network, she got the handshakes with the decision makers that she needed to meet in her chosen markets. Carol was always clear on Strategy #1: Send Clear Signals. She knew her value to other companies, and she could describe how she would make a company successful. Carol was, and is, passionate about her work, her products, and developing a company (and herself, as a result). People loved this confidence and focus.

Within two months Carol had landed three contract assignments with three different companies. She listened to their needs and carved out jobs ranging in content from improving a distribution network and product development to managing a start-up sales operation, all within time parameters that she specified.

Carol knew that this wasn't a long-term situation. She nearly killed herself working three jobs for a couple of months until she knew which companies to eliminate. They all offered her full-time jobs. She selected the best fit, and she is now the corporate vice president of a growing operation.

Carol is a great example of how successful you can be not looking for formal, approved jobs. She uncovered a company's problems, and then presented her skill set as the solution.

Important point: Don't say, "It sounds like you'll want to build strategic alliances to minimize your up-front costs in product development. Why don't we create a job here? I could take responsibility for it and be your first vice president of business development." This statement starts off fine, but the last two sentences are completely on the top side of the Marketing Circle, focusing on your needs instead of theirs. Take the emphasis off job creation and talk about results. You'll be hard to resist.

Do say, "It sounds like you'll want to build strategic alliances to minimize your up-front costs in product development. I have some specific companies in mind that might be worth considering as alliance partners. Would you like to get started?"

They'll be salivating. You focused on their needs, the bottom side of the circle, and demonstrated that you can start solving their problems immediately, a minor investment considering the potential returns. Your objective is to treat the incidentals of creating a job as a minor sidebar to getting started on solving their problems and improving their results.

You also used a strategy I call "dangling a carrot," based on the proverbial way to get a donkey to move forward. Tie a carrot to a string, hang the string from the end of a long stick, and then dangle the carrot in front of the donkey. In this case, corporate results are the carrot, and you want to keep the employer moving forward. The carrot you dangled was that you "have some specific companies in mind that might be worth considering as alliance partners," meaning you have names and relationships already in place. What you *didn't* do, however, was tell the employer all your ideas. *You aren't hired yet. Don't give away all of your carrots.*

There are plenty of unscrupulous employers who interview high-quality talent or ask consulting companies to invest a lot of time in proposals, and then decide not to go through with the hiring or the project. Granted, there are often perfectly honest, acceptable reasons why they don't, but you shouldn't give them all of your ideas anyway. Reserve some of your inspirations, connections, and relationships until after you are hired. Remember the risk mentioned earlier, when the employer is wondering, "Why buy the cow when the milk is so cheap?"

You don't have to work three contracts simultaneously, as Carol did, to see which company is the best fit, but, like dating several people before getting married, working for all three companies meant she knew which management team and industry offered the most long-term potential before she settled down. It's sometimes hard to tell true chemistry by interviews alone, when everyone is on their best behavior.

Look for the Pain

Good news! When predicting target company and market needs to create jobs, you have plenty of tools at your disposal. Doing the "reading and talking" work in How Do I Know What Their Needs Are? at the end of the prior chapter will get you started. The other piece of good news is that if you'd like to grow in your current company, you have insider information. Decide how you can help make your company more successful by selecting the problem that you'd like to work on, then stepping forward with a proposal. Since people rarely take the initiative to create major solutions and/or take on more work, you'll influence your reputation right there. If the answer is "yes," you'll expand your relationships, your reputation, and your skills in the process. Should you want to move up in your operations job, for example, ask your boss if you could take a look at reducing average product cost. If you can develop a process that reduces costs without sacrificing quality, not only will you make a name for yourself within your company, but you will have a notch in your belt should you decide to leave.

If you're in transition, you'll have to work from the outside to identify the pain that potential employers feel. It's not hard if you study your target markets, since most companies in each industry group will be feeling some of the same pain. If you want to change your industry or function, identifying needs and getting to know the people looking for solutions in your *new* market is essential. These searches require networking even more than your typical round hole–round peg searches (staying in the same industry and function), and you'll want to be clear about why your square peg status adds value. "When new industries are in high growth modes, they seek talent from existing industries to speed their development. You need to be sure that you can be found and are building a peer network that includes people well positioned" to bring new information in your direction, according to ExecuNet's 2009 *Executive Job Market Intelligence Report*. As you become well versed in the vocabulary, relationships, and latest problems of your new industry and function, you can start to make yourself look like a round peg—a very important transformation. Finding the pain gets easier when you ask open-ended questions in casual conversations, and when you track trends, you're on top of big generators of work that will turn into jobs.

Ask "Where Does It Hurt?"

Asking people what they see as the problems in various industries makes for fascinating conversation. You can do it as social chitchat, with your colleagues, with friends, or with big cheeses. Anytime, anywhere. Everyone has an opinion. You're conducting informational interviews without people knowing it, and they'll have a receptive audience for their viewpoints. The following three types of questions are for use in general social situations; refer to Strategy #4: Build Sustainable Networks for more questions better suited to informational interviews. Learning to ask the right questions is an important part of tracking trends, which in turn drives job creation. You'll know when you've hit upon the right question when you spark helpful information in response. Many times I've heard executives blame others for not being helpful. Upon examination, it was the questions they were asking that were at fault. They weren't easy enough to answer.

Always having a "cocktail party question" at the tip of your tongue for informal situations can help you grow; it's easier to think of one ahead of time than to create it on the fly. These are the questions that will start interesting conversations in casual, conversational, social settings and elicit information about industry concerns. They focus on the other person's industry, and ideally they overlap with your function.

GENERAL

"What do you know about Company X?"

"Laura, you've been selling to Company X for a while. What are they like as a customer?"

"Al, do I understand correctly that you've been a Company X customer for years? Has this worked well for you?" (Coming into a meeting with customer feedback is especially powerful. Keep the names of the customers confidential, however.)

INDUSTRY PLUS ECONOMY

"What's going to happen to microelectronics, given the recent economic changes?" (This is very broad. Tailor your question to what's been happening in the economy.)

RECENT ADVANCE PLUS INDUSTRY NEED

"How is rapid throughput screening affecting your drug development pipeline?"

There are a couple of points to consider before you plunge in:

- Don't press too far in a social situation. If you've just met someone, or have run into a distant acquaintance on the soccer field or at church, it may not be appropriate to stay on a heavy topic for too long. Besides, you'd rather talk to them in a work setting where you can gather environmental networking and cultural information as well as learn about potential business problems. If things start to get interesting, ask whether they have a business card on them and if you can call them at their office. In the meantime, switch back to a lighter topic, like the goal their daughter just made.

- What do you do with the information once you have it? Each person that you talk to about the mutual fund (or manufacturing, or electronics, or whatever) industry will have her own opinion. Helpful people will tell you exactly what's happening and what you should be doing. Thank them, then take it all with a grain of salt. It's just like résumé feedback. If you base your actions on what each person tells you, you will be knee-jerking both your résumé and your analysis of problems and needs in your industries forever. Look for recurring themes and form your own opinions. That's part of what makes you valuable.

The themes that you identify will not only outline a company's needs (the bottom side of their Marketing Circle), but they also will allow you to ask increasingly sophisticated questions about the nature of these problems. If you're changing functions or industries, start using the new vocabulary and ideas you're collecting to ask more penetrating questions. "How's the new health care program affecting your department?" evolves into "How have you decided upon the best encryption systems for your medical records?" You're on your way to becoming a round peg.

TRACK THE TRENDS: BEFRIENDING GOOGLE AND THE MEDIA TO CREATE WORK

Another way to identify a company's needs, or the early stages of them, is to scan the information that passes in front of you with a whole new perspective: "What's changing?" You're not jumping wildly into different areas of research; you're analyzing what is going on around you and how it is affecting your profession, industry, and organization. Shape these changes into questions. "What are you doing about the new restrictions on executive compensation?" asks a human resources professional about a trend in his profession (he happens to be an expert in compensation). "Do you think that different quality controls should be introduced into manufacturing operations outsourced to other countries?" is a question that reflects an industry trend. "What sort of features can differentiate our smart phone from the latest iPhone?" is one that multiple telecom organizations continue to ask. This is important work and makes for stimulating conversation with colleagues. You're doing market research. You're doing trend analysis.

The Power of Trends

Why is tracking trends important? Your future lies there. If you want to direct your career instead of just reacting like a pinball to what other people plan for you, you'll need to stay informed about shifts in business in general and in your area in particular. You can't afford to ignore this. The engineering support people still doing drafting with pencil and paper mentioned in Strategy #1: Send Clear Signals were let go all at once because they were obsolete. If they had kept track of trends, they wouldn't have been caught flat-footed, without the right skills, in a competitive marketplace.

If you want to stay in control of your career, *don't expect your company to track trends for you.* Companies should track industry trends, and the better ones do, but good career management means that you are making your own conclusions about how the trends affect you. Your company is not tuning in to what works best for you as an individual. You can't afford to wait for them to take action. You have to know what's going on in your field to protect yourself. Staying well informed on an ongoing basis means knowing:

- What skills are important for the work you want to be doing?

- Who is the competition? What are they doing that's so good? That isn't so good?

- What's happening on a global basis, and how will it affect your profession, industry, and company? This includes evolutions in technology.

- What's happening on a local basis with business trends, companies moving into town, promotions in other companies, contracts awarded, business restructurings, and so on?

- Who are the major thought leaders in your field, and what are they saying?

Does tracking trends sound like more work to do? Think of it as an enjoyable necessity, like a wonderful meal. It's intellectually stimulating to be in front of the pack and be thinking not only about what problems are emerging, but about the best way to respond to them. You're connecting dots that others aren't even seeing. You're the visionary leader.

> Don't expect your company to track trends for you.

Where to Find Trends

What are your sources of information? Do you read the daily news, the *Wall Street Journal,* business magazines, trade magazines, professional association publications, and relevant websites (you can even request that updates on specific topics be sent to you every day)? TV and radio count, too; along with the Web, they are the fastest-breaking sources of information. Do you ask leading questions of your network? Choose some of the following sources and ask some of the following questions to consistently stay on top of what's going on:

- Read general news or business publications such as *Business Week,* the *Wall Street Journal, The Economist, Barron's,* and *The Harvard Business Review.* Staying informed of world events as well as business events will let you know the coming pressure points. This is more than *reading* the news. It's projecting, "What does this event mean for us (in manufacturing, financial services)?" You'll be considering outcomes other people aren't, predicting where work will be created, and eliminating blindsides of "sudden" market changes.

- Read publications in your profession such as *Banker and Tradesman, Lawyers Weekly USA, IEEE, JAMA,* and *HR Magazine.* If you aren't sure what they are, ask senior-level people in your market research meetings about their preferences for publications and professional associations. Read these journals. Go to their meetings. On a national level, what topics are in the table of contents and on the program's agenda? Those are usually hot buttons.

- Read publications in your industry such as *The Chronicle of Higher Education, Retailing Today,* and *Advertising Age.* These will give you a feeling for trends that will affect your competition and your company and result in job creation or elimination, not to mention corporate success. Ask different people the same question about how an event will affect your industry. If their thinking confirms yours, you may be on to something. Shape your ideas into trend questions when talking to decision makers.

- Predict trends within companies of interest. Look up the accounting and legal firms of your target companies in directories such as *Standard and Poor's*. If you know the CPA or lawyer managing the account, you may get some feedback that is not "public information." Read your target company's (biased) website and what the media is writing about your target company. Check the Internet, use InfoTrac at your library, or do key word searches on the archives on a business magazine's website. These don't always show up on Google.

- Check out business research websites, such as www.hoovers.com, www.valueline.com, www.google.com/finance, www.vault.com, and www.factiva.com. They can give you comparative research about competition and industry rankings.

What's the best way to stay informed without using up too much of your time? Given the glut of information these days, this requires some strategy. Think of arranging "two-fers" (such as going to social media seminars to stay ahead while taking a potential customer with you), "no-brainers" (your home web page could be the *Wall Street Journal* or another news source, so you'll see breaking news without thinking), or "plants" (people who are sworn to email you whenever something hot happens in their area, and you reciprocate). Important: This is not a one-time assignment. Staying in touch with life outside your current or future company is an ongoing assignment. Becoming a news junkie has its rewards.

What are you looking for when you're gathering information? You're looking for change. Change creates opportunity. "Microsoft 7 could give economy boost" is a headline that should make your ears perk up if you're in hardware or software or sell, install, train, or maintain Windows products. Ideally, you knew earlier that it was coming and initiated discussions with target companies before there are headlines that will be turning into job openings on Monster.com. What you may downplay as your "working knowledge" of a new operating system could be "expertise" as far as other people are concerned. You're in front of a trend.

Even when there's a disaster, the change is making someone money. The October 3, 2009, issue of *The Economist* (page 82) points out twice as many firms jump from industry laggards to leaders during a recession and that the Depression created conditions that allowed Revlon, Hewlett-Packard, DuPont, Procter & Gamble, Polaroid, Pepperidge Farm, and others to be born or to create dramatic growth. In the recession of 2009, three groups of winners were identified: 1) established giants with cash and sound management, 2) companies with a record of innovation, and 3) companies that repositioned themselves. "You can't save your way out of a recession; you have to invest your way out," according to Craig Barrett, Intel's former CEO. That's the type of thinking that will allow you to grow if you're on the team. That's the type of leadership you deserve. Find it or create it yourself.

Once you start looking for change instead of job openings, your horizons are unlimited. As one client said, "I can hardly get through reading the news anymore. I'm seeing so many more leads than I used to."

HOMEWORK

Track Your Trends

List your three to four top target markets. You can transfer them from the ones you listed in Strategy #2: Market for Mutual Benefit. For each market, list trends that are happening either within it or within a specific company in that industry. Are there ways that you could take advantage of these trends to benefit your target companies?

PACKAGE YOUR TIME: NOT USING THE "J" WORD (JOB) TOO EARLY

What type of work do you want to create—full-time, part-time, consulting, retained, or contract? You don't know yet. You might have a preference, but that's a hidden agenda for now because it's on the top side of the Marketing Circle. Your main priority now is to get employers hooked, to convince them that *you're* the solution to some of their challenges. Keep the conversations focused on results and outcomes. Once they're engaged, you can suggest ways to package your time. Propose what's in the *company's* best interests. If you're having a conversation about problems to be solved, not job openings, and you both agree that the new product needs a new marketing brochure, that's a project. If what's needed is designing the marketing strategy behind a product line, however, that's a different story. You may use one work style to get into a company, then move to another once you're in and more firmly entrenched. Going from consulting to full time or vice versa is not unusual: try before you buy and you might just become so valuable that the company can't afford to lose you.

The main point is not to jump to the "J" word, *job,* too soon. Job seekers have a tendency to chase a job or "opportunity" from the beginning, when a company is "not hiring" or "doesn't have a job in your area" and to forget about the advantage of getting the camel's nose in the tent. I've worked with people who are consistently hired during recessions, hiring freezes, acquisitions, and other "low yield" times because they're uncovering problems to be solved first, then worrying about that "little procedural part" of the formal hiring process after the sale is closed. When an employer knows that he doesn't have any "approved requisitions" or budget for new employees, using the "J" word early on can shut down a conversation prematurely. Wait until both of you agree that there's a problem that you both want to solve, and then decide the best way to package it.

You'll find that there are more ways you can work with a company now than there were ten years ago. Although a full-time, on-site employee is still the norm, there are other interesting models as well. In *The Age of Unreason* (Harvard Business School Press, 1990), Charles Handy foreshadowed this trend when he said, "Eighty percent of the value [of a company] is carried out by people who are not inside their organization. . . . All nonessential work, work which could be done by someone else, is therefore sensibly contracted out to people who make a specialty of it and who should, in theory, be able to do it better for less cost." What is your specialty? Once you have a decision maker talking about her needs, you'll know how to package your time and your specialty to meet her needs (and yours). Remember? You're the jack of all trades, master of two. Those two can land you consulting gigs as well as build your reputation as an expert when you're employed full-time.

"The book you're working on sounds really interesting," a former editor of a medical journal told an author. "I'll bet that it's going to take a lot of time to research your topic." The editor liked doing research on a freelance basis, and she was open to full-time employment as well. See how she was leading the witness? If the author said, "No, I have most of it done already," it would remain an interesting, friendly conversation. If he said, "Yes, I'm swamped," she could ask, "Do you want me to free up some time for you? I might be able to give you a hand." The discussion would stay on his side of the circle. You leave a graceful exit for a "no" so neither of you feels awkward, which is important for long-term relationships.

Because of the new ways to work with a company, you no longer have to wait for an approved, funded, full-time job offer to get started working. In fact, you may be more likely to end up with that full-time offer if you remove the immediate pressure of a hiring decision and just start getting the work done. Make sure that you're both clear on the scope and duration of your work before you plunge into some of these creative alternatives. These are some of the various models you'll see in the workplace:

- **Temp to Perm.** You may start off in a temporary position then move to a permanent one (what a euphemism—who's permanent these days?). After a defined period as a temporary employee (possibly on a consulting or project basis; be clear about what you're signing on for), you may become a full-time employee. The trial period works both ways: you're evaluating them as much as they're evaluating you, a level playing field.

- **Full-Time for the Short Term.** You may start off working full-time— they're in a crunch and need a major quality initiative installed in manufacturing by the end of the year—then back off to consulting for them in the first or second quarter. The fact that you will cut back your time later should be clear up front. You may want to get some cash flow going while you're in transition, or you may prefer working in spurts. Your challenge will be to continue your campaign while someone else wants you 120 percent of the time. If you don't keep your campaign alive while consulting, you'll be starting from scratch at the end of the company's crunch.

- **Interim.** Closely related to the above, a variable-load structure is an interim arrangement. You'll see it frequently with CFOs. You work full-time for a specified duration and then you're done. This could be until the company finds the next CFO or until they complete a specific transaction. Some professionals are interim executives for a living. If you can live with the marketing part of it, the flexibility and financial rewards can make it worthwhile. Executive Interim Management, www.eim.com, does executive-level interim searches for companies, but beware, the supply of candidates always exceeds the demand.

- **Short-Term Consulting or Project Assignments.** You may carve out projects or consulting assignments with no interest in regular employment. These projects should be well defined and have measurable outcomes. Otherwise, they could drag on forever and the client could ask you to include additional assignments at no cost (known as "project creep") without adding any value for you. Beware of putting all your time into an assignment that's going to end shortly. Protect your time and yourself by continuing to stay in touch with the marketplace.

You may create a consulting arrangement because you like being self-employed and want to be a free agent, as Daniel H. Pink labeled independent consultants in *Free Agent Nation* (Warner Books, 2002). Marion McGovern even founded a company around brokering independent consultants called M Squared (www.msquared.com). In *A New Brand of Expertise* (Butterworth Heinemann, 2001), McGovern states, "When we ask our consultants why they decide to hang out a shingle and go into business for themselves, the overwhelming desire is for control. . . . Whether it is control over where they work, like Curtis [Flood, the major league baseball player who refused to be traded to Cleveland], their hours or their vacations, overwhelmingly, it is a desire to make work fit into their lives and not vice versa." McGovern works with experts who choose consulting as their function rather than with professionals who consult between jobs. Her concepts feed into Handy's prediction that a company won't need to hire non-core employees, but will use outside specialists to cover these functions. Maybe you would like to be one.

You may decide to consult as part of a short-term strategy. Jack did this masterfully. An experienced president and general manager, he turned down a full-time offer from a company, but he asked if he could work out something on a consulting basis. He offered to give them 50 percent of his time so both sides could evaluate whether they had a long-term fit while he was relieving them of some short-term pressures. That was the honest message that he presented to the company, but Jack wasn't sold yet on the management team being the right fit for him. He managed two lucrative consulting assignments while he evaluated both management teams, and he kept his campaign going at a reduced rate. When he tells a company "no," he'll try to refer them to a potential replacement. This part of his professional behavior contributes to his reputation and continued referrals. Jack didn't want to be a consultant for the long term. He used it as a means to an end and as a way to buy time.

- **Part-Time.** Beware of this title. Many part-time positions include benefits. That's the good news. The bad news is that work under this heading typically pays a fraction of work called "consulting," even though the actual content may be similar. "Part-time" can also mean full-time work for a finite period (more of a project-type assignment), or less than forty hours a week for an extended period. Many part-time jobs are repetitive, lower-level work and pay on an hourly basis. That doesn't mean they are *bad* jobs; they're an essential part of a company's operation. Work part-time if you like the job content and the overall working arrangement, but try to predict if it will affect your brand and know what you're signing up for.

- **Create Your Own Combination.** This is the fun part about the workplace now. There are so many work models that you can often negotiate what you want *after* you've hooked them. (See Strategy #5: Negotiate in Round Rooms for more on this.) If you're currently employed, you have the liberty of proposing different ways to deliver your work. Just stay on the bottom side of the Marketing Circle and focus on the needs of your boss and your company ("more cost effec- tive," "free up some space," "research shows higher productivity with telecommuting").

You're not discussing any of these options with potential employers yet. Right now, you're just trying to engage the decision maker, to make him or her realize that you are *the* person they have to have. There are direct parallels with fly-fishing. You have cast your fly into the stream by starting the conversation with the company. You are now "presenting the bait" by showing that you under- stand what they're doing and can make or save them money. You haven't decided if you're going to panfry or grill your catch yet; it's too early. Just get your tar- get to nibble. Once the big fish accepts the bait and agrees that, yes, they really need you to step in and get them through the end of the fiscal year, you feel the tug on the line. When the employer says something on the order of, "Let's get started," you set the hook. "How would it work if we set this up as a consulting arrangement for the first ninety days? You'd have more flexibility, time to decide if we're a fit, and maybe even a little less paperwork up front so we can get to work faster." You'll get into compensation (discussed in Strategy #5: Negotiate in Round Rooms) shortly.

"VOLUNTEER" OPPORTUNITIES

Creating a job by helping a company without a specific job opening in front of you sounds like volunteer work, doesn't it? You don't want to introduce volunteering too early in the conversation, however, unless you want the work for the pure joy of it. We'll talk about establishing *value* first, because that's what you want to do. Establishing your value shows a company how you can make or save them money. They are more likely to offer compensation if you can show that you're going to bring in more than you would cost. You're not going to use the "V" (volunteer) word too early because you value your time, but there are occasions when volunteering might be a good strategy. Here are some guidelines to use if you sense that a potential employer is happy to have your ideas but doesn't have, or won't spend, the money to make you official.

- First, don't start creating a job just anywhere. Be selective. Approach the top three or four firms that look like they have potential, and then narrow down your list as you gather feedback from the decision makers. You may be willing to volunteer some consulting time for your top choice, but don't overcommit your most limited resource— time. It's hard to do consulting work for more than one company at a time and still carry on the rest of your job search. Be choosy.

- There are only a handful of reasons for taking the risk of working pro bono. If the company name would brand you and you can use it to increase your credibility, if you would acquire a new skill for your campaign, if it would restore your confidence, if it would let you make an industry jump that would be hard to do otherwise, or if it would give you connections with some important people in your field, then give away some of your time. Ten to fifteen hours per week is plenty.

- Set a time limit. "I'll get you off the ground with this portion of the project, then we'll sit down in two months and evaluate where we are. Does that work for you?" Otherwise, you could be sucked into a volunteer's black hole.

- Create an agenda that describes what the company needs and how you can help in the future while working on your current project. Drop some hints. "Do you want to take a look at how you could set up that compensation program when I get done here? I see several ways that would avoid the high fixed overhead on these salaries. I'll put it on the agenda for us to go over." You're not inventing work; you're spotting needs and responding to them. By the time you get through with your project, you will have built a new job description.

GROW WITHIN YOUR WORK: CREATING ANSWERS WITHIN YOUR CURRENT COMPANY

You're already building your New Job Security. You know the importance of being clear about your direction, keeping on top of changes by tracking trends, and compiling materials (résumé, bio, Companies of Interest list, PAR stories) to articulate your accomplishments gracefully. You know how to increase your options by solving problems rather than concentrating on official job openings. It's time to identify a model for the long haul—one that sustains and nurtures you as you work—as well as the let's-get-the-next-job phase. Once we look at how you can continue to keep yourself in touch and competitive while you're working, we'll come back to look at how this "systems" approach sets you up for shorter transitions and the Job Pipeline.

Directing your own growth as a professional is the ongoing, fun challenge that drives your career throughout your entire working life. Continually learning and improving will keep your engine tuned for when you want to speed up, make fast maneuvers, or, eventually, slow down. *You* decide how you will grow. The four main ways to grow are:

- Develop Yourself
- Reshape Your Current Job
- Uncover Job Openings
- Create Jobs

These methods all exist within your current company. You can start planning ways to develop yourself right now. When you leave your company, only the second concept, reshaping your current job, goes away. The other three ways to grow are not only available to you, they are essential. Using all these pistons simultaneously will give you greater power and more choices. Let's talk about how to develop yourself, reshape your current job, uncover job openings, and create jobs within your current company first. If you're currently in transition, look for a boss and a corporate culture that will support this growth.

Develop Yourself

If you are satisfied with your current position but aren't doing anything to challenge yourself, you could be getting a little stale. Complacency can creep in quietly, so congratulate yourself for recognizing it and responding. Don't wait for your company to take care of you. Decide what will keep you at the forefront of your function and profession and what you truly enjoy doing, then go do it. This might mean completing coursework, learning new software, selecting a mentor, leading a project—you decide what behaviors will move you toward mastery of your field, build your reputation, and benefit your company at the same time. If you can persuade your boss that attending the annual meeting of your professional association will improve your performance, let you collect some competitive information, and raise the profile of your company, you've just used the bottom side of his Marketing Circle to present a win-win proposal. Maybe he'll pay for the trip. If not, do it on your own time. It's like showing up for the first time at your new health club. You've thought about getting in shape for a long time. Now you're actually going to invest in yourself and follow through. New behaviors will start changing your outcomes. Some of your plans could overlap with reshaping your current job. So what shape would you like to be?

Reshape Your Current Job

If you basically like your work, your boss, and your organization but you feel like you've reached a dead end, reshaping your current job may be worth consideration. Maybe you find that the same stack of papers sits forever on your desk, or the same items are perpetually on your to-do list, or you avoid going to certain meetings because they take you away from something you would rather be doing. Face it. You don't like doing those things you're putting off. Is there a way, *in the company's best interest,* that you could shift your job content so it would be more meaningful for you? You might even do better work if you were more excited about it. In the following example, Iris shifts her job content while building external relationships to increase her alternatives.

Iris was the director of distance learning at a large West Coast university. With a doctorate in educational technology and extensive experience in a field that was just taking off, Iris was in demand. Her current job, however, was proving unbearable. With a combination of multiple administrative duties running a rapidly growing program and teaching responsibilities that kept her constantly online (that's how distance learning works), she rarely came up for air. When she did, she would find that her less busy colleagues were undermining her success, working on taking over some of her responsibilities or claiming her progress as theirs. Not a pretty scene. Was there jealousy? Perhaps. Iris didn't have time to figure it out.

Iris had been with her university for many years and had multiple supporters. If there was ever a time to start reshaping her work to get rid of some of her day-to-day responsibilities and to set herself up to do the type of work she loved, this was it. She found funding for some administrative help that relieved her of some of her routine chores, delegated some responses to emails to save more time, and then headed straight for developing her professional skills and reputation. The two reinforce one another. She did some consulting work with schools to train teachers in technology. She was a guest speaker at a national professional association meeting, and she lectured in other countries. As she grew, so did her reputation and outside connections. The internal squabbles faded as she moved beyond the reach of her colleagues, both by shifting her job description to get rid of some of the more repetitive work and by increasing external validation that muted some internal politics.

Iris not only reshaped her current job, she also opened up many more possibilities for herself. She was spending more time on the creative, thought-provoking work that she loved and was also attracting outside attention that reignited her university's appreciation of her.

Iris's career management machine is purring. She has positioned herself internally and externally so she has options and is constantly enhancing her competitive strengths. You don't have to be looking for an outside job to develop this momentum. The expertise and reputation that you need to be considered a hot commodity benefits you whether you want to grow in your current organization or in another one, so start now. You might be so pleased with your redesigned position that you decide to keep it.

Gaining the world's recognition of your competence doesn't need to mean moving up the ladder. You may not want to climb it. Growth can mean increasing your expertise within your function and profession, including mentoring others in your area. Some companies have dual career tracks so you don't have to move up into management to continue your professional or financial growth. Technical expertise is critical to a company's maintaining its competitive edge and should be nurtured in all respects. As Beverly Kaye, a noted organizational consultant, says, "Up is not the only way." If you want to reshape your job to encompass more of your passion, consider how you're going to help make the company more profitable by doing so and your boss just might listen.

Before restructuring your current job, you need to anticipate any possible objections. How could you change your job so it would be a win-win? What portion of your job could you give to someone else, or outsource, so you would have more time to concentrate on what's important to both you and the company? Caela Farren, CEO of MasteryWorks, the organizational career management consulting firm, suggests that you give the 20 percent of the work that you don't like to someone else who would see it as a developmental opportunity. How will this benefit the company? Will they save money? Develop bench strength? Make better use of staff time because duplication of work is being eliminated? Determine what will motivate the decision makers, and you'll often get your way. Their motivation usually centers around profitability (surprise, surprise).

You may have a shot at restructuring your current job because you are proposing to give away some of your work in order to take on a killer opportunity for the company. Stepping into an acting position, managing a project or transaction, or turning around a crisis are all finite jobs that you could take on for a change of pace, after you've proposed how your current job will be covered. You'll need to decide up front whether you'll want your old (or upgraded) job back so that can be part of your planning and negotiations. With a finite job, you can build skills that support your career direction, you won't be getting stale, and you will promote your reputation by taking risks and succeeding. Just make sure that you have a path back out of the project. Avoid getting caught in this great-job-but-what-am-I-going-to-do-now trap. Plan ahead.

Uncover Job Openings

If you can't grow any further within your current job, it may be time to look around. Maybe your boss doesn't encourage change, your division is being closed, or you have acquired and practiced all the skills that you need for the next level and the next level just isn't open and isn't going to be in the foreseeable future. Is there any work within the company that you'd like to tackle before you consider leaving? An additional path to growing within your work is to uncover a current or emerging opening in a different department or division. You can network into a position or volunteer to help a new group on a minor project so they can see your talent firsthand. You'll know how to handle your current boss . . . explain how it meets her needs or the bottom side of her Marketing Circle. A good boss will support employees who go after more responsible positions outside their current area or who lend a hand on a project; an employee's continued success reflects well on the boss's reputation. If your boss doesn't support your efforts outside her area, keep a lower profile so you can get to know others while still doing your job back home. You're not going to go far with that boss anyway.

People often stay with their current company even when they don't like it, usually for economic or security reasons. Ideally, you're with a company that has a mission you believe in, that has a logical long-range vision of how it will compete and grow in its industry and the overall economy, and has a management team that you would follow into battle. (You do, daily.) If this is the case, you'll undoubtedly be able to grow within your company, even though your present department or function may not give you the options you seek.

Create Jobs

We've already discussed the fourth way to grow professionally—to create jobs. This is the process of spotting needs and addressing them. Combine all four methods of professional development—developing yourself, reshaping your current job, uncovering existing jobs, and creating jobs—and you'll see that it's not a binary system, it's a continuum. It's not *work* versus *no work*; instead, it's about deciding what you need to continue to grow and how to achieve it so that everyone benefits.

Growing within your work is the engine that moves your career forward. You'll want to maintain that engine on an ongoing basis. Most of the time, you'll be expanding your skills within the context of your current job, keeping yourself competitive when you're employed rather than waiting until you're in transition to start making yourself marketable. Odds are, however, that sooner or later you will be in transition, whether it's your choice or the company's. So what's next?

What's next is to create jobs and uncover existing jobs to maximize your alternatives. You know how to do both. You know how to identify needs to create jobs and to use ads, search firms, and networking to uncover existing ones. You can do this confidentially, while you're still employed, or openly, when you're in transition. You can do this within your company and within your target markets. The efforts should be *simultaneous* rather than sequential. "Wow," you say. "How can I find interesting job openings and create jobs at the same time? Isn't that a giant time commitment?" Well, which takes longer: applying for existing jobs and either finding out you didn't get them or are being ignored for much longer than you thought humanly possible and then having to start over on the next round of job openings, or taking the initiative to create something that you enjoy doing without competition, while spending 3 percent of your time (the response rate for ads) on applying for existing jobs?

> Working on creating new jobs at the same time that you are applying for existing jobs yields the fastest results.

Creating jobs and uncovering existing ones are mutually reinforcing activities, too. You'll find out about both—existing jobs and needs and connections within companies—during your ongoing career networking (for more on this, see Strategy #4: Build Sustainable Networks).

STUFF YOUR JOB PIPELINE

Have you ever seen an annual report of a biotech company? Often there will be a picture of a pipeline in it. It's a common metaphor in biotech because those who fund the companies are well aware of the importance of having drugs in all stages of development, from initial discovery to the final stages of clinical trials. If a biotech company doesn't have multiple drugs in different stages simultaneously, the elimination of one drug due to unpromising results, which happens frequently, can cause the company and its investors significant financial trouble. A giant hole has been created in revenues. I've been there to do the outplacement after this happens. Also, if drug development is all clumped in the same stage, for example, all work is in the initial discovery phase, then resources—time, talent, and facilities—are pushed past the breaking point. The gap until revenues are generated is too great for the company to tolerate. The concept of a pipeline will work for your search as well. You can analyze where the gaps in your campaign are and shift your activity, just as a company can. To get a visual idea of how creating a job and applying for an existing job can work together, take a look at the Job Pipeline.

The Job Pipeline

Additional blank, printable copies of this Job Pipeline exercise can be found at www.thenewjobsecurity.com.

The goal is to keep your Job Pipeline filled. Activity within your Job Pipeline has the potential of developing into real jobs. You're working through the phases of gaining an employer's interest, setting your hooks, and negotiating offers. Things are happening. It takes some work to move inside of it, however. Let's see how the Job Pipeline can give structure to your job campaign.

Filling the Job Pipeline

Early in your job campaign, you're outside the Job Pipeline because you're not ready to approach potential employers yet. You're defining your goals, defining who needs what you have to offer, then communicating your value and skills to others through your résumé and conversations. This is part of Strategy #1: Send Clear Signals. You want to be the one who decides where you're headed after doing your research. Start gathering information as we talked about in Strategy #1: Send Clear Signals and Strategy #2: Market for Mutual Benefit, and then move toward the major decision makers as your clarity and connections start to gel.

Once your direction and message are clear, you're ready to set up meetings with decision makers. When applying for an existing job, it's fairly straightforward. You have uncovered a job opening and moved to the beginning of the Job Pipeline.

When creating a job, you may not know if you are generating interest until you actually see sparks of life from the listener. You will be meeting with people frequently as you gather information. How do you know which meeting will click? Often you don't, except that one may have more potential because of the *level* of the person you're meeting or your *interest* in the company. Always be prepared, as if there were a real job opening, making sure that you're conversant in the company's issues and market challenges. You are always listening for actual needs in meetings, and you can position yourself as an experienced problem solver (if you are) should you find some. That will definitely move you into the pipeline.

Your objective at the end of an initial meeting is to land the next meeting, not to get a job offer. Just move the process forward in the Job Pipeline. At the end of the first meeting, questions like, "Do you want to pencil in some time next week to get together? I can have some ideas together for you by then. What's your schedule like?" work well. It's a soft sell. "Pencil in" is nonthreatening, but it gets you on the calendar.

The middle stage of the Job Pipeline, both for creating a job and applying for an existing job, is to get the employer committed to you. This does not involve hard selling on your part. I often see professionals who want a job so much that they spend their precious time with the decision maker *talking*—about themselves, about how many exciting things they've done, about their last company.

That's a hard sell. By the way, your goal is to spend 40 percent of your time talking versus 60 percent listening during an interview. Surprised? Sales professionals working with potential customers use even higher standards, often spending 70 percent of their time listening. Pushing the product (you) is the natural tendency when you truly want something, but just the opposite approach is more effective, especially at senior levels: inquiry works better than advocacy, and asking questions is more effective than selling. Let the decision maker have center stage. Not only is it a stroke to their egos to have their opinions solicited, but most decision makers think interviews go better when they do most of the talking! The real reason you want them to do most of the talking, however, is to glean the information in their heads and learn how to best present yourself. If you can get them to talk about their needs before you launch into your own background, you can customize your presentation. Otherwise you're firing your cannon before you know where the target is. You could spend a lot of time telling them how you've brilliantly integrated an acquisition when that is the furthest thing from their mind. You just made yourself a square peg, regardless of how relevant the rest of your skills are. Listen and ask first; talk later.

The middle stage, therefore, involves asking open-ended questions (more about this in Strategy #4: Build Sustainable Networks), pinpointing the need, throwing in some quick examples of how you've addressed these issues before, and then steering the conversation into concepts rather than detail. Asking "How are you going to respond to the new Dell product introduction?" will engage your decision maker in something he enjoys thinking about. It lets him see that you know what's going on with the competition and sets you up for a quick anecdote about how you dead-ended someone else's new product with a superior one of your own. This approach is much better than, "How many days a week would I be on the road?" That question belongs at the end of the Job Pipeline, when they're committed to you. In the middle stage of the Job Pipeline, you're setting the chemistry for your relationship and showing that you not only have a grasp of their issues but know solutions to them.

When you reach the final stage of the Job Pipeline, you should subtly start to make your presence felt. If you're applying for an existing job, you may still have competition at this point, so you want to be helpful rather than presumptive. Ask to meet with the people you'd be supervising, provide unsolicited testimonials, or volunteer to contribute to a project they're working on or to go on a sales call with one of their people. You're increasing your presence in the company and increasing the number of people you know, "broadening your base in the account," as salespeople would say. Did you see the *Seinfeld* episode when everyone in one company thought Kramer worked there because he kept showing up?

Becoming more involved during the final stage of the Job Pipeline shows people firsthand that you're the best choice.

Evenly Distribute Your Job Pipeline

When you first start looking for a new job, you're delighted with *anything* that goes into your Job Pipeline. "Yes!! A meeting that might actually lead to something! Hurray!" You're right to give yourself a pat on the back, but don't relax yet. Keep doing your research, keep initiating conversations with new companies, and keep adding relationships to your Job Pipeline. The strongest job campaigns have activity in all phases of the Job Pipeline—the beginning, middle, and end—to ensure that you have *options* coming out of it.

As your campaign progresses, map the stages you're in with different companies and see where you need to increase activity. Remember to give yourself a break when you're first starting to research companies. You're not going to have anything in the pipeline yet. The following Job Pipeline reflects approximately three months worth of work for Richard, an environmental services professional.

Where would you say that Richard needs to shore up his campaign? You can see that he has a lot going on outside of his Job Pipeline, he is doing well with

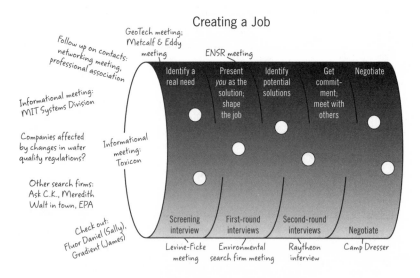

The Job Pipeline

initial interviews, and he has one initiative that is in the final stages. You can also see that Richard is running into some challenges converting initial meetings into second- and third-round interviews. The Job Pipeline can also be used as a diagnostic tool that shows you where you may need to tweak your approach or redistribute your time.

The Job Pipeline Has Holes In It

Notice how this is a perforated pipeline, with holes all along its surface? You already know what's coming out of those holes, don't you? Some companies that you've been considering. It happens. You're going to eliminate them some of the time, and they'll eliminate you, too. That's the main reason that you need to make sure that your Job Pipeline is always being fed, even when you think it's full. Things have a way of disappearing, and you want to make sure that some results are coming out of the other end. Analyze companies that have slipped out of the Job Pipeline, and then put them in your tickler file to revisit in a month, when the dust has settled. Are they still viable options? Or have they had their funding cut and moved onto something else? Remember when you were on the other side of the desk, how finding a new person was important but not a raging fire that you had to stomp out right away? If you haven't experienced an outright rejection, circle back around later. In the meantime, keep your pipeline filled so you have choices when you want them.

It Ain't Over Until It's Over

When things get serious with a company, when you're actually into negotiations about your terms of employment, what is your reaction to starting any new initiatives? Frequently I hear, "I'm not going to follow up on this lead yet because my interviews with Global are going well. I want to see if this one plays out before I start anything new." Red alert. It may save you some psychic energy now not to start anything new, but you've just increased the amount of pain you'll feel and the length of time you'll spend searching later should Global not come through or you not like their compensation package. You may have to leave some dollars on the table, too, since you'll have no leverage in your negotiations with Global if you don't have any other alternatives.

Deals have been known to fall apart at the end. Some of the most awkward cases I've seen are people being told on their first day of work that something happened and their offer is being rescinded (maybe there is no funding, the company was acquired, or an internal executive is moving back from Kuala Lumpur). So sorry. Thanks anyway. Now you have to restart your campaign. Some companies hire zealously and then have to stave off starting dates for new employees when business drops. They ask new hires not to come to work for them right away but to spend six to twelve months doing something else, often with financial incentives attached. Some companies offer partial pay for doing community service work in the interim. Talk about the land of the living dead. A year off might be personally fulfilling, but you will have lost professional momentum.

The point is to keep priming the Job Pipeline until you've started your job. Do you have to keep plugging new companies in at the same rate as before you started negotiations with a good company? You can slow down the rate if you are in negotiations with several companies, but not just one. Those midstage companies that haven't quite made up their minds become increasingly important now. They are your safety net if your first choices don't materialize. Don't neglect nurturing them in the heat of negotiations. You want to have more than one company competing for your attention at the end of the Job Pipeline. This serves multiple purposes, primarily clarifying your choice and providing leverage to increase your compensation. The challenge is to get the offers to come out at the same time. Strategy #5: Negotiate in Round Rooms will give you ideas about how to get your offers on the table simultaneously while still maintaining good relationships with the companies that you'll eventually turn down (one of your better problems).

THE BOTTOM LINE

Wow. Look at how far you've come in this chapter alone. You're really in the thick of things now and creating your own New Job Security. You've seen that the easily visible jobs, from job postings and search firms, are not under your control and your chances of landing one aren't great. That doesn't mean to ignore them, but to keep them in perspective. You've tracked how jobs are born out of need, out of problems waiting to be solved, and you know that you can go upstream from publicly visible job openings and create a lot more opportunities for yourself. You also know how to uncover a company's needs by asking people and by tracking trends. And regardless of whether you or your company decide that reshaping your current job or moving within the company is an option, you will be growing professionally, which will continue to develop your options externally and internally. If you're constantly tracking trends, listening for needs, developing your skills, and seeing how you can help others, you'll be as nimble as a sports car on the autobahn.

STRATEGY #4

BUILD SUSTAINABLE NETWORKS

"Our lives are connected
Like waves upon a shore
Sometimes with a whisper
Sometimes with a roar
Sometimes we think we leave no trace
But sometimes less is more."

—"FACETS OF THE JEWEL" BY PAUL STOOKEY
OF PETER, PAUL, AND MARY

"I'd like to network with you."

How does it make you feel when someone says that to you? I've asked this question of hundreds of professionals in my networking seminars, and the reactions are much the same: they cringe. We don't like "confrontational networking," when we're cornered and have no escape.

The word "networking" has a mixed reputation, although the activity itself does not. I've upgraded its reputation from "bad" to "mixed" in recent years since social networks have tilted the playing field toward the positive side, but what's the difference between then and now? Control. When someone you don't know well approaches you and asks to network, you might feel like you're being taken advantage of, or that you're being put in an awkward situation where someone will want three names from you before they'll leave. Using social networks such as LinkedIn, however, you're in control. You decide to whom and when to respond.

On the other hand, if you feel like you *should* be networking when you're with other people, you might feel "one down" because you hate networking. You're used to being the one *giving* the help, or maybe you're concerned about seeming less than knowledgeable about a subject when you've always been the expert, and the power balance has shifted. Well, we're about to change all that. Face-to-face networking is about to become a pleasure on its own, and online networking can grease the skids when you choose for it to do so.

You already know that networking is important. Not only has it become a popular media topic in the past ten years, but you've been using it for forever. When was the last time you found a babysitter out of the Yellow Pages or on the Internet? A doctor? Are you already on the networking sites LinkedIn or Facebook? You may have landed a job through networking, and you may have read the research about the dramatic effect that our networks have upon our work success and health, even. It's true. The odds are with you. Using your network wisely is a muscle you can exercise and develop if you haven't already. Outplacement and alumni career services surveys report that 65 to 85 percent of job seekers find their jobs through networking (see the pie chart on page 73), so let's look at which barbells will build up the right muscles in the right way.

Not to worry. This isn't going to hurt because you're actually going to be *helping* people. If you have a tendency toward shyness, are an "I" on the extroversion/ introversion scale of the Myers-Briggs Type Indicator, or gravitate toward working with ideas more than people, the 65 to 85 percent may look daunting to you. You're likely to prefer doing in-depth computer research on companies before you approach them, sending out direct mail, posting your résumé on job boards, or contacting search firms hoping that they'll find opportunities for you. Unstructured socializing, multiple emails and phone calls, and approaching people that you haven't met before are not your idea of a good time. There are plenty of presidents and CEOs just like you, but you'll have to consciously go against a few of your natural inclinations during your transition to new work. Very few people pull down great jobs strictly through research. Using emails only for initial contact and to set up meetings rather than for trying to move an employer through the whole Job Pipeline is a good place to draw the line. Forcing yourself to do less research up front, get in front of new people with a good Elevator Story, and help them with their goals will help you head toward that 65 to 85 percent range.

Networking is not just for between jobs any longer. That's the focus of this chapter. We'll talk about how networking is "sustainable" once we've set some other ideas in place. First, let's look at how networking's beginnings are causing us some problems today, as well as some new approaches that will make your networking more powerful.

NOT YOUR GRANDFATHER'S NETWORKING . . .

The concept of networking evolved from work on informational interviewing created by John Crystal and Richard N. Bolles, two brilliant career theorists. They described the advantages of talking to someone who is doing the type of work that looks interesting to you rather than that person's superior. In order to interview this person, you would ask someone whom you both knew for an introduction. Voilà! A network was born.

If you'd like to tap into the research that is evolving on the relationships between networks and job change, start with Mark Granovetter's *Getting a Job: A Study of Contacts and Careers, 2nd edition* (University of Chicago Press, 1995), in which he defines that initial contact you just made as "some intermediary known personally to the respondent, with whom he *originally* became acquainted in some context *unrelated* to a search for job information." In other words, a friend gave you the name. There is some fascinating social psychology beneath what you're doing, but we'll come back to that later.

The original insightful idea of purposely building a network for information morphed over time and has been abused. People started asking potential superiors for informational interviews, promising that, "I'm not looking for a job. I'm just looking for information." Guess what? Everybody knew that that wasn't the truth, so the people who had been kind enough to grant the interviews felt mistreated. The idea of interviewing people about their expertise was so good, however, that the demand from job seekers continued to build until some companies set up policies that employees weren't allowed to give informational interviews due to time constraints. That brings us to irritated companies and overloaded, abused interview givers. Not a pretty place to start, is it?

One easy solution, before we get into more complex ones, is to change your vocabulary. Don't tell someone that you want to network with them unless you're online in a social network or at a meeting specifically designed for that purpose. Don't ask for an informational interview. Always be honest. Say, "I don't expect you to know of any openings just because I'm calling." This is true, and it takes the pressure off of the listener, but it makes it clear that you have an agenda other than pressing for names and openings. And you do. To set up the meeting, you can say, "Can we get together for a cup of coffee?" Or, "Can I pick your brain about how you think deregulation is going to affect us?" Or, "Can we trade ideas on hot small-cap companies?" You haven't asked to network or to have an informational interview. You haven't triggered any knee-jerk reactions, and you don't sound like you're going to take up too much time; you're on to the *business* question, and you're more likely to gain a receptive audience. If you need to refer to the meeting with others, call it a "market research meeting," since it's accurate and doesn't raise hackles. When you see the terms "networking meeting" and "informational interview" in this book, know that they're shorthand we can use among ourselves, but when you're out in the field setting up your conversations, increase the receptivity to your approach by changing your vocabulary.

. . . OR EVEN YOUR BIG SISTER'S NETWORKING

Talk about career whiplash. Networking has changed dramatically in the last few years, so stay tuned. It's going to keep changing. It's the distribution channel—that is, how you access your network—that has made the big leap now that the Internet is so integral to network management. Whether it's face-to-face or online, however, real people are thankfully still at the core, so a lot of the moves you already know are transferable. Keeping up with the changes and how they'll affect your career management will be part of your ongoing trend tracking that we're going to talk about next. The new networking includes the concept of gathering information, which Bolles and Crystal introduced, but it emphasizes the relationship and the reciprocity between the two parties. *The new networking is a barter system based on the exchange of mutually valuable information,* regardless of whether the connection is online or off. You just defanged the networking monster of asking strangers for leads. You're peers who are helping each other. Combine that with your taking the initiative by offering something of value first, and the playing field is suddenly level or tilted in your favor.

You, and the person to whom you'd like to speak, both have areas of expertise. You're equal partners in the conversation, regardless of the organizational levels between you. You can be of help to this person. Your challenge is to figure out how. Remember your marketing for mutual benefit homework? Spend some time thinking about the needs of the company or individual you're approaching before you make the initial contact. Before I pick up the phone to call one of my clients, I always consider, "What can I do to help this person?" You get a more positive reception, and you are creating a relationship rather than a sales call.

Thinking of what you can do to help other people, leading with their needs and staying there, not only drives the Marketing Circle so you can get your own needs met, but it also shifts the power balance inherent in the earlier style of networking. This shift makes networking much more palatable than it used to be because it feels good to give and it makes your targets feel good to receive; they'll keep coming back for more. Are you hearing the first notes of the "sustainability" theme playing? You're still the expert; you're still the person who is helping others. With online forms of networking, helpfulness is expected and the norm.

You'll be ignored after a while if you do nothing but take (or sell) instead of giving. A senior executive can practice the new networking and keep his dignity intact. A mid-level professional can get the attention of someone at the top of an organization because he has ideas to make her more successful. At entry level, the game is a lot more open than it used to be. Regardless of level, you may be giving more help than you're getting when you begin or at any given point. That's okay. You're building a relationship and a reputation.

In the earlier style of networking, you, the person seeking information, would approach a Learned One asking for names and referrals. He had the power; you were the supplicant. Now you approach him as a colleague on a level playing field regardless of the number of levels between your title and his, because he needs your information just as much as you need his. Let's talk about what you have to offer that will be of value.

ATTRACT EMPLOYERS BY SURFING YOUR VALUE WAVE

It's always amazing to me how many incredibly talented people aren't aware of what they have to offer. Your assets are often more obvious to others than they are to you. You should now have an idea of your competencies and strengths from Strategy #1: Send Clear Signals. Additional strengths will surface over time as you continue to get feedback from others, review old performance appraisals, and analyze job openings. "I have everything they're looking for," you'll say after reading some ads. Your strengths are right there in black and white. Pick out your top five strengths that you enjoy using and the marketplace values, and we'll use these in the Value Wave in just a minute.

Strengths alone don't win you the beauty contest though, do they? After figuring out what you have to offer, you need to integrate your talents with a company's needs in order to catch their attention. You are (or are becoming) familiar with company needs having done your research on target markets. Company needs are the second part of your Value Wave. Remember, the better you keep the conversation focused on increasing a company's profitability in your discussions, the more they'll pay attention to you.

There's another wave, a larger force behind company needs, that you may catch even before the decision makers in a company do. It's the trends that are hitting an industry. The need to be profitable is a constant, but market trends will shape *how* a company is going to be profitable. Your secret weapon: know what's happening in an industry and you can predict the needs of companies in that industry. Your agenda for market research meetings (a.k.a. informational interviews) will not need to change dramatically for companies within an industry since a lot of the questions can be similar (reacting to global competition, offshoring, regulatory changes, etc.), and your up-front research for each company will be lessened. You did your *industry* research and learned to track trends in Strategy #3: Stop Looking for Jobs. These insights ensure that you come across as a visionary leader who can actually make a difference, a leader who may well know more than the potential employer does about his markets but isn't wise about it. You're just asking interesting questions. (Damning but true. Employers can fall victim to being insulated and not being as forward thinking as you. Could General Motors be an example?) Your "currency," in all senses of the word, makes you valuable.

> The new networking is a barter system based on the exchange of mutually valuable information.

Now that you have a sense of industry trends, a company's needs, and your strengths, you're ready to navigate these three waves to more powerful conversations in your networking meetings.

- Overlaying industry trends: "Would you like to talk about ways the strategic alliance that you're pursuing could be used to develop markets for your filtration instrumentation in some new sectors? It looks like there is going to be a growing demand in defense and government labs, and I have some ideas about how you could go after that."

- Building in company needs: "It sounds like you're in the process of developing some strategic alliances that will broaden your product offerings. I have some experience with that."

- Your strengths: "I have strong marketing skills."

Take a look at one client's Value Wave (opposite) to see how the conversation becomes increasingly powerful as industry trends overlay company needs and an individual's strengths. You're subtly opening up the possibility of creating a job.

That question to the far right of the wave is a big deal. These are the types of questions that you can be shaping for your markets and companies that will make them sit up and take notice. You'll get meetings when there are "no job openings" or hiring freezes. Does it mean that you'll get jobs? Not necessarily. Does it mean that you'll get new relationships and ideas, new ways to help people, and maybe even some consulting work? Absolutely. Be known before you're needed.

The question at the end of the Value Wave and the conversations it can open up are your payoffs. Spend some time creating thought-provoking questions at

Catch Your Value Wave

Industry: Filtration instrumentation
Function: Senior operations management

Industry Trends	Company Needs	Your Strengths	
• Demand for evaluating the quality of air and water due to terrorist activity	• Increase the volume of production of instrumentation while maintaining high quality	• Process reengineering • Managing multisite manufacturing plants	You, Setting up a Meeting: "I wanted to see if we could get together. My guess is that you could be facing a production crunch before long if you're going after the increased demand for environmental instrumentation. New orders could be falling in your lap overnight and I may have some ideas about how to streamline your processes so you can maintain and grow quality while ramping up production. Do you want to get together next Tuesday for coffee?"
•	•	•	
•	•	•	
•	•	•	
•	•		

two levels, one for companies in the same industry, and one that's your "cocktail party question" as described in earlier chapters. What can you ask random people that you meet socially, at networking events or wherever, that will help you to move forward? Bill, the client in the Value Wave, could have asked people, "What companies do you think might actually grow as a result of increased security against terrorism?" He'll need to cherry-pick the responses, but he may get some answers from unexpected places that will let him go upstream to get connections in the job creation process.

Now for your own Value Wave. Fill out the three columns in the "Catch Your Value Wave" homework and then convert them into questions that you can use with decision makers. They'll be wondering where you've been all of their lives.

HOMEWORK

Catch Your Value Wave

1. Fill in your function and one of your target industries at the top.

2. Work either "up" or "down" the wave, whichever is easier for you.

3. For the industry trends wave, be sure to include macrotrends outside your industry that will cause changes within your industry, such as global economic shifts and changing governmental regulations.

4. For the second wave, a specific company's needs, you'll find that many of these will be transferable to other companies within the same industry. Some will be immediate, such as meeting a deadline. Some will be oriented toward the future, such as product development or execution of the company's strategic plans. Capture as many of both as you can. You won't have perfect information, but make your best guesses.

5. Record your strengths in the third wave.

6. Surf the waves! Develop some questions that will demonstrate your value to decision makers as they position their company to capture opportunities. You just happen to have some ideas about how to do it. Bonus points for creating a "cocktail party question" in the process.

You may want to complete a separate "Catch Your Value Wave" for each industry that you've decided to approach. Your message may need to change. Not only will industry needs vary, but company needs and the strengths you showcase may shift as well.

WHAT NETWORK? GETTING A SYSTEM TO EXPAND YOUR BRAIN

Now that you're armed with the concept of networking as a successful bartering system and you see the value you can add to a company by anticipating and harnessing trends, what are you going to do next? You're all dressed up with no place to go. It's time to start networking.

But where is this infamous network? Do you feel that other people have stronger networks than you (network envy) or that yours is somewhere between weak and nonexistent? "I don't have a network," or "I've used up my network," or "I've recently moved to town and have to start a completely new network" are frequent regrets that I hear from professionals, but these challenges are reversible and within your control. Rest assured, you *do* have a network. However, you may need to uncover it, like King Arthur parting the mists to see the Lady of the Lake's stronghold.

Structuring Your Network

To bring your network to life, you'll want a contact management system that can grow along with you. Picking out a system now that you like for tracking names will save you time and improve your work results for the rest of your career. A tall claim? Not really. Software can help you remember details, come up with names you've forgotten, and remind you to do things that might otherwise fall between the cracks. Although paper-based systems work, they're more cumbersome and don't allow you to cross-reference the names of the administrative assistants and everyone else you've met at a company as easily. "But I don't have any system!" you're saying. Great. You're not going to have to unlearn bad habits. Plunge in.

You probably have contact management software already. These programs are databases that keep track of the names, contact information, events, and tasks that you feed into them. Initially, they were used by sales professionals to keep track of customers. You'll basically be doing the same thing. This sort of software can keep track of your personal relationships, from holiday card mailings to soccer team memberships, as well. You'll really be on top of things. A president of one company can't believe that I remember her birthday every year. I don't. The reminder function in my software does.

Outlook is one contact management program that many people already have on their computers without knowing it; it's bundled with Microsoft Office along with Word, PowerPoint, and Excel. Check your computer to see if it's there. Or you may want to investigate other contact managers. ACT! is another popular choice. If you want to sync up with a BlackBerry, an iPhone, or another similar smart phone, make sure the software you select will be compatible.

Tracking Your Contacts

Pick out a system to use for tracking your contacts. Don't spend too much time analyzing which one is perfect because this task can become a black hole. You can always switch later if you need to. Begin by entering a couple of names to get the process started.

Okay, So I Have a System

Now to the "who" part of network development. It's time to start entering names into your database. Which names? Begin with the professional contacts that you're in touch with fairly frequently. Start a new card in your contact manager for each person, and enter what you know about him.

Sample Entry

Full Name:	Mike Mayfield
Last Name:	Mayfield
First Name:	Mike
Job Title:	Director of Product Development
Company:	Field Systems, Inc.
Business Address:	124 West Street
	Longview, TX 12354
Business Phone:	(765) 432-9876
Business Fax:	(765) 432-9825
Mobile:	(123) 456-7890
Email:	mike@fieldsystems.com

Talked to on 1/8. Said to call in 2 weeks.

Admin: Leslie Howe, 765-432-9873. Talked to on 12/5. Is going to Colorado for holidays.

Mike's thinking about acquiring some new drilling technology. Follow up.

If you spend time filling out every little blank on each card in your database, it will take forever. Capture whatever is readily available in your brain and keep going. "Wait a minute," you say. "I have hundreds of people in my cell phone and stacks of business cards. Isn't this going to take a lot of time?" Absolutely. You may want to hire an assistant on an hourly basis to feed in the backlog to get you started or you might buy a card scanner. Otherwise, just enter recurring professional contacts and add others when you have the time. This is a lifetime reference tool you're building, so getting information into it is important. Tip: If you have Outlook, when you receive an email, open it up, highlight the email address (if you like the person), and right click. Select "Add to Outlook Contacts" and it's done for you.

Most contact management programs have a really handy function: an empty field where you can make notes. In Outlook, it's the white box in the lower right corner. You can record the dates of meetings with the contact, the name of the person who introduced you, his expertise, his admin's and children's names, and so on. This is your cheat sheet. If you can't remember a person's name, search on a key word and it will come up. However, your contact system is only as good as what you feed into it. You may hire someone for several hours a month to help you update your contacts as they change. It will take less time to maintain once you're up and running.

If you think you don't have a lot of contacts, and your list fizzles out once you have ten names, you're on the tip of the iceberg. Don't screen too tightly when you're deciding upon whom to enter. They don't have to be a big cheese to warrant an entry, nor do they need to live locally or be a close friend. Just go back to your Rolodex, your business cards, your calendar, your Referral Triangle in Strategy #2: Market for Mutual Benefit for names of vendors, competitors, and customers, and more people will keep springing out. The art is to capture the names as they pass across your radar screen.

Whether you feel like you have too many contacts to enter or not enough to sneeze at, don't worry about "finishing" your database soon. It's never finished. It's a work in progress, and it will continually provide support for your career growth. Get a good start on it now, and then add to it as you can. It's time for you to start talking to some of these people rather than spending all of your time in front of a computer screen.

Social Networks: Boy, Are You in Luck

The evolution of social networks is *the* major change in the landscape in the last few years, and they're continuing to evolve every moment. They can dramatically improve your sources of information and your career management results. If you're not using them and your competition is (and, I promise you, they are), you're at a disadvantage. Using them is fun, too. You can find people that you haven't seen in years, from high school friends to former employers and neighbors, as well as meet new people with similar interests. You will discover ways that you can help each other that you never would have known about before. Don't worry. They don't have to be a huge time sink unless you allow them to be. This book isn't a primer on how to use them; those already exist, and the tutorials on their own sites make using them fairly easy and safe. Here, however, I will give an overview of the pros and cons of the three dominant ones, and provide ideas about how to use them to build your reputation, your knowledge, and your entrees into companies.

What is a social network? The term has been used by social psychologists for ages. It's a social structure made up of individuals or organizations that are connected by one or more themes, such as friendship, beliefs, family, interests, or business. There are hundreds of social networking sites on the Internet now, allowing people to find or meet each other quickly, no matter where in the world they are located, but we're going to stick with the three that are changing how people manage their businesses and careers. In descending order of *career* relevance, they are LinkedIn (50 million users globally), Facebook (350 million users globally), and Twitter (44.5 million users globally). Let's look at each of these three, and at what they can (or cannot) do for you.

Launched in 2003, LinkedIn describes its core mission as "keeping you informed about your contacts and industry, finding the people and knowledge you need to achieve your goals, and controlling your professional identity online." This is the social networking site that focuses on business and will be the most useful professional network for you. Being able to see not only your own network, but who among them is connected to someone you'd like to meet, makes this service invaluable. You can contact them outside of LinkedIn (which is more personal) to see if an introduction makes sense. Kate Brooks, director of the Liberal Arts Career Services at University of Texas at Austin is clear that "having a strong LinkedIn presence is becoming more important. Several recruiters this year have said that they're doing the bulk of their recruiting through LinkedIn," both actively and passively. You know that from Strategy #3: Stop Looking for Jobs, as well as from some LinkedIn groups that you may have joined already. Joining their interest groups that relate to your field, once you have your feet wet, will help your reputation continue to spread and will allow recruiters to find you more easily.

Facebook, with 350 million members and growing, on the other hand, "helps you connect and share with the people in your life." In other words, it's not about work; it's about people's personal and "private" lives. Do you need to be on it? As far as career management is concerned, it's not as important as LinkedIn, but it doesn't hurt. Work is popping up on it in overt and covert ways, so stay tuned. Companies *do* use it to check up on you, so if you're doing anything silly in your photos, you may never know what killed your application at a company. Photos should *always* be ones that you wouldn't mind your mother seeing. If you're saying, "Boring! That defeats the purpose of Facebook," see the information on "digital dirt" below (page 127). Kate Brooks agrees. "A Facebook picture should still be professional since it can be seen even when everything else is hidden." Since this site is truly more about life than work, we won't spend as much time on it here, but just be aware that the two cross over. Elizabeth Bernstein of the *Wall Street Journal*, in an article titled "How Facebook Ruins Friendships" (www.online.wsj. com, August 25, 2009), points out that "our online interactions can hurt our real-life relationships. . . . People you know can be bolder online, displaying sides of their personalities you've never seen before." If you're swearing that you're too old, too mature, or too smart to enter the fray, realize that the boundaries are shifting continually and even old, mature, and smart people are showing up in greater numbers on Facebook. Use your hard-earned discretion and judgment about what you post and what is visible to the outside world so that you won't need to reverse any hasty comments or impressions later on. Facebook and LinkedIn are good ways to find lost colleagues given that people typically leave their company within three years.

Twitter allows you to "Share and discover what's happening right now, anywhere in the world." From following the 140-character "tweets," or updates, of people you choose to "follow" (including recruiters and industry giants) on your cell phone or computer to creating your own group of followers to send your tweets, Twitter *does* have its place. As Kelly Golnoush Niknejad proved when she founded a Twitter-based site that became the only way that news could be sent out of Iran after the postelection news shutdown in 2009, Twitter can be an important tool. (By the way, Niknejad has now entered into an editorial partnership with *Frontline*, the PBS public affairs series. Talk about perfect execution of Strategy #3: Stop Looking for Jobs, and looking for a problem to be solved instead!) Most of our uses won't be as dramatic, but Twitter is worth paying attention to as its uses unfold. If you sign up for an account and follow a couple of people you respect for a while, you'll make a decision. Recruiters love it because it's free as well as faster and more personal than posting an opening on a job board; MC Hammer loves it and claims that Twitter has revitalized his brand and business; you might love it if you're thinking about writing a blog but don't want to spend much time on one. If you start participating, keep your tweets professional and positive. The drill is to offer tips, resources, links to relevant news, events, or ideas of value to your market, and not to sell yourself.

I was dismissive of these sites at first, thinking that they were strictly geared to young, hip users and entry-level employees, but they, and I, have changed. Upon interviewing executive search firms, recruiters, senior-level job candidates, directors of career planning at universities, and corporate human resource professionals (among others) for this book, the message is clear. They're using all three sites to find, learn about, and monitor potential candidates and current employees at all levels. Not being on LinkedIn, at a minimum, sends out the message, "not plugged in," and thus might reinforce a belief that you're "too old" or "not comfortable using the Internet to develop relationships." Sign up for LinkedIn and then you can decide about the other two. Staying on top of quickly evolving technology not only is important to grow our careers and maintain an up-to-date image, it's also sort of fun.

The Pros and Cons of Social Networks

Tidy classifications of "pros and cons" or "do's and don'ts" don't really work well for social networks. The answer is always, "it depends." Considering the implications of the four areas below and how you want to be known before you plunge in can lead to improved choices, visibility, and reputation over the long term.

- **Companies can find you.** According to Jennifer Scott, Principal at HireEffect, 80 percent of recruiters (agency, independent, and corporate) use LinkedIn to source candidates. It's free (let that word and its implications sink in), and they're tracking both passive candidates, ones that aren't looking for jobs that they find with keyword and interest group searches, and active candidates who may be tracking *them* down. (See the info about job postings and search firms in Strategy #3: Stop Looking for Jobs.)

  Remember how you did the research in Strategy #1: Send Clear Signals, about the key words in job postings of interest to your markets or from interviews with your colleagues on "the four most important skills" they'd be looking for? You built them into your résumé so it's skimmable and scannable, and embedded them in your Elevator Story, right? Now it's time to embed them in your profile on the social networking sites, your professional headline on LinkedIn, and in your choice of interest groups. Make yourself easy to find! If you make your profile settings as public as is reasonable, including putting your phone number or email on your profile so an employer can contact you by Googling you rather than needing to join LinkedIn, you've just helped both sides. My client, George, had a nonsolicit, an agreement with his former employer that he couldn't ask any of his former clients to follow him to his next firm. George put his new contact info on his LinkedIn profile that popped up on Google and, voilà, people could track him down at his new location, easily and legally.

- **Reputation . . . make it or break it**. *Any* potential employer is checking you out now on Google, LinkedIn, and Facebook, at a minimum. They can't afford *not* to since they're the easiest tools for performing due diligence. According to ExecuNet research, 44 percent of recruiters have eliminated candidates as a result of information found online. Even your current company is probably checking you out, too. The groups you've selected to join on LinkedIn, the crazy pictures you've posted on Facebook, rants against your company or boss—this information is *never* private. Never. It's fairly simple for others to work around your privacy settings and, after all, you're posting information, pictures, and opinions on the *Internet*. Did you think it was really going to be private?

"Digital dirt" is a great expression coined by Kirsten Dixson in *Career Distinction: Stand Out by Building your Brand*. Google yourself and see what comes up. Is there "dirt," or entries that do not build the brand that you would like, especially on the first page of Google? What about your credit rating or information about legal or marital disputes? It's all out there. You can set up a Google alert if you want to track when your name pops up on the Internet. Stacey Rudnick, director of MBA career services at the University of Texas at Austin, teaches a required course to first-year MBA students that includes managing your online presence. She suggests Googling yourself on a regular basis (including using www.images.google.com for pictures), thinking of who you're connecting with, considering how your privacy settings are structured, and, most importantly, making sure your information is *consistent*. Remember Debra Cohen's research at the Society for Human Resource Management in Strategy #3: Stop Looking for Jobs? More than 93 percent of their HR members said that they are "less likely to hire" if "information on the applicant's profile contradicts that provided on the résumé, cover letter, or CV." If the stories differ, is that person trustworthy?

Should you be the victim of digital dirt that isn't accurate, either bury it, delete it, or differ. "Bury" is pushing a highly ranked Google link further back onto later pages, where it won't get noticed as much. Burying a link can be done by your publishing material about your research, your blog, or your insights on professional trends. "The more information you post about yourself," says Kate Brooks from

Career Services at the University of Texas at Austin, "the less likely any negative information is to show up when your name is Googled by an employer." Unsolicited testimonials, that is, friends or clients who volunteer third-party testimonials about you that are frequently viewed so they appear on the first page or two when your name is Googled, are even better. "Delete" you can often do with comments on your wall on Facebook, and "differ" is contacting the source of the "dirt" and enlisting help to have the tone of the comments changed or reversed. A phone call saying, "I'm really trying to set a professional tone on my wall because I'm starting a job search. Could I get your help?" is much more likely to elicit the response you need over retaliation or defensiveness. Taking the fight outside, so to speak, out of the social network to a direct connection, shows your maturity and wisdom . . . and it gets results.

- **Promiscuous networking.** It's easy to connect randomly and casually on all three sites. If you're in any way a public figure, people who have heard you speak at a meeting or read about you may ask to link to you. Someone you meet at a party may want to friend you. You may extend the same casual invitations to others. Who wouldn't want George Clooney as a friend? Do you really know these people though? Are they safe (will they protect your boundaries and identity), and are their connections safe as well? Do you really want all of these people to have access to the inner workings of your network or your life? If the answer is "yes," link away, but I'm going slowly. I personally use two filters when deciding whether to connect with someone: I need to know the person fairly well and to feel comfortable with writing a reference for the person (not that I will for everyone, but I want to be able to should they want one). Given the amount of time I'm going to spend on each site (finite), the awkwardness of "un-friending" someone if necessary, and the importance of maintaining the brand that my clients value, I want to build something that's sustainable from the start. After all, this should be a long-term network for each of us. A cleantech investment banker, Bic Stevens, told me that if he isn't sure about accepting an invitation, he asks the person to call him so they can get to know each other better first, a practice that is both polite and a good idea.

    Lauryn Franzoni, ExecuNet vice president and executive editor, concludes in the 2009 *Executive Job Market Intelligence Report* that "There's a big difference between purposeful networking and 'friending.' Do you want to meet the people who can bring you closer to your career goals, or do you want to collect names? It's about cultivating your community, nurturing your network and maintaining meaningful—and reciprocal—connections." Quantity does not equal quality. Check back with the next edition of this book, since the effect of promiscuous networking that online social networking encourages is still being discovered. In the meantime, use your judgment before clicking "accept."

- **Value share.** In social networks, as in life, it's not just about you. Even given the 140-character constraints of Twitter, the etiquette is to help each other instead of shamelessly promoting your own goals. "Retweeting" someone's message is a perfect example of a three-fer. Jennifer Scott of HireEffect defines "retweet" as forwarding to your followers any information you find useful that other people have tweeted you. "Not only will the person who authored the tweet be thankful, but so will those who see the message as a result of your generosity." The original sender, the forwarding person, and all his followers benefit. If you find yourself as the originator of a tweet that is fortunate enough to be retweeted, remember to thank the forwarding person for retweeting your message. Doing good deeds pays off at many levels on all of the social networking sites as well as in your personal network and job creation. Surprised?

WORKING THROUGH YOUR NETWORK'S LAYERS

Randomly talking to important people may be hazardous to your career. I've often seen recently laid-off people, who want a quick fix, approach the biggest "ace" in their contact network first to see if they can be hired ASAP. The emotion is totally understandable. The strategy isn't. When you approach your aces, you want to be clear about what you can and can't do, what the bottom side of the marketing circle means for them, and where you can add value. You may have one trip to the well, and you want to be prepared.

You prepare yourself by working through the layers of your contacts. Now that you have identified some of your contacts for your contact manager and, possibly, LinkedIn, sit back and take a look at them. You'll see that your network is stratified into three layers. The comparison of these layers to the rings in a target has been used for years to explain how the different levels of your network function.

Networking Layers

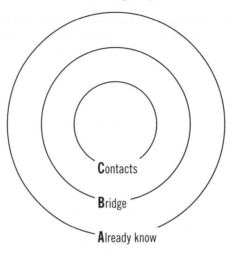

Contacts

Bridge

Already know

- **A Level:** The outside ring is the people you *already* know. These are people that you can go back to many times. You can ask them dumb questions, be undecided or unclear about what you want, pick their brains, and listen to their opinions. They won't send you away or get tired of you because they truly care (think family and friends). What do you want from them? You're investigating what's hot and what's not in various companies and industries and where there may be potential growth, and they may have some ideas. If you can visit them at their offices to talk about possible recommendations and contact names, you'll typically get more detailed information than you would on the golf course. You might start a conversation with an A-level contact in an informal place, then follow up with a more formal one where you can practice your informational interviewing skills. These people are important; they're your main support during your job transition, so think of their needs, too.

- **B Level:** The middle ring consists of people who create a *bridge* for you. These people work in organizations of interest to you, but they aren't in a position to make decisions about you. You may have been referred to them by A-level people. You need two things from B-level people: names and needs. "Who should I be talking to, and what keeps him or her up at night?" Of course, you're not going to get helpful information if you don't establish a relationship first, so treat this as a market research meeting, which it is. Anyone from the chief financial officer to the shipping and receiving clerk has opinions about how the company and the CEO are doing. Take all their input with a grain of salt, but build their trust; you have just developed a new relationship, and they may be able to influence others on your behalf.

The job seekers in highest demand are often those who have spent some time with and learned from various B-level people. They have learned about the industry's problems from a variety of perspectives. They often know more about the competition than the company does, so they can turn around and "sell" the industry knowledge they've accumulated. They're not giving away trade secrets, but they can talk generically about how trends are playing out and about creative approaches to problems.

- **C Level:** The inside ring consists of *contacts*. These are the decision makers that you've been waiting to meet, often introduced to you by a B-level person. These are typically tough people to break through to without connections. Your objective with these people is to form relationships, ideally through brief meetings, where you can ask some leading questions about challenges they're facing, then dangle carrots—your ideas for potential solutions. When you were setting up the meetings you probably promised that you didn't expect them to know about jobs just because you're calling, so stay on the subjects of market research and problem solving at the beginning. CEO's don't even know about all the open jobs half of the time, but they *do* know talent when they see it. In the meantime, your job is to focus on their needs, dangle carrots, and see if you can lead them to the *next* meeting, where you'll "pull together some ideas" that address their needs. You didn't think you were going to get a job offer in one meeting, did you?

Seeing the layers in your network should make it easier to identify who you can start talking to now. Move from the outside in. Warning: the boundaries between the three rings are permeable. Think carefully about the order in which you want to approach people. A-level people, ones that you already know, may also be C-level people, or decision makers, as well. Hold off a little on contacting them. B-level people may be C-level people in disguise. Timing is everything. As you refine your information and improve your presentation, you'll get better. You'll know when you're ready for prime time.

Whose Handshake?

The flip side of working your way into and up the corporate food chain is making sure that you're perceived at an appropriate professional level. Executives often share a concern that doesn't get voiced because it's an awkward subject. "Whose handshake do I need to get the C-level person to pay attention to me?" In other words, to get an introduction, should you use the name of the B-level person you visited who is five levels away from the CEO, but who knows the CEO somewhat from a committee where they crossed paths? "It depends on your options," is the answer. If you meet a CEO through a friend that she made while sitting on another board, odds are that you will be trusted and accepted quickly. LinkedIn is brilliant with showing you the connections between yourself and your target decision maker that you never would have discovered otherwise. They even have a "degrees of separation" graphic that tells you the names in your network that link you with him or her. Isn't technology wonderful? Take it outside of Linked-In for your more important connections. In other words, talk to (preferably) or email your link between you and the big cheese for additional information and to ensure that any introduction that might be given is more personal and enthusiastic than a form request on a social networking site might be. Evaluate which of your handshakes will be the most effective before asking for an introduction, regardless of whether it's online or through your current network, and ask your best shot for the introduction. Doing something nice for her in return will keep those bridges strong.

Breaking Through: Catching the Uncatchable Person It's time to set up a meeting with a B- or C-level person you don't know yet. Boy, have some of the approaches I've developed and tested in the past couple of years combined with using email made getting to the top easier! I'm getting close to a 100 percent response rate now from people that I don't know firsthand. Let's assume that you're developing a Companies of Interest list (a.k.a. Hit List) as in Strategy #2: Market for Mutual Benefit. Let's assume that you know your Value Wave and the challenges that your target industry is facing. Let's say that you've shared your Companies of Interest list with your A-level connections already and you haven't discovered any connections there or on LinkedIn with Jeffrey Strong, CEO of AllClear Financial, one of your favorite companies. By the way, pat yourself on the back for having gotten this far.

You have two options before you cold call. One is the business section of your public library or your alma mater for a printout of the top officers in AllClear Financial. (If it's small and privately held, AllClear may be able to hide fairly well.) Add these names to your Companies of Interest list. Your connections may know either Jeffrey himself, or someone in his company, the bridge level, who can get you to Jeffrey, assuming that they and you choose to do so. Building internal champions never hurts. Ask your A-level friend to do an "e-intro" (i.e., send an email to both you and the B-level connection, introducing you to each other). It's fast and painless, and you can take it from there on your own. People are using these e-intros fairly frequently now. The second one is the easiest source of all, the "degrees of separation" information on LinkedIn described in Whose Handshake? above. One of my clients was able to start conversations with 100 percent of his targets when he combined his current relationships with those of his secondary and tertiary connections that LinkedIn makes visible. Pretty cool, huh? Just remember to take it outside of LinkedIn when you're asking someone for an introduction so you can make it more personal and pick up any subtle clues.

So you have the introduction . . . or you don't. What do you do next to get conversations with some of your Companies of Interest about their developing needs? Breaking through is next . . . finally.

The Email Approach You're ready. You have a target that you'd like to meet, a referral name (preferably), and you know where her pain is from your trend research. Use email as your primary approach. This is the norm now and gives you the highest odds of getting a response. You can break through to senior-level people more easily, they can open it when they're receptive rather than being caught off guard by a phone call, and they can circulate it to others with a single click. (Beware of the dark side of this fact. Remember that everything you say is public information.) If you're not comfortable with computers, take some computer courses. Regardless of whether your administrative assistant has been taking care of all your email communications for you or you've never learned, the expectations on the hiring side are all the same: email ability is taken for granted. You're hurting your chances and your potential income if you don't become conversant.

Now that we're on the same page, let's get on the same subject line. Subject lines of emails to people you don't know well are critical now. Let me say that again: *Subject lines are critical.* In this world of TMI (too much information), it's your one shot at getting someone to pay attention. Anything that is too generic, too cute, or too "sales-y" won't work, but the "double hook" I've developed will break through.

Let's look at a hypothetical example to serve as a model for breaking through to the decision maker for job creation. You've learned that Amazon.com is opening a new distribution center near you and you've tracked down their VP of operations from the Internet, your crackerjack librarian in the reference section, or LinkedIn. This would be the person to decide if a job were going to be created, so you start with an email. In the past I've recommended that you do this by phone, but that's changed. Email is ubiquitous now and typically makes it easier to break through, so the phone is now the back-up strategy.

Base Email Format

To: john.q.public@amazon.com
Subject: Katherine Williams referral, July 23 PM?

Hi John,

Katherine Williams said to tell you "hello." We were talking about your coverage in *The Supply Chain Management Journal*. Congratulations not only on the article, but on Amazon's growth and the cost control that opening the new distribution center in Iowa implies. Welcome to the neighborhood.

I've been setting up warehouses and inventory centers for retail operations for years and thought you might be interested in hearing more about what's going to happen with your highway access in Iowa once the cold weather moves in. Perhaps I can spare you some logistical nightmares I've seen others experience and potentially save you some construction costs if you'd like to go over some ideas before you get too far along.

Should we set up a conversation for the afternoon of Tues, July 23? If so, tell me your preferred time and telephone number. If not, tell me a time that works for you. I look forward to trading ideas.

Rex Trailer
C: 319.343.8765

See how you stayed on the bottom side of the Marketing Circle, meeting the VP's needs the entire time? You also politely challenged him, as we talked about in Strategy #1: Send Clear Signals, by introducing some information you weren't sure the VP knew about, how winter weather will affect the company's transportation scheduling. Even if the VP has people working on this already, he shouldn't ignore ideas from an expert who lives in the area. That was the carrot you dangled, your expertise in a potential problem area for him. If he does ignore your offer, you can write him off with a clean conscience, maybe using connections that develop later on to circle back around. In the meantime, he had his chance, and you learned what he'd be like to work with. Odds are that you'll hear back, however, especially since you have Katherine in common.

Finally, and most importantly, you took initiative and did everything possible to elicit a response. This is my *base email format* that you'll hear about again and can use when you want to move a relationship forward. You do three important things with this format: 1) You use a "double hook" in the subject line. The subject line is all most people will see of an email. If it doesn't intrigue them, they won't open it. They don't know you and there are other fires on the desk. The first hook is a name in common or, failing that, the topic, "Highway access for new distribution center, July 23 PM?" The second hook is the date. They'll have no clue what the date means and will typically open the email just to make sure they haven't missed something. 2) You don't attach a résumé. That's a dead give-away. Hiring someone is not on their brain at the moment, and you're after the broader target of job creation. They may not open the email or the attachment if it smacks of a job approach. 3) You also end with an action step so they'll have it on the top of their mind as they finish the brief email. Instead of a vague "Can we get together?" or "What works for you?" you've taken control. You haven't asked *if* you can get together, you've just asked *when*. Being specific with a date proposal just saved him a lot of time and decision making, too. The fewer decisions the recipient needs to make, the more likely the meeting is to happen.

Will anything come of this? You don't know. Might you volunteer your exper-tise with no job offer or compensation? Absolutely. That's a risk you run. But you're not giving them all your ideas or your time. If you actually end up doing some short-term work together you'll reserve some of your good ideas, because you still want them to "buy the cow." So the disadvantages of taking the initiative in starting a relationship are the risk of rejection and the potential waste of some time . . . not bad trade-offs for the possibility of getting into a good company that "isn't hiring" at the moment.

The Phone Approach The July 23rd date that you proposed in the above email has another advantage: you just set up an imaginary deadline. Bravo! You now have a structure that allows you to call John or his admin without being too intrusive. The overall strategy is to follow up an email with a voice mail. You've tried an email approach and it hasn't worked (so far). Don't read too much into it. It could be anything from John being out of the office to his spam filter to a deadline to the email being lost in cyberspace. The next step is to take advantage of your imaginary deadline.

It was July 20 when you proposed July 23 for getting together or talking on the phone. Refresh your memory before you pick up the phone; you'll probably be leaving a voice mail. You'll need three things: the name of the person who referred you and/or the "pain" that you used for your first hook in the subject line, the carrot you can dangle that John might want, and the date you proposed to talk or get together. If you'd like to do a little research on John ahead of time, bonus points. You're set. Pick up the phone and just do it

Call the phone number you have at night first. Listen to the message without leaving one yourself. Some messages have the admin's name and phone number on it. Grab it. That person is the best person to follow up with when possible.

WITH ADMINISTRATOR OR HIS OR HER VOICE MAIL:

Hi, Susan. This is Rex Trailer. My guess is that you control John Public's life, and I have a question. I sent John an email last week about some design considerations he's going to run into with your new distribution center in Iowa. I'd proposed talking this Tuesday afternoon, and I'm not sure if that's on his calendar or not. Could you check for me? (If voice mail, leave contact info.) I'm at 319.343.8765 or rex@tractortrailer.com. Thanks.

If she answers "yes," your response is "Great. Does 2:30 work? What's the best phone number? Thanks, Susan."

If she answers "no," your response is "That's okay. It may have gotten buried. May I forward the email directly to you and ask you to let me know if that time works? I'm holding off on some other things in the meantime. If there's another time that would work better, just let me know. Thanks, Susan."

WITH NO ADMIN, LEAVING MESSAGE ON JOHN'S VOICE MAIL:

Hi, John. I'm Rex Trailer, Katherine Williams's colleague and the retail supply chain guy in Iowa. I sent you an email last week about some design considerations you may want to keep in mind early on, given our weather where your new distribution center in Iowa is being built. I've been right in the thick of some challenges in this area. I proposed that you and I talk on the phone on Tuesday afternoon. Does that work for you? If so, let me know if 2:30ish works and your preferred phone number. Look forward to talking. I'm at 319.343.8765 or rex@tractortrailer.com.

That isn't too hard, is it? Given that you prepped before you picked up the phone, you're set even if the decision maker answers—a nice problem to have.

Before you start leaving emails and phone calls, I need to share with you a major pet peeve of mine: no contact info in messages. Have you ever gotten a voice mail message that says, "How's next week? Give me a call." Click. Not only do people have multiple phone numbers these days, unless you have a chip implanted in your brain, you have to go look it up! The harder you make it for someone to return a phone call, the less likely they are to do so. Putting a phone number in your email auto signature is wise, too. It makes you look more professional and gives the reader choices about how to respond *easily*. Don't ask your targets to spend their time and energy looking up your number. Odds are they won't bother. Leave it slowly and clearly at the end of each message. If they're retrieving your message while driving down the highway, they're more likely to remember the phone number if it's the last thing they hear rather than the first.

Integrating Approaches for the Capture There will be plenty of times when people don't return your emails or calls. They were going to send your résumé to a friend of theirs who absolutely needs you . . . then don't. They don't follow up after a great meeting even though you left on a high and they promised to get right back to you. It's not fair, but get used to it. If you don't assume that you're going to hear back from anyone, you're in better psychological and strategic shape. Most of the time it's not about you, even though you feel it is. Whether it is caused by an "erosion of etiquette," as an executive in transition described the phenomenon, or simply overload, the results are the same: no news. Your job is not to hold your breath waiting for the promised follow-up but to have an action plan in place and other initiatives you're pursuing simultaneously.

Getting the decision maker to take the next step, whether it is setting up the first meeting or negotiating the final clause in a contract, is both an art and a science. Brendan knew how to do both.

Brendan really wanted to work at SymmCo, the industry leader in data storage. He had left his position as director of regional sales at an international health care products manufacturer with sparks flying on both sides. To move up in that company, he would have had to relocate to corporate headquarters, a long way from his family, so he chose to leave the well-known company and look for another job.

SymmCo, however, was not lacking for job applicants. Its products had a strong reputation, and its employees had been making a lot of money on stock growth. They were hiring, but what did Brendan know about data storage? His industry background wasn't a fit at all. His functional background, sales and marketing, was of interest to SymmCo, but they wanted salespeople who knew their products and their customers, ideally someone from the competition with current customers in tow. Brendan wasn't a "round peg, round hole." This would be a tough sell.

Brendan, though, was good in sales for a reason. He was professionally persistent, didn't take things personally, and consistently focused on the bottom side of the Marketing Circle, helping others. People liked him.

He started penetrating SymmCo by talking to A-level contacts, people he already knew, learning the names of B-level people, and setting up meetings with them. Everyone was fairly responsive in the first round because of the strength of his referrals' relationships with them. The hard part didn't come until later.

Brendan's first meetings went extremely well. He determined the company's and industry's needs and showed them how he could help. Had they looked at the health care market? Had they thought about the giant opportunity it would be for SymmCo? The data storage requirements for the health care industry are enormous, and Brendan had been selling to a lot of people who might need it. (Notice how he switched products but played up the same customers?) He might have some ideas for them.

People were biting. SymmCo is a large company, so there were multiple places that Brendan might fit. His bridge-level people referred him on to other people. He didn't want to narrow his options by pursuing only one opportunity early in his relationship with SymmCo. He wasn't sure where he was best suited in the company, plus he wanted to keep a little competitive pressure going. He pursued the next round of meetings, and things kept going well.

He began homing in on three separate opportunities: he was creating two, and one was a new opening in a growing department. The two he was creating would be at higher levels with more challenging work than the official opening. No surprise there. His favorite choice was a marketing opportunity to start up a health care vertical; his second choice, still interesting, was in channel management. The problem was that the decision makers weren't getting back to him; the marketing people were promising action but not delivering, and his second-choice group was pursuing him. Turning down a potential channel management job could be risky because the marketing position might never materialize. This is where the strategy for breaking through to the right person came in handy.

Brendan left a phone message for his potential marketing boss. "Hi, Jack. This is Brendan Span. I need to follow up on our discussions to see what your timetable is. I'm truly excited about the potential for building a health care vertical and would love to work out something with you. In the meantime, I'm having some discussions about another opportunity within SymmCo in the channel sales area, and there's another department that has expressed some interest in me. Since I'm most interested in what you're doing, however, I want to finalize things with you first before I pursue any other options. I could really use your insight on this. Could we set up a time to get together next week, maybe Tuesday morning?"

Brendan was open and honest about talking to others within the company, but he also used it as leverage to get his first choice to move faster. As a result, Brendan wound up with several offers. Not only did he land the marketing work that he wanted, he negotiated for additional stock options and a more favorable base and bonus package. His rationale was that he was making a long-term career commitment and wanted to yoke his success to that of the company. He broke through the foot dragging and got the attention he wanted by finding ways to motivate people. You can do the same.

Brendan's story demonstrates the advantages of the "multiple warhead missile" strategy. Instead of depending on one relationship and one series of meetings to generate an offer, Brendan pursued multiple approaches simultaneously—not hard to do within a large company Not only did he prime the Job Pipeline outside of SymmCo in case his efforts there imploded, he also primed it with several initiatives within one company to build internal competitive pressure. You can build a buzz about yourself and your name will get around, which is just what you want. The art is to keep the buzz positive. You should avoid playing one side against another, sharing information that might not be appropriate to share, or, conversely, withholding information that should be shared. "John, Arthur made me an offer today that I'm going to accept. I wanted you to be the first to know because your opportunity sounded like a lot of fun, and I appreciate the time you spent with me. I may have some names of other candidates for you." You're being upfront, you're ensuring that one of your champions hears the news directly from you, and you're still volunteering to help. It wouldn't hurt to ask John out to lunch shortly after you've started your new job to keep your network broad and engaged.

Additional strategies for breaking through to your C-level person include:

- **Call until you "catch 'em."** When are most people in their offices? Call before office hours, after office hours, and ten minutes before the hour. Meetings typically start on the hour, so call them ten minutes before. *Don't leave any messages.* Call sporadically until you catch the person. When you finally get the person, do not vent your frustration. Making someone feel guilty will backfire. Move right to your future. "Glad I caught you. Let me tell you what I'm calling about."

- **Create arbitrary deadlines.** If you say in a message, "I'm going to be in your area next Wednesday or Thursday and want to see if we could grab a cup of coffee," you're imposing a preferred time constraint. Leave eight other companies in that geographic area the same message and work out the specific times later. If you're flying to Chicago for either pleasure or business, the subject line in the email becomes, "In Chicago on Sept 20. Have time in PM?" A trade show where a company you're targeting should be visible can be shaped into a deadline (they need your help there), as can multiple other media, professional association, or business introductions that benefit *them*. See how Strategy #2: Market for Mutual Benefit, combined with imposing an arbitrary deadline, can help you break through?

- **Dangle a "client" connection.** If you're attending an upcoming meeting with a client or a potential client, or are meeting with an influential person or someone in the government, you can use this to your advantage. "Tom, I'm going to be meeting with Siemens next week. I know that you've been talking to them about your new sensors. I can't guarantee that we'll discuss them, but if you want to get together ahead of time, I'd like to hear what you're working on." Once again, you want to be forthright, but if you really think this company has great sensors and that Siemens would benefit from learning about them, your meeting definitely will catch the attention of the person you are calling.

- **Befriend the assistant.** An assistant can be your ally for forever, so treat them with humor and respect. "Jo, is it true that you're the real reason Nancy is walking through brick walls these days?" Making this person chuckle scores on both sides of the Marketing Circle. You're meeting their needs by acknowledging their legitimate importance, and you're building your reputation as a result. Since they are the keepers of the schedule and the hidden persuaders, you want them in your corner. If you pass their screen, you may land either an in-person meeting or a telephone appointment. Not bad.

- **Don't leave a lot of messages.** As Paul of Peter, Paul, and Mary said in his song quoted at the beginning of this chapter, "Sometimes less is more." You're a professional. You're not desperate. Leave too many messages and you risk becoming an in-house joke. You'll know when to back off. If you try the above approaches and you still haven't hooked your C-level person, he truly is uncatchable. Don't take it personally. He probably isn't tuning in to his mother either. Keep moving.

On the plus side is that the number of people you actually can connect with will go up as will your number of meetings. You can use voice mail and email to move your career forward, leaving messages with carrots and proposed meeting dates without ever seeing or talking to each other until the agreed upon time. It's faster and more efficient than messages saying, "Sorry I missed you. Call me," which have no next steps except playing telephone tag forever. Moving the relationship to "real time" as soon as possible is the objective. If you're under thirty-five years of age and grew up on email, force yourself over to the phone and in-person meetings sooner than you'd like. The human touch is what makes things happen.

THE DOG HAS CAUGHT THE MEAT TRUCK: YOU LANDED THE MARKET RESEARCH MEETING

Congratulations. You've broken through to the decision maker, dangled some carrots, and set up an appointment. Victory comes in small steps, so pat yourself on the back with each one. It's time to start preparing for the meeting, but don't drop everything else. Your Job Pipeline is still hungry and needs ongoing initiatives to feed it as you move some of these earlier relationships further down the line.

Who's in Control?

You asked for the meeting, right? That means that you're the one in control. If you've asked to go out for breakfast, lunch, or coffee (stay away from dinner or drinks; they're too long and too complicated), that means that you're supposed to pick up the tab. It also means that you're the one with the agenda and the questions.

You can develop your meeting agenda now. What questions do you want to ask this person? ("Do you have a job for me?" by the way, shouldn't be one of them.) Most of your questions will be conceptual questions that are intellectually engaging and fun to consider. "How is the change in health insurance coverage for employees affecting your overhead?" works better when speaking to a compensation professional than "How much vacation time would I get if I worked here?" Your questions can subtly demonstrate that you know the challenges of the industry and the company. About 60 percent of your questions can be used in meetings with other companies since you're working by target market instead of pinballing with random companies. You have comparative data about trends, issues, and needs in your industries. (What a great springboard you now have for writing articles, blogs, or tweets, as long as you respect confidentiality!) The remaining 40 percent of your questions will be tailored to the specific company.

Prepare Your Funnel

Now is the time to do some in-depth research on the company that you'll be visiting. Use my One-Third, Two-Thirds Rule. You'll want to do one-third of your research up front to even get the meeting, but if you sink a lot of time into researching a specific company and then can't land a meeting, you've just wasted your time, a valuable and finite resource. Do two-thirds of your research after the meeting is set up. This is research that will benefit you with every other company in the same target market because they're all competing against each other and you may be of interest to all of them. When you were researching trends, we talked about sources such as your library, professional associations, the Internet, and colleagues, so plunge in. The stakes have just gone up.

Use these same resources to look up the person or people with whom you'll be meeting. Finding common links with this person will get you further in these initial meetings than knowing everything on the balance sheet. Word of mouth is a great resource, and you can be creative about how you use it. Find a bio of your target through the Internet and note where he did his undergraduate and graduate work. Do you know anyone who graduated from SMU around 1982? Do you know someone who worked at a former company of your target's? Facebook and LinkedIn can come in handy with both of these. Can you find any information about your target's hometown? The possibilities are endless. But don't scare the decision maker in an initial meeting by sharing everything you may have learned about him. The idea is to lower his defenses with a common connection rather than sounding like a stalker.

As you're doing your corporate and individual research, specific questions will start emerging for your agenda. The questions will vary depending on your function and industry, but remember that this is not a job interview. Questions that apply pressure to hire you will backfire. This is all about relationships, helping others, and gathering information about their needs. You don't know if this is a frog that you'll be kissing or the actual prince(ss), but you'll walk away with a new friend regardless, warts and all.

Think big when building your agenda. What are some icebreaker questions? What are some conceptual questions you could ask about their industry? Here is where you mentally engage them and show your grasp of their challenges. You then proceed to narrow down the topics into company-related questions, such as where their bottlenecks and major time sinks are (inoffensive ways to ask about their problems).

The agenda you're designing works like a funnel. It starts with a broad opening and narrows down to specifics. In the middle part of the funnel, you're poking around to determine the company's and the industry's needs. If there is no expressed need, you won't be able to create a job right away with this person. Your fallback objective is to acquire a new relationship, referrals, marketplace information, and trends, though an occasional golden nugget—a problem someone has that you can solve—may slip through.

It's time to start writing down agenda questions for your market research meetings. The questions you develop will provide you with a valuable comparison base, helping you to decide which company attracts you the most. You might also gather some useful research data for publishing an article with one of your professional associations. What questions would you like to ask in your meetings?

HOMEWORK

Market Research Meetings

Brainstorm seven to ten questions that you'd like to ask in a market research meeting.

It's harder than it sounds, isn't it? Below you'll find some ideas, but I asked you to think of your own questions first for a reason. Your questions should target your industry, the company you're visiting, changes going on in the economy, and the individual you're interviewing. Any list of sample questions could sound canned, so be sure to customize yours.

Sample Questions for a Market Research Meeting

Put into your own words.

Icebreakers
"Have you been at _____ for a long time?" Use clues in the environment. Bring up your mutual friend.

Industry
Projections for the industry: is it growing, stable, declining? Short- and long-term projections? Are they cyclical? What new development do you see coming that could affect the success of the field? What are the biggest challenges this industry will be facing in the future?

Company
What companies do you predict will do well or poorly over the next five years? How do you see your company as a place to work? Who are your toughest competitors and why? How did you get started?

Area of Interest
What type of background is typical of a successful _____ [your area of interest] in your company? What are the four most important skills that someone in this position should have? Would my background be appropriate? What type of job titles would be used to describe this type of work? How core is the work that these people do in delivering against the company's mission? Will this type of work be in demand in the future? Where do these jobs typically lead?

Needs
What are the two to three biggest issues that you'll be facing in the next year? What type of skills will it take to address these issues?

Recommendations
What is the best approach to be considered as a serious candidate for _____ [your area of interest] positions? Are there other fields or types of jobs that I should be considering that use the same skills? How do you find talent when you're looking for it? Are there search firms that you use that you think are particularly helpful? Which companies have the highest likelihood of needing someone with my background?

Names

Does this list give you additional ideas for your agenda? Capture your ideas while they're still warm. Add them to the homework section above as potential questions to ask. Your agenda is well on its way.

In addition to your agenda, you'll want to have completed your earlier assignments. This is where the market research meeting and interviewing overlap. What if you actually stumble on some problems that you could solve or an actual job opening that might be of interest to you? Eureka! You don't want to be caught unprepared to demonstrate your strengths. Worst case, this company is a dead end for the moment, but the person is willing to be helpful. You have a great referral source and you can pull out your Companies of Interest list *after* it has become clear that this company isn't going to be a "hit."

Before the meeting, have ready:

- Your Elevator Story.

- Five reasons why the company you're visiting needs you (or your best shot at it, given your research). The point is to think from their side of the circle, why *they* need *you*.

- Five brief stories (PARs) to demonstrate that you can deliver on these five reasons for hiring you.

- Your résumé and your Companies of Interest list. Bring out the résumé only if asked. Bring out your Companies of Interest list about two-thirds of the way through the meeting if it's clear the current company will not be a fit.

With these tools in your tool kit, combined with the research you've done on the company, you'll be prepared for most interviews as well as market research meetings. You know your product (you), and you know your consumer. You'll be prepared for everything from "Tell me about yourself" (your Elevator Story) to "Why should we hire you?" (the three most compelling reasons of the five PARs for hiring you, followed by asking if that's the type of background they're looking for). You won't be caught flat-footed. Remember, however, that you asked for a market research meeting and, unless it's clear that it's an interview, you don't want to pull a bait-and-switch and pressure anyone for a job. This will hurt your reputation and curtail any referrals. Regardless of the outcome, you're getting valuable information that you can build into market trends and aggregate for future conversations and expertise.

THE MEETING: THE BIRTH OF A NEW BEST FRIEND

The main reason to prepare well before a meeting is so you can demonstrate your competence, of course, but also so you can relax. You want to start a new relationship, not flog someone to deliver three names before you leave. It's the informal party model: you're deciding whether that person is someone you'd like to have a long-term relationship with, and in the meantime you're talking casually, helping him with his goals just as he is helping you with yours.

Three main points will help you optimize your return on this investment: your opening, the shaping of a job, and your closing. It's all about meeting some new people, being genuinely curious about their work, listening for their needs, and seeing what you can do to assist. Piece of cake, right?

The Opening: Your Two Leading Questions

A lot of these ideas also apply to job interviews, not surprising considering that the mind-set that works best for both is one of curiosity and openness, that of a potential investor instead of a job supplicant. I won't dwell on the mechanics here. ("Groom the receptionist. Go to the restroom ahead of time and make sure you look presentable. Dress conservatively. Get a real grip when shaking hands, not just the fingers.") There are interviewing books such as *Knock 'Em Dead* by Martin Yate (Adams Media, current edition) if you want more details. There's just one recommendation that I can't resist making, however: take a notepad with you. Have you seen those pads with leather binders that are fairly unobtrusive? They work well because you can have your agenda on the top page of the pad and your résumé and Companies of Interest list on the bottom of the pad, where they stay unbent and out of sight until you want them. Just make sure that these documents aren't attached to each other so your Companies of Interest list doesn't fall out when you're telling Company A that you've never wanted to work for anyone else.

The first question is the icebreaker. Whether you start your conversation when you are presented at the door of his office or the two of you are walking to his office together, you need to be prepared with some ice-breaking questions. Think fast: what is your mutual interest? You know the answer: the person you know in common. Start by asking, "How is Jack doing?" or something related to Jack that would be of interest. If you don't have a personal connection, you can decide while you're waiting in the lobby what type of question would work for starters. (The weather? Their stock price? Traffic? The Red Sox? Something in the news?) Go with your instincts and keep it informal.

The second question might refer to something that you pick up from the office environment. You'll probably see pictures of the kids (always a good lead-in), awards, or memorabilia that will tell you more about this person as an individual. Have you heard the story of the interviewer who had a giant fish tail mounted on his wall? Anyone who didn't ask about the fish tail was immediately disqualified from further interviews. The executive decided that if such a major trophy was ignored, the candidate wouldn't be inquisitive enough to fit in with the company's culture. Whether or not it is fair, people certainly *have* been hired because of similar interests, whether it is fishing, basketball, golf, or military service. Forget whether or not it's fair; it's common ground.

Shaping a Job

You may have promised that you'd take only twenty minutes of this person's time, so you're moving quickly by the middle part of your conversation. You have your agenda, and you're choosing the questions that seem most relevant. You're listening well. When the person you're interviewing seems engaged in the conversation, ask questions that will uncover the problems that could be fodder for job creation:

- What are your bottlenecks?

- What keeps you up at night?

- What are the two biggest time sinks for you in the next couple of months?

What you've just done is found three separate ways to say, "What sort of problems are you having?" If, however, you ask directly about problems, the temperature may chill. Companies, or people, rarely like to openly admit to problems. These sample questions are less threatening. Invent your own using your own wording and sprinkle them throughout the conversation.

As needs or problems emerge, ask questions that help you sense whether or not you might have a shot at creating a job:

- "It sounds like you have your hands full with that."

- If you're feeling especially intuitive and have some insights that the target may not, try out an observation. "It sounds like political issues are keeping you from meeting your deadlines."

- If you're getting agreement, that's a green light. Proceed with, "I've had some similar experiences turning over political roadblocks to get back on track. Tell me about what you've done so far."

- You can follow with a story (PAR), but make sure that it's short, relevant, and uses the vocabulary of the company you're talking to.

- If they're still with you, ask, "Would you like me to get some ideas together for you about different ways that you could meet those deadlines?"

- If "yes," then proceed to, "Why don't we touch base early next week since time is of the essence. How's Tuesday morning?" For bonus points, you might add, "I could make the meeting a little more relevant if I incorporated some ideas from your CFO and CIO before we sit down. Would that make sense?" If it does: "Could I get you to send them an email to tell them I'm coming and cc me on it? I'll know that I can go ahead and contact them without you needing to think of it again."

If you get this far in a meeting, reward yourself (cheap, legal, and low calorie). This is a process you'll want to replicate elsewhere.

These leading questions asked toward the middle of the meeting followed by your suggestion of another meeting will give you a good reading on whether or not there is a prayer of creating work within this person's area. Notice that you did not mention a job or pay, or the idea of employment or consulting. Right now you're just trying to help them. If the next meeting goes well, then you can start talking about how to structure the work. Get your hooks set first.

As mentioned in Strategy #3: Stop Looking for Jobs, you're taking a risk when offering to give away some of your time. Don't throw the offer around lightly, because your time is precious. Only use this strategy with your favorite companies, and ones that don't have the right type of opening staring you in the face. The other risk you run is the "why buy the cow when the milk is so cheap?" one. If you give them all your solutions in meetings before you have set up any agreement, you undercut your value. On top of that, telling a company the "right" way to solve their problems in your first meeting is dangerous. You don't know their history or what they have attempted so far. Saying, "This is what you need to do" in a first meeting could sound superficial or naïve. Doctors always ask questions, listen, and find out your history before they make a diagnosis.

If you actually spark your contact's interest in creating a potential job, you don't need to settle all of the details in the first discussion. Pace yourself. You should have plenty of time to decide on the scope of the work in the next few meetings. As you're reaching an agreement, tell him you'll draft a plan (things will go faster if you take the initiative) so you all can meet his deadlines. Note that you just stressed the bottom side of his Marketing Circle—moving quickly—to help keep him motivated. It's a good idea to include a review period in your agreement, three to six months out. Ask your friends in human resources, employment law, or professional consulting to help you structure an agreement if you don't already have one. The briefer it is, the better.

You won't explore developing a job in most of your market research meetings, however. You'll most often be meeting with B-level people to gather information. Your goal now is to head for referrals to C-level people in target companies.

Referrals to these senior-level decision makers must be requested with a light touch. They're based on trust. They're like a letter of recommendation, reflecting the judgment of the referring party. Your contact will only recommend you to her colleagues if you are competent and helpful and won't waste her friend's or boss's time. To push too hard for leads is to run the risk of looking like a machine that is using other people rather than trying to help. People will back off. There will also be times when your networking connection genuinely doesn't know anyone in your target areas, so don't assume you will hit home runs with all of your meetings. Advancing one base at a time, with some walks and doubles, will get you to home plate just as well.

There are two ways to ask for referrals: through your general conversation about companies and by referring to your Companies of Interest list. Let's say that you're talking about what companies are hot, and why, and which companies should be integrating more quality controls into their offshore manufacturing (your business question that uncovers more targets for you). Maybe some contact names within these companies have been volunteered. If not, try, "It sounds like an interesting company. If you know someone there who it makes sense for me to talk to, I'd appreciate a connection." Now stop talking and see what happens. This question should flush out leads if there are any to be had. You may need to reassure your contact that you don't expect people to have jobs just because you're calling but that you might actually be in a position to offer them some helpful ideas.

Your ace in the hole is your Companies of Interest list. Reach for it if the company you're visiting isn't going to be a target and say, "I'm particularly interested in two companies that you mentioned. I'm going to follow up with them. Let me share with you the types of companies that I've been thinking about so far and see whether you have any opinions about them." Decide before the meeting whether the company you're meeting with should be on the list.

Give him time to review your list. It's amazing how well this works. Imagine someone giving you a list of thirty companies and twenty names that you could easily skim instead of asking you for suggestions of where there might be work for someone with her skills. The Companies of Interest list shows that you're not depending on other people to define your interests. It also helps him help you because it allows him to brainstorm networking connections quickly and easily. When deciding on individuals to add to your list, choose executives from your target companies who could influence your selection, whether they are board members, top officers, vice presidents, or directors. Why have names of individuals on your list as well as company names? How many times have you gotten to know people at soccer games, church, or dinner parties and haven't paid as much attention to their professional affiliations as to their personal ones? Your contact who is seeing your Companies of Interest list is as likely to make an association with an individual's name as he is with a company's. "Susan? Oh sure, I know her. Our kids play soccer together. Is that where she works? Let me give her a call."

Classy Closings

Keep track of the time. Note when you're within three or four minutes of the time that you promised the meeting would end. You'll look less professional if you run over your time limit without acknowledging it. "Teel, I asked for twenty minutes of your time when I set up the meeting, and we're nearly there. How are we doing with your schedule?" Let her choose whether to wrap up or continue, which is much better than having her silently resent your eating away her time.

At the end of a market research meeting, you'll want to do two things: review the action steps and clarify how you can return the favor. In the heat of a meeting, your contact may be magnanimous about volunteering to undertake various initiatives for you. After the meeting is over, however, the best intentions are often not fulfilled, so go for the "close" while he is in front of you. "Thanks for your willingness to give Bill a call on my behalf. I hate to give you more things to do, though, so would it be easier if I got his contact info now, then I'll follow up with him and use your name, or maybe you could shoot him an email now and cc me? You won't have to think of it again." Note: You focused on the bottom side of the Marketing Circle by emphasizing how you will save him time, plus you waited to hear the response to make sure he was comfortable with this. Take as much initiative as you can to help the person deliver.

Asking how you can return the favor of someone sharing their time and information is a classy step that will separate you from the rest of the pack. You may hit on some way in which you can be helpful before or during the meeting, so listen for clues. After all, you're becoming a gold mine of marketplace information and connections. You may pick up on a need that you could pass along to a third party. "Oh, you're renegotiating your insurance coverage? I know someone who does a great job with risk management if you're looking for ways to limit your liability. Would you like me to have Bob give you a call?" That's a win-win-win situation. If you don't have any helpful ideas to offer by the end of the meeting, ask. "Now, what can I do to help you?" This simple question will totally disarm your contact because he is accustomed to being asked for help rather than being the recipient of it. If he can't think of anything right away, you continue to try. Just spreading his name around in a complimentary way helps to build his reputation . . . and yours.

Follow Up

"I've given hundreds of informational interviews, yet I rarely get a thank-you note," a president of an advertising firm lamented. "Giving an informational interview is actually more of a favor than giving a job interview, but I get less appreciation for them." Writing a note after a meeting, just like asking what you can do to help, makes you stand out above the average person. Some heavyweight paper and a few handwritten lines are all you need. Include an email address or a phone number that you promised, and then your note will be saved for a while, a visual reminder of you. Funny, we've come full circle. A handwritten note used to be considered less professional, but now it's seen as a gift from someone who took more time to be personal. (Email thank-you's are also acceptable, but realize that you have a choice.)

Whether or not to stay in touch after the meeting is your call. Make the decision consciously. There will be some contacts—people with valuable networks, spheres of influence, and perspectives—that you definitely want to stay in touch with not only during transition, but throughout your career. They would be logical candidates to send a LinkedIn invitation (more on this below). Some relationships will end with your thank-you note. If you say, "I'll keep you posted," at the end of your meeting, it's a good idea to actually do so, especially after you call or meet with one of his referrals.

Now that you know the structure of a market research meeting, the next step is to schedule real ones, if you haven't already done so. Just draft an email similar to the base email format with a date and, hopefully, a referral's name. Start with people who you do *not* anticipate will be major players in your career plans. The objective is to practice your skills. Play it in Hartford before you get to Broadway; you'll get better with these meetings as you do more of them. The skills from these meetings will roll over into your day-to-day life as well. The questions you're asking should not be reserved for job transitions. You'll want to ask questions about trends, competition, and pressure points on an ongoing basis to make career management part of your daily routine. The conclusions you reach and actions you take will become part of your New Job Security.

THE "SUSTAINABLE" PART OF NETWORKING

Finally. The fourth strategy of managing your career is Build Sustainable Networks, but we're just now getting around to talking about sustainability. Why? Because it's important to learn the correct way to network, to help others, before plunging in. Without knowing the right moves, you could burn up or wear out your network, not to mention thwart opportunities to expand it. Like meeting with a trainer when you first start using a gym, you learn the right form and the right exercises so you can get abs of steel without throwing out your back. Consider yourself trained. You know how to arrange meetings; you know how to ask questions informally to gather information; and you know how to help people, without any guarantees of return. Now for the workout.

What: Build Sustainable Networks

Let's look at the what, who, and how of building sustainable networks. The "what" part won't take long. You already know that building sustainable networks means staying in touch with your network on an ongoing basis, not just while you're in transition. How many times have I heard from professionals, "I've learned the hard way. I will never, ever let go of my network again." True relationships are developed neither quickly nor easily, contrary to the rapid "friending" that may happen on Facebook. To hope you can turn on the tap only when you need it and have relationships and connections flow out is to be sadly disappointed. These same professionals who swore their allegiance to keeping their networks alive are often the same ones who, a year later, are bemoaning their lack of time to stay on top of their new jobs and their old networks. There are ways to do both, however. We'll cover them in the sections that follow. You don't want to give up what you've gained.

Who: Double Low Density

Not to worry. Keeping your network alive doesn't have to be too time consuming, even when you're employed; you just need some realistic strategies. There is fascinating research being conducted right now in academic institutions about just what you're doing: building and sustaining networks for work success. Ideas issuing from this research provide a system that will allow you to access people more efficiently, and thus minimize your time commitment.

Professor Herminia Ibarra, formerly of Harvard Business School and now with INSEAD, writes about the importance of consciously building your influence through effective networks in "Network Assessment Exercise, Teaching Note" (#5-497-001; Harvard Business School Publishing; April 11, 1997; p. 5): "Effective networks provide *links to multiple networks*, serving as ports of entry to social and organizational groups to which one does not have direct access. To be 'well connected' in this regard is to position oneself on the boundary of many nonintersecting networks. . . . Density refers to the extent to which people within one's network know each other . . . a high level of density may signal a 'redundant' or 'inbred' network that will not afford them access to new ideas, information and opportunities. . . . Managers with sparse networks advance more rapidly in their careers."

In other words, a sparse or "low-density" network is your goal for career networking. A low-density network includes people in different areas of your life who do not know each other. Part of your value to them is the unique information and connections from different groups that you can share. Dr. Ibarra made a startling statement in an ExecuNet presentation that she gave at a networking meeting I hosted. *"You're more likely to receive job assistance from someone you do not know very well than you are from a close friend."* Surprising? Her point was that you're already likely to know a lot of the same information as your close associates, hence *redundant information,* but people further removed will have access to new ideas and connections that you don't typically run across. She is building on Mark Granovetter's work in *Getting a Job* (Harvard University Press, 1974) and on Ron Burt's work on structural holes in "The Network Structure of Social Capital" (*Research in Organizational Behavior,* JAI Press, 2000), demonstrating that *weak ties are more useful than strong ties for people who are searching for jobs.* These points about the critical role of new people, new ideas, and low-density networks in your career success are major points to build into your planning.

Dr. Monica Higgins, an associate professor at Harvard doing social network research, furthers the work on the structure of relationships in an article called "Changing Careers: The Effects of Social Context" in the *Journal of Organizational Behavior* (Volume 22, No. 6; September 2001; pp. 595–618). She describes what would happen if you only hang around a group of advisors who are "high density," meaning they are well connected with each other. "Advisors who already know each other may be thought of as different 'doors' to the same 'room,' while advisors who do not know each other represent access to different 'rooms.'" You'll want access to those "different rooms" as you decide who to actively keep in touch with over the long term.

What do you want your "buckets," or the groups that you'd like to stay in touch with, to be in building your own low-density network? Your work, family, and friends, as described in K. E. Kram's *Mentoring at Work: Developmental Relationships in Organizational Life* (University Press of America, Lanham, MD, 1988), are the three most obvious places to start. Which groups are your highest priorities? Regarding work, think of colleagues, bosses, subordinates, vendors, and clients from your most recent job as well as from earlier companies. Professional associations can also be very helpful because they take a horizontal cut across a large number of companies for their memberships. Relationships with officers in an active professional association will connect you with their contacts as well.

Family is always an important part of your network. Slice and dice their categories in whatever way is most helpful to you, from the types of work they do to geographic or lineage associations. They're clearly a group you can go back to over and over again.

Friends outside of work can be organized into various categories, from people you went to school with (an important group because you already trust each other, and you can probably still find them on Facebook) to friends that you know through sports, clubs, religious activities, children, the neighborhood, and com-

Diversity Range

HIGH DENSITY

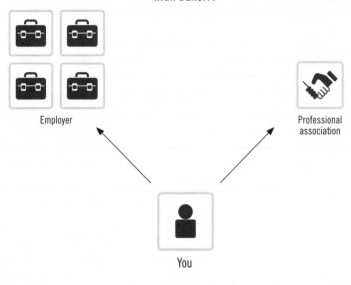

Employer

Professional
association

You

LOW DENSITY

Community

Employer

Professional
association

Family

You

School

© 1998, Monica C. Higgins, Harvard Business School

mon interests. Some of these categories will have surfaced when you first started entering your network into a system earlier in this chapter. Now you can decide which are your top categories to nurture, your low-density groups. Since they won't know each other, to use Dr. Higgins's analogy, you'll be walking into different "rooms" of information as you keep in touch. That's just the point.

If you'd like some structure to define your buckets, use the chart on the following page to identify the top five or six groups of people that you want to connect with over time, and then identify a Key Player within each group that you will help over time and share resources with. Who should you select? Look for three characteristics: someone who is relevant to your work life; someone who is influential, receptive, and not too many handshakes away; and someone who is a low-density networker in her own right. In other words, if your selection is also involved with lots of different groups of people, she will have fresh information to share with you—more insights, more leads, and more connections that you would not have been able to access on your own. You now have a *double* low-density network, since both you and your Key Players have low-density networks, and you are becoming increasingly valuable as a contact because of it. LinkedIn has a model that is similar to this with its third level of connections, so you can use it as an inspiration for the best connectors. Drop the term "double low-density network" at your next party and you'll be the center of attention (sort of like "double secret probation" from the movie *Animal House*).

Your objective is to come up with five to seven names, one or so per bucket, of people who will become your Key Players. You don't want high volume here; you just need different groups represented by well-connected people. You may also want to include a maverick who isn't in a target group but would be a great source of information. Your friend who is a consultant for McKinsey might count because he's inside major companies all of the time. Your CPA, someone you know on several boards, or your thesis advisor might not be in targeted categories, but one of them might be a connection with low-density networks. Keep them in mind as you're selecting your top five to seven Key Players.

HOMEWORK

Your Key Players

Group	Top Five	Key Player Contact Info	How Can You Be Helpful?	Next Follow-up
Former employer, Motorola	Yes	Former boss: Don Jones (djones@ gmail.com)	Emailed him that I heard a potential customer is unhappy with its current vendor, 1/15	March 5

If you identify the main buckets that you'd like to group your network into, the names of your Key Players will fall into place. You may not even know all of the Key Players yet. You may want a relationship with the president of your professional association but you haven't yet identified how you can be of help to him to get the relationship started. LinkedIn (or a slow time at a meeting) may provide you with an introduction to him once you're ready, however. When you have your top choices identified, keep the information to yourself. Announcing to this select group that they've won your contest is like telling someone, "Guess what! I've decided that you're going to be my best friend!" It might make them nervous. You'll also want the flexibility of changing the Key Players in your network as your needs change, something you can do more easily if their initial selection is known only to you. It's your behavior that will change the relationship, and that brings us to the "how" of career networking.

How: Pelicans and Dragonflies

Before we plunge into process, I want to clearly state the values behind what we're doing. Wayne Baker, in his book *Achieving Success through Social Capital* (Jossey-Bass, 2000), could not have said it better. "If we create networks with the sole intention of *getting something*, we won't succeed. We can't *pursue* the benefits of networks; the benefits *ensue* from investments in meaningful activities and relationships." Networking is never about using people. Rookies or people you don't want to hang around may take that approach, but your approach is more honorable: you're taking the risk of helping first, without a guarantee of any return. Since you can't help everyone in the world equally, you have to decide where to spend your time, just like you do when you're developing any friendship.

First, let's actually identify ways you can jump-start your career network so people in it can hardly wait for your calls. Next, we'll talk about structured networking meetings, groups organized specifically for the purpose of lead generation, which will help you broaden your exposure and your support. These types of networks—your hand-selected Key Players group and your structured networking meetings—are examples of the two levels of relationships you'll see in your networking. Some relationships will be more in-depth and others more tactical. In her article "Managerial Networks" (#9-495-039; Harvard Business School Publishing 1996; p. 3), Dr. Ibarra defines these two categories as:

- **Long-term, high-reciprocity ties:** Close bonds and reciprocal relationships ensure reliability under conditions of uncertainty. These include peer alliances that function by exchange of favors, ties of trust and loyalty, and so on.

- **Short-term, instrumental ties:** Many important network ties serve highly circumscribed job-related functions. They are often dissolved when the relationship has served its purpose . . . networks that consist exclusively of close, "important" relationships usually have important gaps from a task-related standpoint.

Translated: You'll want both "deep divers" and "surface skimmers" in your career network. Your Key Players should be in the long-term, high-reciprocity category, plus there may be others that you aren't nurturing quite as actively. Think of yourself as a pelican with this group. Have you ever seen a pelican flying over the surface of the water searching for its next meal? When it spots its target, bam! This bird intuitively makes an immediate nosedive (or is it a beakdive?) into the water. It goes deep, disappearing quickly. Just as you think it's going to drown, the pelican surfaces with a giant fish in its bill. Mission accomplished. You'll want to be a pelican with many parts of your network. You'll want to dive deeply, immersing yourself in your element. Delving deeply into your profession or industry to learn from the experts enables you to become and stay an expert also. The depth of knowledge and the connections that come from these long-term, high-reciprocity ties are part of your New Job Security.

Contrast the pelican's style with the dragonfly's. The dragonfly rarely slows down. It constantly skims over the water's surface, touching down briefly before taking off again, moving continually from reed to water to a piece of driftwood then away. Staying on the surface when you're building a network gives you a sense of momentum. You start setting up meetings with a number of people, generating activity and some leads. "I didn't know networking could be so much fun," newly laid-off professionals report. "If I could just get paid for this, I'd be happy." These short-term, instrumental ties are perfect at the beginning of a job campaign and are essential, to a more limited extent, as your campaign continues and during your long-term career networking. How else do you find out that shipments aren't going out of a certain company's loading dock like they were last quarter? How else do you know that another company is going to outsource the payroll work that you'd like to bid on? Short-term, instrumental ties can feed you ongoing, real-time information.

Don't neglect the pelican's approach, though, if you find that being a dragonfly is seductive. If you're high on the "E," or extroversion, scale of the Myers-Briggs, or gravitate naturally to meeting new people, the dragonfly approach may feel very comfortable. But if you stick exclusively to the dragonfly approach, after a while you will start wondering why nothing is moving forward; there's a lot of smoke but no fire. Although keeping that wide-angle view of what's going on in the marketplace is valuable, you also need the in-depth knowledge of your targeted industries and your profession. Use your networking abilities to network *down and into* your specialties as well as across the marketplace in general. If you stay too broad, you won't have the expertise in any one to two areas that people are looking for. Targeted industry insights will sell you and build your reputation. You'll know what the needs are, which companies are hot, who the movers and shakers are, what the right vocabulary is if you're changing industries, and maybe even the names of some potential customers for them. You've come up with the big fish.

Pelicans Let's look at some tactics for approaching your Key Players. They're similar to some of the ideas in Strategy #2: Market for Mutual Benefit and Strategy #3: Stop Looking for Jobs. No surprise, huh? The care and feeding of your "elite athletes" does not need to be exhausting. It's like keeping in touch with your friends. Sometimes you email them, sometimes you phone them, sometimes you get together. You see and hear things that remind you of a friend, so you invite him to join you at an upcoming event you're attending or give him your ticket if you won't be able to use it. With your Key Players, the content may be slanted more toward common professional interests, but that isn't critical. Golf wouldn't exist if it were. The process is the same, regardless; you're thinking about the bottom side of their Marketing Circle, then following through (no pun intended).

Here are some ideas to get you started:

- Tell them about an emerging business opportunity they might pursue (a perennial top-of-the-list favorite because it relates to increasing profitability).

- Email them an article of interest.
- Send them a book.
- Tell them about a meeting or speaker that they might enjoy.
- Offer to help with a crunch they may be facing.
- Ask them whether they're going to a professional association meeting. Set up a time to get together at the meeting.
- Pass along a compliment you heard about them.
- Say something complimentary about them to others.
- Suggest names or resources for a project they're working on.
- Give their name to a reporter as an expert to interview.
- Help their kid.
- Give them a gift subscription to a relevant magazine.
- Invite them to do something outside of work that's appropriate, such as golf, squash, or dinner with the spouses.

Here are some things you should *not* do with your Key Players:

- Put them on email joke distribution lists.
- Put them on *any* email lists that will make them look like just one in a crowd.
- Contact them constantly.
- Do anything that is too familiar or not politically correct. You probably don't know their values or boundaries yet.
- Give them expensive gifts.
- Call or email just to chat. Have a clear purpose when you contact them, and then you can chat if you like.

Maintaining relationships with five to seven people doesn't sound so bad after all, does it? It doesn't take too much time, and the methods are unlimited. It's fun to be creative about how you can help someone.

What do you do with a Key Player once you have one? Now that you're doing all of these good works, what is on the top side of the Marketing Circle for you? These are the people who can help you stay competitive. You need them while you are employed as much as when you are in transition. When you are employed you are likely to get caught up in the day-to-day details and lose touch with the skills and competencies expected by the outside world, not to mention the shifts in companies and players in the marketplace. Your Key Players can keep you current on this. By asking them questions similar to the ones you asked in your market research meetings, you will keep yourself sharp and updated with valuable information to trade with other Key Players (as long as it isn't confidential). Remember, these people don't know each other, so you have a unique cross section of perspectives. Introducing them to each other is a gift only you can offer and they'll value if they're all big cheeses. Go write an article, a blog, or a tweet and quote your Key Players!

HOMEWORK

Network with Key Players

Go through your planner, your task manager, or your calendar now and write in "Contact Key Players" at regular intervals. Every six weeks or so should be fine. Vary how you contact them (email, meeting, or phone) and your content so that they don't feel like they're on a schedule.

You'll find that you can delete some of your reminders when you come to them because you've just been with Sheryl at a trade show and just talked to Bic about the project he was working on. Great. It's working. Your reminders are simply a safety net so none of your Key Players are forgotten.

Dragonflies The short-term, instrumental tie group has obvious applications when you're in transition, but first let's touch briefly on their advantages when you're employed. These are task-related relationships that dissolve upon completion. Can you think of any dragonfly encounters you've already had serving on teams or projects? Job-related dragonfly encounters are no different. Even though you may not be grooming these people as you are your Key Players, I've seen ten-year-old connections reactivated when they were needed. "Phil, this is Emily Parker from Alpha Industries. We worked together on a project for Beta Sites several years ago. You were setting up the systems architecture, and I was feeding you expectations from the end users. Remember? Can I catch you for a couple of minutes? You did a great job on the conversion, so you immediately came to mind when someone was asking me how we should integrate our information. I have a couple of questions." Later on, you can ask, "If there is some consulting work here, may I give them your name?" You established the connection, you complimented them, you asked your question, then you tried to reciprocate. That's all you need to do. Old and new connections with competent professionals can typically be activated with a simple, clear request. LinkedIn may make finding them easy since their contact information may well have changed. Invite them to link with you, and then you can add them to your own contact management database if you choose. You don't have to know everything in life because you have dragonfly connections to help you out.

When you're between jobs, short-term connections speed up your transition. Just like a mutual fund spreads your risk of loss over a group of stocks instead of relying on a single one, your dragonfly connections will broaden your exposure to the marketplace and lower your risk of missing an opportunity. "Individuals with wide-ranging social networks are more likely to learn about opportunities sooner than those having narrow ones," according to Peter Marsden and Elizabeth Gorman in an article titled "Social Networks, Job Changes and Recruitment," from the *Sourcebook on Labor Markets: Evolving Structures and Processes* (Kluwer Academic/Plenum Publishers, New York, 2001, pp. 6–7). I constantly see proof that people who don't know each other well are still happy to be helpful (Granovetter's strength of weak ties), so don't be hesitant about asking. Just don't apply too much pressure, and be helpful in return.

Your dragonfly connections will supply the information that your pelican group doesn't know. When one of your Key Players says, "I've heard rumors that the CFO position at Widget may turn over," you research the names of the top decision makers and board members at Widget, then check them out on LinkedIn and email their names to a group of dragonfly and pelican contacts to see whether they have any handshakes with this group. Use the bcc (blind carbon copy) line for your list of recipients if you aren't able to write individual emails; you want to protect their privacy, and you don't want it to look like you're sending out a mass email. A similar approach works well for a small number of job postings that look particularly promising. Go ahead and respond, but put out an all points bulletin to your off and online networks at the same time, listing all the officers and decision makers for the job. This gives you a good chance of finding a mutual contact. Responding to the designated person in the ad at the same time will get you into the proper queue. Networking in at the top will get you into a more powerful group. All you're asking of your network in either case is, "There may be something coming up at Widget that I'd like to pursue. Do you know anything about this company or these people?" Be conscious of how frequently you "go to the well" with questions for your contacts, however. You don't want to wear them out. Either lump together several inquiries in one communication, or couple them with something that is helpful to your contact. You'll want both pelicans and dragonflies to look forward to your messages.

Where do you find your short-term, instrumental tie group? They're all around you. All those people in your contact manager database or Rolodex, that you're connected to on LinkedIn, or that are following you on Twitter that didn't make it to your Key Players group are in it. Anyone you meet socially or through family, work, professional connections, or networking meetings is in it. Networking meetings designed for the purpose of sharing leads are everywhere. The business section of your local newspaper should have a calendar section that lists some. Employment divisions in your state government should have networking group lists. The Department of Labor funds www.careeronestop.org, which has information on networking groups as well as additional career resources. Industry associations and local churches often host such groups. People have figured out that networking is the way to find jobs, so events abound. Test some out and see which ones offer the ideas and the people that help you move forward.

I need to make a disclaimer. I'm highly biased toward a specific networking organization called ExecuNet, which has been mentioned elsewhere in this book. It's a nationwide membership organization of career-savvy executives who earn more than $150,000 in compensation. Most of the members are employed and are keeping on top of trends in career management and skills that are in demand in their fields. Even though you may not be at this level, you may want to learn about its process and start your own networking group for which you define your own parameters (there are examples below). If you're well above this compensation level, its services are even more relevant. Finding senior executive openings and appropriate career support gets tougher the higher up you get, and it provides both. Its nationwide networking meetings allow you to check out company reputations and plug into underground information about what's happening locally. On its website, members can access job listings with compensation over $150K and career management information.

If the above types of networking organizations and events don't meet your needs, then start your own.

James was general manager and vice president of an international instrumentation company prior to its leveraged buyout. He reported that his network outside the company was nearly nonexistent since he had focused all his energies on the company and traveling to his offices throughout the Far East. "How will I connect locally?" he wondered. "I'd really like to have a group of peers who I could share resources with as I go through this transition." He wanted something small and personal, with a constant group of members at his level. Be careful what you wish for!

We defined a group with these characteristics, which were also in James's broader industry of manufacturing, from ExecuNet attendees, my clients, and some of his connections. We invited them to an initial pay-for-yourself breakfast at a nice, centrally located hotel. It worked. James chaired a breakfast of twelve people the first time, where each person briefly presented to and received feedback from the entire group. They continued to meet, developed an email distribution list, gave themselves a name, TBG (The Breakfast Group), shared information and leads between meetings, and grew. It became so large that James's original vision of a small, ongoing advisory group was diluted. The coordinating role passed on to other people over time, and the group continues to evolve independently of its founders.

James, in the meantime, had clearly mastered the job of networking. He tested multiple professional association and industry groups to determine the best use of his time. He then became involved with those of greatest interest to him. He joined a newly formed small networking group that was close to his original goals, a functional group (a CEO group), and several groups that cut across his industry (turnaround, corporate growth, and corporate director foci). He balanced his networking time between those who were in transition (they typically know where the action is) and those who were employed (the ones creating the action). James is now president of a company and is seen as a resource by companies and individuals as the guy with connections. His BlackBerry is golden.

Another newly formed networking group that James joined had a different model. John, a senior vice president of human resources with extensive international corporate experience, formed Hilltop Group. His mission was to have an ongoing group of very senior-level professionals with international experience who were committed to remaining in the group when employed. The group, which has a constant membership of the same ten people, started off meeting in one another's homes once a month on a Saturday afternoon. They now are scattered all over the world, still stay in touch, some work for others in the group, and they're all successful. James has a "board of directors" for his career management for the long term. What a good idea.

There are two main points from James's story that may be useful in your career networking. One is that you can create your own networking group instead of, or in addition to, attending already-established groups. You decide whether you want a short-term group that dissolves as people get jobs or a long-term group that people stay in when they're employed. Ask people to attend a pilot meeting to see whether there is a need, and, poof, you may have just created something. The second point is the advantage of maintaining a balance between the pelicans and dragonflies. James has some of both, and you can, too. The proportions may vary from times of transition to employment, but the combination will give you both breadth and depth. You're on top of things now. Your back is covered by your group.

SIXTY-SECOND NETWORKING
WHEN YOU HAVE NO TIME

No, this has nothing in common with speed dating. Instead, it's an efficient way to manage your network when you think you don't have time to do so. "Gee, Robin would be interested in that article," passed through my mind as I was reading something on www.wsj.com. Bingo. I punch the email icon, type her name into the email address field, write a ten-word note to Robin, and the article appears in her inbox. You've just reached out and touched someone with little effort. Embedded in this example are the three easy steps to sixty-second networking.

1. You've already identified your Key Players and have some sort of schedule in your calendar for contacting them. You've set up your structure.

2. Here comes the sixty-second part. *All you have to do is keep in touch with your five to seven Key Players.* When the reminders pop up for your first follow up, do something that's quick and easy. Passing on a lead, forwarding an article, ordering him a book, referring some potential business, or recommending him as a speaker doesn't take long.

3. Many of your follow-up contacts can be coupled with a networking question. Your email might say:

Lydia,

I just took the liberty of giving your name to Tom Richards, who sets up the program for the ACA conference. I thought you'd make a great speaker. If you don't hear from him soon, give me a call.

I have a question for you. Besides the ACA, do you have any favorite professional associations? I'm looking for the most senior-level ones in our industry, and my guess is that you'll have some inside information.

Thanks. I hope you're doing well.

A subsequent email could invite Lydia to join you at an association meeting. That isn't so bad, is it? As you continue to develop your relationships, you can insert your side of the Marketing Circle in your conversations. Hey, you've just offered Lydia a plum and have her attention. It's time for a trade.

This doesn't need to take long. Inviting them to meetings you'd be going to anyway along with Key Players from your other buckets is a three-fer. You have fun and make good use of your time, they have fun, plus they get to meet each other . . . one of the main values you can bring to *their* career management.

THE BOTTOM LINE

So, you've come a long way in this chapter, in particular by clarifying the values behind sustainable networking that Dave Opton, the founder and CEO of Execu-Net, articulates so well: "The underlying philosophy of networking is about giving without expectation. If you're not prepared to put your needs aside and help others first, you'll quickly wear out your welcome by asking for too much, too often." From the values to defining how networking has evolved, to setting up a system for your own network, to actually breaking through and meeting with new people who can provide you with information, you now have the strategies and a process. You know how to structure a long-term career network that keeps you connected with both the off- and online world, with a limited time commitment, while you're employed. When you're in transition, your network is like an accordion. Your Key Players give it the ability to expand rapidly. Sounds like you've mastered this career networking thing, doesn't it? That's a big deal.

STRATEGY #5

NEGOTIATE IN ROUND ROOMS

"Money is better than poverty, if only for financial reasons."
—WOODY ALLEN

Negotiating is like spinach. We know it's good for us, but we avoid it. When I give negotiating seminars, I ask a room full of executives to raise their hands if they've ever negotiated their own salary. No more than 20 percent will raise their hands. I then ask them if they've ever negotiated a contract. Nearly 90 percent will raise their hands this time. Why the disconnect? Why are we so comfortable working out terms for products, services, and even the acquisition and divestiture of entire companies but not with working out terms for our personal compensation? You would prefer negotiating a deal for your company than a deal for yourself, right? If you feel that negotiating your compensation is too personal, and that you'd just like to get through it and on to the job, you're not alone. This discomfort has existed since Adam failed to negotiate a counteroffer with Eve. You could be missing out on more than apples, however. Your income, clout, and reputation are at stake, so let's increase your comfort level with pricing the product (you're the product, remember?).

In this chapter we're going to focus on negotiating an incoming compensation package, because that's when you have the greatest leverage with a company. Some ideas about pricing your services if you're creating a job are at the end. Just because these examples focus on the early stage of your relationship with a company, however, doesn't mean that you can put your negotiating skills on the shelf for the rest of your career there. Negotiating, as you will see in the following examples, is omnipresent in daily life. Read Deborah M. Kolb and Judith Williams's *The Shadow Negotiation* (Simon & Schuster, 2000) for additional ideas about handling the constant negotiations you experience when employed (it's targeted toward women, but the strategies are universal). Consciously develop negotiating as one of your career management skills using win-win outcomes, and your satisfaction will grow as much as your income.

Now, back to pricing the product—perhaps an easier way to think about yourself, because it seems less personal. The first step is to recognize that you're already an expert. According to the *Random House Dictionary*, you've negotiated when you've "arranged for or brought about by discussion a settlement of terms." This means you're actually negotiating all the time. Have you ever bought a car? A house? Raised a teenager? A two-year-old? On the job front, whenever you worked on teams or projects, or with customers, vendors, or bosses, you have negotiated. Closing contracts with other companies, labor unions, or funding sources are more obvious forms of negotiating. You are making trade-offs with people, time, space, resources, money, and responsibilities to reach your goals and the company's goals. Your own compensation package deserves at least the same amount of energy.

A second point that may encourage you to negotiate more frequently is that companies expect you to do so. If you're working on a salaried basis, especially if you are at a senior level, negotiating your package is expected. After Bob finished his compensation negotiations with his new boss, he stopped by the human resource director's office to tell her about the deal. Bob reflected his mild surprise that the CEO had acquiesced so quickly to Bob's wish for a higher base. "We already had the money in the budget," the HR person said. "We would have been disappointed in you if you hadn't asked for anything more."

You're establishing your competence and your reputation by asking about other compensation options before signing. You have value, the company will benefit by hiring you, and *you're not going to lose the offer* if you explore alternatives to the first proposal. That is the most common fear, "I'll lose the job if I ask for more." Au contraire. Ask for more correctly and you just may get it, along with a little more respect. After all, if you're going to be representing this company and *its* best interests to the outside world, don't you need to demonstrate that you can represent your *own* best interests in a professional manner?

WHAT ARE ROUND ROOMS?

Round rooms don't have corners you can paint yourself into, or straight lines that intersect at only one point. You want the same conditions for your negotiating: lots of options and ways that you can intersect, or reach agreement, on compensation so both you and your new employer are satisfied.

Broadening the base of your negotiating—getting away from a narrow focus such as, "I made X dollars in my last job, and I need to earn at least that much in my next job"—will actually help you to achieve your goals. (That specific concern will be addressed later in the chapter.) The point is that if you're relaxed and open as you discuss your compensation, seeing it as a business deal, then you may come to an agreement that serves you better than the original offer. Stating a specific salary requirement, for example, could lose you money. Maybe they were going to offer more and you'll never know. Stay loose at the beginning of your financial discussions, drawing out other people first. The main characteristic of broad-based negotiating is that there is more than one possible outcome to the negotiating process that could satisfy both you and the company. Give the employer more than one way to say "yes."

You will be broadening your scope in three different ways as you negotiate:

- Broaden what you're asking for: it's not just about the money.

- Broaden how you talk about your compensation if you're quoting your salary history or future expectations.

- Broaden the number of ways an employer can say "yes."

Like a triangle resting on its longest side, you will have more stability and a greater chance of success if you and the decision maker have multiple choices and options during negotiating. A triangle balancing on one point, a "we have to do it this way or I'm walking" attitude, will topple. Your goal is to secure a job offer, and you're more likely to achieve that by keeping your presentation broad and flexible until the numbers start getting fairly specific.

PREWORK: IT PAYS

Before you even get close to talking about money with a company, you'll want to develop three pieces of prework: your Marketing Circle, your timing, and your compensation figures. Your financial results will be closer to what you had in mind if you're prepared. Let's look at your Marketing Circle first.

Your Marketing Circle

You thought through the Marketing Circle for your target company prior to crossing its threshold for the first time, right? Your needs are represented on the top side of the circle. You know what is important to you in addition to being compensated fairly. This information will help you test whether a job is truly a fit for you and where you might have some flexibility in your negotiations if you need to make trade-offs.

It's the bottom side of the Marketing Circle, however, that has probably gotten you where you are today, entering negotiations with a good company. Responding to a company's needs is even more important when it comes to negotiating. If you want the company to offer you more, why should they? A salary is rarely increased just because you want it to be, or because you made more at your last company, or because you have two college tuitions to pay. Those concerns are on the top side of the Marketing Circle. Instead, plan how you're going to help pay for yourself—with your breakthrough research skills that will finally allow them to get their products to market, with your project management skills that will motivate teams to do more with fewer resources, with your treasury skills that will ensure that the funding will be there when it's needed. You just moved to the bottom side of their circle. Figuring out why you're worth more is part of your preparation. You need to be able to verbally express your value and not assume, "Surely they knew that." Don't expect them to wonder if you're worth more than they offered you. That's your job, and you'll want a defensible position.

Jack Benny Timing

Have you ever seen a video of Jack Benny, the famous comedian, performing? He was a master of timing. The key to his success was his pauses. He would stand there on stage with his arms crossed, waiting for the audience to get the punch line before he said it.

> Mugger: Quit stalling—I said your money or your life.
>
> Jack Benny: I'm thinking it over!

The audience roared. You can consciously time your statements about money as well. The "when" and "who" of money conversations will have a direct result on the "how much." When do you want to talk about money with a company? Take a page from Jack Benny's book. Pause. The answer is "as late as possible." Putting off discussions about money will increase your chances of getting more of it. Why? You haven't set your hooks yet when you're starting to get to know them. At the beginning, they don't know that you're the answer to their prayers, so you're easy to discard. If you quote your current salary in response to a compensation question in your first interview or over the phone, you've just given them a reason to eliminate you. Your answer will be too high or too low, period. If it's exactly what they were going to offer, you just positioned yourself too low. If your former salary is too high, they'll decide that they can't afford you. If your salary is low, rather than thinking that they would be getting a good deal, employers often feel like they're getting someone too junior or inexperienced. You lose with any answer. Talking about money early on, therefore, is *not* to your advantage. It pigeonholes you. Should you need any further inducement to hold off on monetary discussions, ask yourself, "Have I ever seen employers find additional money for someone they really wanted to hire?" My surveys show that the answer to this question is a resounding "yes." Employers don't go rooting around for additional money after just one meeting, however. They'll wait until they are convinced that you are indispensable and that the investment would be well worth it. That commitment develops toward the *end* of the hiring process, not at the beginning. You've moved from being a commodity to a necessity.

Who should bring up money first? This is part of your timing strategy also. The answer is, "Not you." You have nothing to gain by introducing a loaded topic early on. You might even give them reasons to exclude you. They'll get around to the topic if they're serious, so bide your time. There's an old adage in negotiating: whoever mentions numbers first loses. It's true. Ralph knew the rule. He was talking to a Fortune 500 firm about the presidency of one of their divisions, and salary wasn't brought up during the first four rounds of interviews. By the time the company introduced the topic, guess how many other people the company was interviewing? Zero. Guess how much leverage Ralph had now? A lot. The decision makers really didn't want to go back through a pile of résumés and start all over again. They wanted their problems solved, and finding a cheap group president wasn't one of them. Ralph knew that the conceptual sale had to be closed first—they had to see him as their solution—then the compensation discussions would be fairly easy. He did well.

Although all of this makes sense, you're still asking, "Aren't I wasting my time if I don't find out from a company early on whether we're in the same ballpark?" The answer you probably already see coming is, "No." If you think a company and its management team have some potential, talk to them without bringing up money. You're not wasting your time. Worst case, they become good practice for you, what I call "garbage interviews." As you proceed, you'll find that some companies aren't good fits for you, but you can still try to help them and refer them to a candidate if you can. Not only will you build your reputation, but you'll build your interviewing and negotiating skills so you're ready for prime time when the right company emerges. You get better with practice. The best case is that the company can actually afford you and you continue interviewing, or, if it can't afford you, the company refers you to an emerging internal position in another division or to one with another company. I've frequently seen people referred to more appropriate, higher-level positions within the company that weren't advertised externally. You never would have made this inside connection if you hadn't accepted the interview. In this instance, timing your compensation conversation is everything.

Five Sets of Necessary Numbers

Determining your salary requirements is the third leg of your prework stool.

Calculate Your Lowest and Highest Figures For your lowest figure, decide what your absolute minimum salary is. This is the amount that you need just for your ongoing expenses. This is not something that you'll use in a discussion. It's your private safety net. Determining this figure now will help you make wise decisions in the heat of the moment, when you're being wooed for a start-up venture where you eat air for the first year with the promise of back-end rewards.

For your highest figure, think of the highest salary you have ever made. Add in any bonus you earned there. If you received one every year, choose one of your better years. Add in a modest allowance for your benefits. I recommend a modest allowance instead of the actual dollar amount because these figures can get really large, which can skew the grand total you're calculating. Human resources professionals report that salaried employees typically receive more than 30 percent of their salaries in benefits such as 401(k) plans, health insurance, life insurance, vacations, and stock programs. An average number is fine here because you might sound too expensive otherwise. Add them all together and see what comes out.

> There is more than one possible outcome to the negotiating process that could satisfy both you and the company.

The following sample works with salaries from $25,000 to over $1 million. Insert your own figures.

Best salary	$95,000
Bonus	$9,500
Benefits	$10,000
Total	$114,500

The next step is to take this number and round it off. You can present the above package, for example, as being in the "low six figures" or "low one hundreds." Both statements are honest, accurate, and not too detailed. This is exactly what you're looking for with broad-based negotiating. These figures reflect your previous compensation package or your overall compensation and will be correct if you need to get into a discussion of your salary history. Notice that we haven't added any stock options that you may have. I love stock options because they're so vague. They're hard to quantify quickly, and that will work to your advantage. The examples coming up shortly will give you some other ways to present your earnings, but remember that you only want to get into this subject if it works to your advantage, not as a base from which to plan your next salary.

Establish Your Market Value What are you worth? If you don't know the going rate for your services other than your most recent salary, you're a victim in waiting. You'll be basing your new salary expectations on your old salary, but who's to say if that one was accurate? If you're changing functions or industries, or if you're doing some consulting, your old salary will not be relevant. Time to do some homework.

Standard economic theory on pricing a product (you) is "what the market will bear." As long as a willing buyer and a willing seller agree on a price (typically at a point of some discomfort for both), they have a deal. Learning what the market is paying for your competition is a good place to start. This doesn't mean that you can't price yourself higher or lower than your competition, but you need to be aware that you're doing so and with good reasons. If you're just starting in a field, you may lower the going rate a little. If you're an industry guru, you may decide to exceed the going rate. The company gets what it pays for, and you can explain what that added value is.

How do you find out what you're worth? As you track the skills you need to stay competitive, the companies that are hot, and the trends in your industry, your worth is but a question or a website away. You should determine your market value now, and then check it occasionally while you're employed to see if it changes.

Ways to quantify your market value:

- Ask colleagues. As you're gathering information from people who will *not* be hiring you, ask them for the going rate for your type of work (or for the work that you'd like to be doing). *Going rate* is a nonthreatening, noninvasive term since you're not asking about *their* salary.

- Check out websites and job boards. Some job listings, like the senior-level postings on ExecuNet.com, will include salaries. Ignore geography during this research. You know that jobs in San Francisco may pay a little more than those in Austin, Texas, due to differing costs of living, but you're looking for trends rather than specifics. Another great resource is www.salary.com.

- Contact the national office or website of your professional association. They often do salary surveys.

- If you have a contact, ask a consulting firm that has a compensation and benefits practice, such as Mercer or Towers Watson. They often do salary surveys for their clients so companies can benchmark their salaries against the norms. This will take some networking because it isn't public information, but you might get some insider information from either the consulting side or the client side.

- Ask reference librarians in business libraries (including universities) for their favorite salary sources.

- If you're considering consulting, talk to other consultants about how they would charge if you did some work together. This has to be legitimate! I know what my competition charges because of the many referrals I've sent to them and received from them. You already know not to give away their confidential numbers to others, however.

- Look at business publications. If you're at the highest level of a company, business publications such as *Fortune, Business Week,* or the *Wall Street Journal* will often report what CEOs make. Read the articles for background information, but take them with a grain of salt.

- Ask search firms, my favorite source. They typically won't talk with you unless they're screening you for a specific job, but if things are slow or you can network in, they will know real-time market information for your geographic area. If they're screening you for a specific job, don't pull out your salary research questions; you need to sound focused on their opening instead. It's when neither of you are trying to sell the other on anything that you will get more useful salary norms.

- Human resource professionals at large companies in your industry should have some comparisons if you ask them about the "going rate" in your field.

- For publicly held companies, check out the salaries of their top officers at the Security and Exchange Commission's Edgar database (www.sec.gov/edgar.shtml) if you are, or are hoping to become, a top dog.

- Set up informational meetings and job interviews. Once you start getting out into the marketplace, you will receive direct feedback on what you're worth. You'll learn the salary ranges for jobs that you're interviewing for and can leverage this (without quoting company names) when it's helpful.

Does this give you some idea of how to collect your data? In that case, you're ready to go to work. Start thinking about your market value *now*, before someone catches you off guard with a salary question. You don't want to miss an opportunity.

HOMEWORK

Collect Job Data

Collect compensation information for at least five jobs similar to the one you'd like (or already have). You won't always get complete information, such as info about stock options and bonuses. Just capture what data you can. If you're going after different types of jobs, collect compensation information for each type of job.

Now that you have a feeling for the going rate, or what the market will bear, for your work, you'll have an idea about how you should price yourself in your negotiations. People typically make their biggest leaps in salaries when they change jobs, not when they stay employed with the same company and get the same 3.5 percent increase that everyone else does. You won't know whether you can make a big salary leap until you do your homework and maybe even get out and do some job interviewing. Using the old argument that "I have to match what I was making" demonstrates narrow thinking. It's history and it's on the top side of your marketing circle. Saying, "The other opportunities I'm looking at are in the X range" is much more persuasive. It's market based, honest, and suggests that there may be some competition for you.

Track Compensation Trends If you're going for a job in senior-level management, you'll benefit by knowing the main trends in compensation in your industry and geographic area prior to your negotiations so you can leverage them. Within all six areas of compensation—salary; variable cash; long-term equity; perquisites; retirement and asset protection; and severance and change of control policies—there are continual shifts according to Tom Wilson, CEO of The Wilson Group, a company that works with boards of directors and top executives to develop and implement integrated incentive compensation systems. The shift from a high salary to variable comp, that is, a lower guaranteed base salary and more compensation based on results and performance, has been going on for a while. How you want to react to that shift will depend on your values and your reading of the economy. Tom describes a shift from stock options to restricted stock taking place in compensation plans as well. What percentage of which would be your preference, given your tolerance for risk and the flexibility of the company? You'll typically receive twice as much of either when coming into a company versus what you'll receive when you're an employee, says Wilson, so ask while you have the leverage.

Another shift involves the *measures* of compensation that are valued, which will fit perfectly with your thinking about marketing for mutual benefit. Once again, it's not about you, it's about your target company's *customers*. Keep their customers in *your* sight and your target will keep you in *its* sight. Instead of measuring units per hour for manufacturing, for example, a company will measure on-time delivery to customers and their satisfaction, Wilson points out. Use the same language when you're asking for an increased bonus payout and you may have a double reward: you'll be more likely to get it and you'll be showing that your values are aligned with your company's best interests. His research indicates that supplemental life insurance and long-term care—possibly the new 401(k)—are growing in use, and your prayer of getting a company car is going out the window. To evaluate other compensation trends and their impact, ask the same sources that you used above in establishing your market value. If you keep an eye on these trends when you're employed, you can protect your company and yourself from economic swings by having the right incentives in place at the right time.

Get Insider Information Tracking down information about the compensation of the executives at a company you're going to be negotiating with will give you a source of hidden strength; you'll know when enough is enough. (Asking to make more than your boss makes is typically poor form.) If your target is a publicly held company, you can find the compensation of the top officers and its board on the proxy statement in the company's annual report. It's in the Security and Exchange Commission's Edgar database (www.sec.gov/edgar.shtml) and is essential reading. The company will be surprised if you haven't checked out publicly held compensation information so that you know how to position yourself in relation to its executive team.

In addition to the general market norms mentioned above, search firms are another source of information on specific companies, especially large ones that are more likely to have your target companies as clients. When I was connecting some great employees with search firms after a company layoff, I learned that the company having the layoff was known for paying their people really well. That's helpful information for your negotiating strategy. Those working for search firms also know which companies don't pay well and which ones go through boom-and-bust cycles. Connecting with these people will take some networking, but you know how to do that. Don't forget your double low-density network and LinkedIn, either, for learning the word on the street about compensation norms in your target companies.

Former employees are a third resource you can tap prior to a specific negotiation. Just ask them what the "going rate" or "norms" are for salaries in your area at their former company, then keep their feedback confidential. Integrate this information with the other sources of insider information you've gathered and you'll know what sort of flexibility a company is likely to have.

Define Your BATNA Roger Fisher and William Ury's advice in the classic negotiating book *Getting to Yes* (Penguin, 1991) is still right on the money: "The reason you negotiate is to produce something better than the results you can obtain without negotiating. . . . What is your BATNA—your Best Alternative to a Negotiated Agreement? . . . If you have not thought carefully about what you will do if you fail to reach agreement, you are negotiating with your eyes closed." In other words, pinning all your hopes on one company with one specific compensation package is both psychologically and professionally risky. This is the point of keeping your Job Pipeline filled, so your alternative choices will emerge at approximately the same time as your impending offer does, giving you some leverage in negotiating (not to mention job choice). If other companies aren't getting serious, what are your alternatives? Continuing your search is an obvious one; doing some contract or consulting work, or maybe starting something of your own are other choices. Maybe being semiretired or volunteering is your BATNA. Money isn't everything. Regardless, thinking about courses of action *other* than the one you're starting to negotiate will increase your confidence and comfort. You don't want to risk making an unfavorable agreement because you have no fallback options. If you are negotiating salaries at several companies, so much the better for your decision making and leverage.

THE LANGUAGE OF NEGOTIATING: SAYING THE RIGHT THING AT THE RIGHT TIME

Now that you have done your prework, let's look at a standard compensation structure and at a standard process for negotiating, and then we'll look at some exceptions. As you may already know, most medium to large companies have compensation systems in place. Similar jobs are grouped together into similar salary ranges to make sure people are paid consistently for similar levels of expertise and responsibility. When there is an official job opening, it is slotted into a specific band with a salary range attached. Now here's the trick question.

> When you're interviewing for a job, if you're quoted a salary range that goes with the job, which of the following are you being told?
>
> > a. the whole range
> >
> > b. a portion of the range that corresponds to your experience and previous salary
> >
> > c. the bottom quartile
> >
> > d. a range that reflects their interest in you

Roll of drums, the answer is "c." In most companies, if they quote you a salary range at all, it's typically in the lowest quarter of the whole range. Is this deceitful? Not at all. People already in that range expect their compensation to grow with their experience, and that's what the top of the range is reserved for. If you come in at the top of the range, there is no room for an increase later. Yes, you might be able to upgrade your salary range, but it isn't an easy thing to do. Job content has to meet certain criteria to merit a range change. Aiming for a higher-level job is usually faster and easier. Even though there is usually more money in the overall band than what you're being quoted, that doesn't mean that a manager is at liberty to fork it over. If you want a shot at getting any of it, you'll have to ask. Now for the standard negotiating approach. We're going to assume that it's the right time—no earlier than toward the end of a second-round interview, and preferably later—and that you're talking to the right person, your potential employer and boss.

> EMPLOYER: Pat, it looks like you have the type of background that we're looking for. What would it take to get you? (There are two types of questions an employer will ask about your salary: "What have you been making?" [your history] and "What do you want to make?" [your future]. Everything else is a variation on these two themes. These are predictable questions, so practice your answers ahead of time.)
>
> YOU: The money is important, obviously, but it's getting this product with this brand to market and getting to work with this team that have me particularly interested. I'm seeing a wide range of compensation packages

in the marketplace, so maybe we can start with you. What did you have in mind? (You put the money into perspective, showing that it isn't your only driver. You implied that there might be some competition for you by knowing about other compensation packages, and then you ducked, trying to get them to break the ice by quoting numbers.)

EMPLOYER: Well, the range is $93,000 to $99,000 plus benefits and bonus. Is that what you had in mind? (It's amazing how many people will give you the range if you just ask.)

YOU: (Pause.) I'm sure we can work out something. I was hoping for a little more. What sort of flexibility do you have? (There are three key phrases to keep in your tool kit: "Do you have any flexibility?" "Is that in your ballpark?" and "Can you see your way clear to . . . ?" These are three nonconfrontational ways to stay open and ask about numbers without committing yourself. Practice using all three of them.)

EMPLOYER: Not much. What did you have in mind?

YOU: I was expecting a base somewhere in the teens, between $113,000 and $120,000. Is that in your ballpark? (Remember, they're just going to hear the *lowest* number in your range, so don't say it if you don't mean it. You can go 10 percent over the top of someone's range without blowing them out of the water. They're probably quoting you the bottom part of the overall salary range for your level anyway. You can then round up a little from the 10 percent and put your number into a broader band so you don't commit yourself to exactly what you would accept yet. *Asking a question immediately after you quote a figure is important*; you want to get feedback on whether or not they're going to play at your level. If you don't ask a question *right then*, right after you've broken the ice with a number, you're never going to know two weeks later if you don't hear back. If it was the salary, you could have kept the discussions going if you had asked a question. The ballpark one above, the flexibility one earlier, or whatever fits in with the context and gets you feedback is fine. If you don't know your market value yet, you can fall back on your old salary (say, a $115,000 base) if you need a rationale, as long as it's true. It's just a weaker position than, "I'm interviewing for jobs with base salaries between $112,000 and $125,000. Is that in your ballpark?")

EMPLOYER: I doubt it. I can look into it. I can do $105,000, however, and I might be able to do a little more on the bonus.

YOU: Tell me more about the bonus. (Notice that you haven't agreed on the base salary yet, but at least you got him past his earlier range. What's emerging is lower than you want, so table the discussion about the base to find out whether there are other ways to close the gap. Always talk about your salary first rather than jumping into benefits since you'll live and die by it for the rest of your time in that job, but you don't need to agree to it until the end when you know the complete package.)

From Salary to Benefits and Back Again

Now it's time to begin a relaxed discussion about benefits and variable pay. Benefits could include anything from retirement plan contributions to flexible working hours to medical insurance to stock options. Human resources can tell you about the standard benefits. Your boss is the one to ask for any exceptions. Decide on your top benefits priorities ahead of time. Your boss may have the time and energy to discuss up to three benefits, depending on their complexity, but don't wear down the new relationship by fighting for the country club membership unless it's integral to your success.

Ian knew he had already maxed out on his salary negotiation. A major university had extended a job offer for the chief marketing position and Ian wanted to close the deal. The position had been newly created, and the organization knew the job was important to its future growth. The search committee had already upgraded the position several times because the salary originally offered didn't bring in candidates with the experience necessary to work with their board of trustees. A higher salary level would bring in a different caliber of applicant, but now the budget was strained.

One of the major search firms was handling the search, so Ian got feedback from them during the early stages of his negotiation. He asked for several thousand dollars over the university's quoted salary and they agreed. He knew they were jumping through hoops to deliver this, so he dropped salary as a topic. Next he brought up benefits. Now that he was in his late fifties, Ian was interested in moving out of the for-profit world to achieve some of the intangible benefits a nonprofit organization could offer.

"I'd like to talk with you about the vacation time that is allowed with this position," Ian said as they started getting into the details of the package. "I already have a family commitment for this fall, and I need to honor it." (He and his wife had made plans to go to Europe, but Ian didn't need to get into the details.) "Is there a way that I can work out an extra week's vacation in October? I'll make sure everything is covered before I go."

> "Sure, we can handle that informally," his new boss reassured him.
> If you don't ask, you'll never receive. Ian ended up doubling his
> vacation time and, in addition, his relocation package. During his benefits
> discussion, he went for things that were either nonrecurring expenses or
> that didn't cost the organization much but meant a lot to him. Smart guy.

Ian talked about his salary first, then moved to a discussion about benefits. If you're talking with a for-profit organization, the order of topics would be the same, but the content can change. Variable pay options like bonuses, incentives, and profit sharing weren't relevant to Ian's nonprofit position, but they may be relevant to you. Since companies aren't obligated to pay on these agreements unless the company is doing well, they may be more likely to grant your request. If you're looking for a way to close the gap between what a company is willing to pay in salary and what you were expecting, think "variable." Be sure you cover these issues before you start discussing the less tangible, non-cash (at least not in your pocket) benefits. Most of these are routine (insurance, day care, tuition reimbursement, sick leave, etc.) and are best left for a human resources discussion unless they're one of the top three items you'd like to negotiate, as retirement contributions and vacation time often are. Just remember that there is a finite amount of energy you and your future employer are going to spend negotiating, so spend that energy on the most important points first. Once you have the benefits and variable pay options roughed out, you can circle back around to the salary discussion.

> YOU: I appreciate your pushing up the percentage on the bonus and the
> 401(k) plan contribution. It sounds like there are only two things still on
> the table: whether you can see your way clear to the $113,000 salary we
> discussed and the stock options. I would submit that the $8,000 dif-
> ference between our numbers, and I'm going with the lower end of my
> range, is a drop in the bucket compared to what we're going to bring in
> as a result of the product rollout we've discussed. Can we work with the
> $113,000? (Even though you were discussing benefits at this point, note
> how you put the salary back on the table at the end of the meeting with a
> specific number attached? You chose the low end of your range expecta-
> tion in return for bonus and retirement plan increases. You also pointed
> out how you were going to pay for yourself by doing a good job with the
> product rollout. This is a "show me the money" strategy that gives the
> employer an argument to use with others on your behalf. If your future
> boss can't answer you right away, offer to get back to her in two days,
> giving her time to see if they can shake more money out of the budget.

You want to keep the momentum going at this point. When you call back, before you get into a conversation, ask, "Where are you now in your thinking about the salary and stock options?")

You've just finished most of the standard negotiating process at this point. If things move forward in your follow-up phone conversation, it's a nice touch to go back and finish the negotiations face-to-face. Use the same approach if you receive the offer in a letter. In both cases, there may be some odds and ends that you'll want to resolve with the company, and it's better to do so in person. It's much easier to tell you "no" over the phone than it is in person, isn't it?

ADVANCED NEGOTIATING PLAYS FOR CATCHING CURVE BALLS

You're bound to run into some curve balls when you're negotiating your compensation package. You can anticipate and prepare for most of them ahead of time.

When They Want You to Propose a Figure First

There will be some occasions when your tactic of asking the employer to break the ice by quoting numbers first won't work. They'll ask you to go first. They may be well trained or lucky. Regardless, if you've ducked once and it hasn't worked, it's time to be forthcoming. Just present your compensation so it works to your advantage. The following dialog assumes that you are talking to the right person (your hiring manager) at the right time (the second round of interviews or later).

EMPLOYER: Susan, what sort of salary have you been making?

YOU: I've had a good, but somewhat complicated, compensation package. Since your package will be structured differently and I'm sure you pay competitively, can we start with what you had in mind?

EMPLOYER: We're open. You first.

YOU: Okay. My package has been in the low six figures, with stock options on top of that. Is that in your ballpark?

EMPLOYER: Could you be a little more specific? What is the base salary?

YOU: My base was $100K, but I've been talking to several companies about jobs with base salaries from $110,000 to $125,000, depending on the variable pay. What range are you proposing?

In this scenario, you're gradually backing up. The normal response to "What salary are you making?" is to say, "$100,000 annually," and to say it quickly. You now know that immediate disclosure is not to your advantage and will pigeonhole you at your former salary, a number that will inevitably be too high or too low. You ducked in the first round by asking what they had in mind, but since they came back to the same question a second time with "you first," it's time to come clean. You don't want to look like you're hiding anything. The compromise is to give them a straight answer and then immediately show them that you're worth more than that in the marketplace, or give them a "broadband" answer ("My base was in the low one hundreds"). Be sure to follow your salary revelation with a question such as, "What range are you proposing?" so you can see how he reacts before the moment slips away. If the employer says, "Gee, Trey, I'm afraid we can't afford you," you know that you caught a rejection in the making. Try, "I don't know. Tell me what you had in mind first, and we'll see if we can work out something." That will keep you in the running without looking desperate. If you avoid quoting any figures the first time the question is asked, that may be about as far as you can go without looking like you're playing games. You can decide in the context of the interview. Notice that the second time Susan was asked, she answered generally with her whole package, but the third time she gave them the actual base and referred to competitive jobs. She hadn't closed on any other offers at that point, but mentioning them kept her honest and showed the company that she might have alternatives. Not bad. Susan's most recent salary was below what she was worth on the market. If she quoted her old salary alone, a company could have assumed that she didn't have experience at the level they needed, so she answered with her market value as well. It worked. After all, a company does have to compete for talent against the current market norms, so Susan's figures were in line with the other people they were interviewing. If you run into someone who demands to know your most recent salary, and you know your salary is lower than his range, you can say:

"Peter, if it's critical to our moving forward, I can share it with you. My company froze increases for several years due to layoffs. I am choosing to leave due to salary concerns, and the risk is that what I'm worth in the market, which is demonstrated by the jobs I'm interviewing for right now, will be lost with a piece of old information."

See what your interviewer does with that one. You can try it with search firms, too. Notice the room for continued negotiating all through this discussion. Susan did not paint herself into a corner once. She asked questions, she answered with ranges, and she didn't make any specific salary demands. When the discussion moves to benefits, she can decide what other lifestyle decisions will be her top priorities to negotiate, always presenting them from the employer's angle. "I've used some great video conferencing equipment that really cut down on our travel expenses and let us cover a more geographically diverse set of customers. Are you open to how much time I spend on the road if I can still improve customer service and cut travel budgets?" Don't forget to give your employer several ways to say, "Yes." Asking questions rather than demanding absolutes will identify the win-wins without pushing them too far. Propose two alternatives that are acceptable to you, then let them choose, for example, asking for more vacation time while accepting their salary proposal or a higher bonus percentage and a lower base salary. Does this remind you of asking your kids whether they'd rather clean up their room or do their homework before dinner?

Talking About Salary Too Early or to the Wrong Person

Companies need to eliminate candidates for jobs early in the hiring process, especially if they've posted a job and have hundreds of responses. Salary expectations are an easy way to screen applicants. You may get a phone call.

> EMPLOYER: Hi. This is Eric responding to your application to Bolt 'Em. Your background looks interesting, and we'd like to ask you some more questions, but we want to be sure that you realize the salary for this job is $58,000. Is that in your range?
>
> YOU: Hi, Eric. Thanks for the call. I don't know if the salary is in my range. The work looks interesting and is certainly something that I've had a lot of experience with. Bolt 'Em has a great reputation, and I have some ideas about how to keep building it. What I'd like to do is set up a meeting with whoever is doing the hiring, and, if we have a fit, I'm sure we could work out the salary. Do you want to ask me your questions, and then we could see if we should set up a time?

Let's say that you have been making $73,000, so their figure of $58,000 is well below your salary range. This problem might be surmountable, but you don't know this yet. You did, however, follow two important rules in your response: you *didn't* try to negotiate with the person who called you on the phone, and you *did* attempt to get an interview since the company was of interest to you. It's not unusual to get entrée into a company with a lower-level interview, and then get referred to a higher-level, unadvertised opening once the employer sees how capable you are. You didn't have any leads that would help you come in at a higher level, but you like Bolt 'Em, so you decided to go for the bird in the hand. Not talking to just anyone about your compensation is a good rule of thumb. The person calling you on the phone to set up an appointment is rarely the one who will be deciding your compensation. Dodge his questions, and try the "I'm sure if we have a fit, we can work out something" response. The first-level screeners in human resources need to eliminate people to winnow down their pile. The more material you give them, the more reasons they can find to eliminate you. Don't let a premature salary discussion be one of them.

If your first interview is with human resources, it isn't unusual for them to screen you by asking about salary history or asking you to fill out an application with salary questions on it. You want to be charming, but you don't need to cross all of the T's on this one, either. If asked about your compensation by an HR professional, try, "I've had a good income. I'd rather hold off on salary discussions, if I could, until we get a little further along. I'm sure if we have a fit, we could work out something. Could you tell me a little more about . . . ?" as you redirect the conversation back to the job's content. You don't want to trigger a full-blown salary discussion this early in the relationship and with the wrong person, so you want to take the pressure off you by lobbing the ball back into their court. If they give you the range, just nod and say something noncommittal. If they want to play hard ball and say, "I need to know your salary expectations," you have to make a decision. In this case, you could say, "Look. I don't want to scare you off. I've been making a good income, and I don't want to run into any preconceptions if I come in higher than your range. You want the best person, and I want interesting work. Can we see whether we meet each other's expectations before we get into the details?" Another alternative is the above response Susan gave to Peter, which expressed her various concerns for not wanting to answer definitively because he would be operating from old information. Ultimately, however, you don't want to risk irritating a senior HR professional any more than a search firm executive. They're just doing their job by trying to get information out of you. You're doing your job by trying to keep your options open. Their responsibility is to screen out the less qualified parties, and compensation is commonly used as a qualifier. If you need to give them your previous *compensation* information (broader than your salary, since you can include some of your benefits and bonus), state it as positively as possible, mentioning variable pay and stock, and then ask for immediate feedback.

Negotiating Through Search Firms

The partners in the five largest international search firms, described in Strategy #2: Market for Mutual Benefit, are pros, as are many of the executives in the boutique firms. If you're negotiating with a search firm, they'll need to know your salary to present you to a company, so there isn't a lot of point in avoiding that discussion for too long. If you have a very high compensation, your network contact might be able to use it to your advantage to introduce you to a search firm. "Bruce, I have a $750,000 semiconductor company turnaround guy you should talk to. Want to know more?" The people in your network would be better at doing this than you because you're not going to get the attention of the firms as easily as a mutual friend with good connections and it's a little too pushy for you to lead with your own salary. This should only be done with the highest-level firms that work with these salaries. You don't want a rookie who would love to work at your range using your name as a battering ram to get into companies. Whether you are making $75,000 or $750,000, if a search firm presents you for a search and it gets serious, their level of involvement in the negotiation may fade as you progress. Different firms work in different ways. Remember that your ultimate agreement is with your employer, and that is the preferable party with whom to negotiate. They have the authority to make exceptions in their proposed compensation package, and they're the ones who will stand behind the terms. Negotiate directly with the decision makers whenever possible.

Creative Ways to Close Salary Gaps You've wrapped up the benefits phase of your negotiations and are now revisiting the salary base. The employer isn't going to budge from the original number, and you expected a little more. We have a gap. Before you walk away or accept less than you think you're worth, get creative about closing that gap. You may end up considering a different job or shaping a new job; remember Strategy #3: Stop Looking for Jobs. You also may find that negotiating for more than money increases your potential job satisfaction. There is more than one way to skin the compensation cat. Try a creative approach if you'd like to accept a job offer and the salary isn't quite what you had in mind.

Hiring Bonus or "Split the Difference" These are two of the easier ways to increase your base salary. Hiring bonuses come in and out of vogue depending on your industry, the economy, and your uniqueness. If you have a unique skill set that the company really needs, you should ask for one. One approach is to ask regardless of your satisfaction with the overall compensation agreement that you've reached because it's part of the professional image that you want to project. The other approach is, "Carol, we're just $10,000 apart in our salary discussion, so what if I take the difference as a one-time hiring bonus? I'm going to be paying for it shortly with increased revenues, and it's not on your books for the long term." Having it on an annual basis is preferable, of course, but getting it once is clearly better than never.

"Split the difference" is a tried-and-true negotiating tactic that my clients use constantly with success. "Carol, we're just $10,000 apart in our salary discussion. What if we split the difference? We can up my base by $5,000, which I'll pay for shortly with increased revenues, and you can still be within your budget. Does that work?" This would be more rewarding than the hiring bonus, unless you do both, since you get it annually, but use your judgment about wearing down your negotiator. After you've reviewed the other creative approaches below, decide which, if any, will work best with your target company and limit the number of long, downfield passes you throw if you're expecting them to receive all of them.

Add Responsibilities You don't want to give up on your higher salary proposal yet, so focus on the employer's needs and how you can help her.

> YOU: Beth, I understand that $65,000 is the best you can do at this point and that you're facing some constraints due to internal equity and budgets. Since we're only $8,000 to $10,000 apart, I have an idea. You've been thinking about starting Six Sigma for a while now, but you don't have the necessary time to devote to it. What if I get that off the ground for you? You will see returns within the next twelve months that you wouldn't have been able to generate otherwise, and I will have more than paid for the salary differential. What do you think?

Sounds similar to an earlier tactic for raising your salary base, doesn't it? It is. This time, however, you're proposing that you take on additional work to warrant the increase. To use this strategy, look for trouble spots when you're interviewing, such as bottlenecks, competitive pressures, or problems that they don't have time to address. You're doing this anyway as you listen for their needs and consider how you might create a job. You then present a solution to an issue that is important to the employer and interesting to you as a bargaining chip. It's essential that you define a task that is manageable in size and scope, though, because you're just about ready to volunteer to take it on in addition to your new job. Notice how you actually "showed Beth the money" by suggesting how she could afford to cover your salary differential? Proposing to accept additional responsibilities may catch the employer off guard, and she may be surprised into mulling over your suggestion. You aren't looking for additional responsibilities, but you're willing to do it in return for the compensation. See what happens. You attempted to unofficially upgrade the position into a higher salary range, but you avoided the use of the words, "regrade the position." You don't want to introduce new paperwork now, when your objective is to close on a hiring decision. Next year, when you're in and have a good track record, you can request a formal position upgrade.

Combine Jobs If both a lateral job and a lower-level job are open, why not save the company some trouble and make them a proposal?

Ilene was smart. She was talking to a company about one job that looked interesting, but when they got to the salary discussion, she learned that the salary was about 60 percent of what she had been making, lower than she was willing to consider. She tried the standard negotiating process of trying to raise the salary, without sufficient results. Instead of ending the discussions, Ilene got creative. "In addition to the project management job we're talking about, I've noticed that you have a job opening for a team leader, something that I have extensive experience with and could do in my sleep. I have an idea. What if we combine the two jobs? It would increase my credibility as project manager when people see that I have hands-on experience as a team leader, and it would give me insider information on any kinks or personnel issues that might arise with any of the teams. Instead of paying two full salaries and sets of benefits, you could have a better-qualified team leader plus a qualified project manager for 80 percent of their combined compensation. Would that work?

You've just saved them the time of finding two people and the expense of two separate salaries and budgets. Bonus points for being creative.

Reduce Your Time Commitment Lower value should equal less time. If you discover that the job isn't going to come close to what you're worth, you may have an opportunity on your hands. You've already gone through the standard negotiating process, so you both know of one another's salary ranges and that the twain are not going to meet. If you still like the company, make a proposal.

YOU: Tad, let me run an idea by you. This job has been open for a while now, and I'm sure you'd like to get the interviewing process over with

and get back to work. For the salary range you're quoting, you're probably going to get someone with ten to twelve years of experience. I'd like
the chance to work with you, but someone with more than twenty years
of experience won't need five days a week to do the work. If you have
some flexibility about how you package this job, meaning the number of
days you'd need me to be on site, you can get a lot more experience and
higher-quality work for the same price. Are you open to a four-day-a-
week commitment?

If Tad bites, work out an arrangement for a part-time, professional job that is
fair to both of you. The time-honored negotiating rule that you just observed when
you proposed something less than a full-time commitment is to get something in
return for what you're giving up. In this case, you're getting time in exchange for
less pay. Telecommuting could be included in the negotiations. What you want to
avoid is lowering your price while receiving nothing in return. Reducing a job's
time commitment is a great strategy if you're considering an active retirement
or would prefer part-time work. Two conditions will increase the likelihood that
a company will consider repackaging a job: if you are overqualified for the position, and if you are a "known commodity." Being overqualified enables you to
argue that you can do the same job in less time. If you're overqualified but don't
know anyone inside, however, you may not make the interview cut. If the hiring
manager screens you based on your résumé, he will be concerned that you'll get
bored quickly, be too expensive, and quit once you have been trained. Get your
connections talking you up so the company will meet with you and see how
charming you are, not to mention what a valuable asset you would be to their
firm. If you're currently working for the company and are negotiating your
work arrangement, you are already a "known commodity" and have the highest
leverage. You're trained, and they don't want to lose you.

Ask for an Early Review Date You like the company. You want to accept your
employer's offer. You've pushed each other about as far as you're both willing to
go. The only thing that is still bugging you is a $10,000 difference in salary that
has not been resolved. Before you give your final "Yes," suggest the following:

YOU: Thanks, Christopher. I really do appreciate the offer, and I'm excited
about the opportunity. I have just one last question about the salary, if
I may. If I forgo that additional $10,000 we talked about, can we sit down
together in six months to review my compensation? If we're mutually

satisfied with my performance, I'd like to see the $10,000 reconsidered at
that point. Will that work for you?

Note the light touch. You made a proposal and then asked for a response. The worst thing that can happen is that your new employer will say, "No," and you'll say, "It was worth a try. Next year when we sit down, I plan on making that difference look like chump change compared to our progress." If your new boss agrees to a six-month salary review, he hasn't made any guarantees that your salary will actually be increased. Start keeping a regular record of your accomplishments so six months from now you'll be able to demonstrate why you're worth the extra money. Do this on a regular basis, and when it comes time for both your six-month as well as your annual performance reviews, you'll have a track record of performance that will justify your additional salary. Another point to keep in mind if your new boss agrees to an early review: get it in writing. If you don't get this casually agreed-to six-month review in writing, it can vanish in the wind. Bosses leave, forget, get laid off, get promoted. One sentence in your offer letter that says something like, "Bill's performance will be reviewed in June of (year) for a merit increase," will give you a more substantial standing than, "He said so." It will be your job to track why you deserve the increase and to set up the appointment in the sixth month. Early review promises can fall into the cracks, so you take control.

Now that you have five ways to close the salary gaps in your negotiations, add your own variations—apply for a broader range of jobs, and negotiate creatively. Your goal is to get offers on the table so you can make the best choice; it is not to walk away from jobs that offer too little without attempting to turn them into something that will work well for both of you.

The Offer

If the company doesn't automatically put the offer in writing, here's what you say when you have most of the compensation package worked out, but before giving them a final yes. "Could I get you to put what we've discussed into a letter for me? I want to make sure that I've understood everything clearly." See how you put the motivation for the request on your own shoulders? They can hardly deny your desire to be clear. Requesting a letter is a great strategy because it serves several purposes: it gives you the only thing in writing about your terms of employment that you may ever see, plus it buys you time. You may need a little more time, as in the third response below, if you're negotiating other offers before you decide. You're slowing down the first company, and speeding up the others . . . all doable. It's the end game in chess.

EMPLOYER: Do we have a deal?

YOU (choose one): Yes. Thanks for the offer. I'm looking forward to working with you.

Or,

I think so. It sounds great. Can I sleep on it overnight?

Or,

I'm really excited about the opportunity. Thanks for the offer. What I'd like to do, if it's okay with you, is to get back to you next week. I want to make a long-term commitment to you, and, as you know, I was talking to other companies in this transition process. Let me wrap up with them, and I'll get back to you next Wednesday. If you want, I can get started on some of those materials in the meantime. Does that work for you?

This last option shouldn't come as a surprise to them because you have seeded earlier conversations with hints that you've been talking to other companies. If you're not sure, now is the time to evaluate whether you want to choose this option over your BATNA, or over any of your other options that are at least halfway down your Job Pipeline. Call any other companies that still may be high on your list and say, "I really enjoyed talking with you last month. I wanted to give you a heads-up that I have an offer that I need to respond to shortly (or you're in third-round discussions with a company, if you don't want to wait until offer time). If we have anything further to talk about, I'd like to set up a time to meet. I really think we could do some interesting things together, and I want to touch base with you before I do anything rash." Regardless of whether one offer or three offers emerge, that period between an offer's being made and your responding is when you have maximum leverage. Congratulate yourself, but be careful of abusing your power. You don't want to be perceived as someone who is using a company. Getting an alternative offer just to win a salary battle with your current employer is damaging a relationship that you might want later on, and it's not the reputation that you want on the street. Take advantage of the leverage if you want to motivate a preferred company to make a decision, but you don't have to mention the source of your offer if it isn't appropriate. It's normal to take some time to make your decision, but you'll want to treat their proposal with respect and enthusiasm.

If all else fails and you cannot reach satisfactory financial arrangements with a company, it's time to part company. Do so with grace, though. They're probably feeling badly because they can't afford you; don't make them feel worse. "I'm afraid that it looks like we aren't going to have a match," you say. "You're doing some really interesting work, and we may well cross paths at some point in the future. I may know someone else who would be worth considering for the job, so let me know if you'd like me to check and refer over this person. I'd be happy to be of help." Ask that person out to lunch in a couple of months to keep the bridge in place.

Prenuptials: Contracts, Golden Parachutes, Change of Control Agreements, and Stock Options

If you are negotiating for one of the top positions in a company, you will be considering benefits that other employees aren't dealing with—protection for the high-visibility, high-stakes risk that you are taking. These packages are very sophisticated and you'll want to devise your own, possibly with counsel, and get it all in writing before you cross the threshold. I've worked with many executives on the other side, when they're leaving the company for multiple reasons, who wish that they'd protected themselves better on the way in. Noncompetes for an unrealistically long time, no outplacement, limited severance, negative word of mouth, and loss of stock ownership and bonuses are not unusual. The comments of Joe Rich, chairman of Pearl Meyer & Partners until his unexpected death in 2007, are still accurate. He stressed that agreements are "really two-way streets. The general give and take is that the executive gets predefined severance benefits, and the firm gets a clean break. You forfeit the right to sue for wrongful termination." Your options (no pun intended) are so varied and are subject to so many shifting norms that it takes a specialist to stay up to date on all the regulations and valuation methods. It's a good idea to have one in your corner. This could be an expert in executive compensation, such as you might find at a consulting firm specializing in this field, or an employment lawyer who has experience with contracts at your level, or both. I recommend that your advisor be confidential: to have a visible expert early in the negotiation process sets a heavier tone than you want. It could be interpreted as adversarial. Companies often have a compensation specialist who advises the company and the board's compensation committee on equitable arrangements for linking your pay with performance and your wealth with shareholder wealth. The company may provide this person to advise you. Listen to this person's proposals, and then refer back to your own private counsel for advice that is not biased in the company's favor. If you need to bring up your expert, make it clear to the company that you're using her in an advisory mode rather than an attack mode, and have your expert's permission before you use any names.

To be clear about the best interests of your advisor, follow the money. The majority of employment law and compensation practices have companies for clients, not individuals, and will not want to get involved in anything that even hints at a conflict of interest with any current or potential corporate client. There is an additional category of practice called executive advocacy that focuses strictly on the professional's behalf and is worth checking out. James Hartley, co–managing partner of Shilepsky O'Connell Hartley and an executive advocate, emphasizes the importance of getting the contract right going *into* a company rather than trying to alter agreements during the heat of a merger or acquisition, a change in control, or an emotionally charged termination. Both are doable, but whenever possible, err toward the former, while the company is still courting you.

WHAT ARE YOU WORTH?

Now things are getting fun. If you've just created a new position—whether it's full-time, consulting, contract, or interim work—the compensation doesn't exist yet. That's the exciting part. Setting your price is like finding water with a divining rod; it is as much art as science. If you have the skills to listen for needs and shape a job, setting your compensation should be the easy part. Your approach will depend on the type of work you have defined. If it's full-time employment, it shouldn't be too tricky. The company will have norms in place, if not an actual compensation structure, and the process outlined above will work. Knowing your market value and BATNA is important so that you aren't susceptible to off-the-wall proposals. From the initial, "What did you have in mind?" to asking for a letter at the end, you're now negotiating as a potential employee. In this book, we're approaching consulting as a means to an end (full-time employment) rather than as an end in itself. If you start having fun along the way and decide that you want to stay with consulting, go for it. Read books like *Million Dollar Consulting: The Professional's Guide to Growing a Practice* by Alan Weiss (McGraw-Hill, 2009) to get more of a flavor for the function.

Here we're looking specifically at how to price yourself when you're between full-time jobs doing short-term consulting to create relationships, back into a company, build your skills, bring in some income, or stay in the flow. People will expect you to have standard rates and will also assume that they aren't your first consulting client. You'll want to respond with confidence, even if you don't reply with a specific figure right away. Before someone says, "What are your rates?" have an answer planned. "I don't know" doesn't count. As you're thinking about your consulting rates, keep three things in mind: benefits aren't included; you don't get paid for days you don't work; and you're still looking for a full-time job. Your decisions about your rates and availability should reflect these. To get some idea about the rates you should be charging, consider the following seven points.

- **Know Thyself**

  Even if you're just planning a one-time consulting project, you don't want to be too casual about your rates. You're stating your value and defining your reputation when you set your fees. Catherine priced her consulting work well in a temp-to-perm proposal. She took the annual salary she would be receiving should the job become permanent and substantially rounded it up for her project pricing. The company responded with, "We're excited about your ideas, but your consulting rates are more than we can afford. We've decided that we'd like to offer you the position as an employee now rather than in three months. Are you interested?" She was. She'd priced herself to achieve her objectives and modified them to become an employee. In addition to knowing your rates, you need to know what you're selling. Consultants have specific areas of expertise that people need. You may be an expert in strategy, accounting systems, lean manufacturing, or training. However, calling yourself a general business consultant won't do. If you're positioning yourself as a management consultant, you're grouping yourself with a lot of people who aren't sure of their expertise as well as some killer sharks who work for the world's best-known consulting firms. Is that where you want to be? You'll discover that highlighting one or two of your skills will attract attention now and will eventually set you up for the type of full-time employment you want. "Jack of all trades, master of two," as discussed in Strategy #1: Send Clear Signals, pays off in development of consulting work as well as your growth as an employee. Claim your areas of expertise! You can pick two that are interesting, then start reading and writing about them so you become more visible and build your reputation. It will be easier to find work if you're specific about your expertise and easier to price yourself, too.

- **Know Thy Competition**

  Just as you need to know your market value when you're looking for employment, you'll want to know the going rate for consultants in your field. You might underprice yourself otherwise. You may decide to charge a different rate than the norm (rarely lower!), but you should know what your differentiators are and why you are worth your price. You may be worth more than the average turnaround consultant, for example, if you have actually directed successful turnarounds as a line manager. How do you find out what the competition charges, let alone what your rates should be? Do what you did with salaries: gather data. You can find information in the following ways:

Refer to your own experience. Have you ever hired a consultant in your area of expertise? Do you know people who have hired them? Track down what they charged using the "going rate" question. Make sure that you're comparing apples to apples. Consultants who are part of a firm will typically charge by the project (often a hefty price) and will have overhead that you may not. It's good to know how the larger consulting firms as well as the independents set their rates. They are all part of your competition.

Ask your double low-density network. Combine your question about "the going rate for an IT consultant" with some information that would be of interest to your network and send out an individualized-looking email asking for their pricing experience with consultants. Lumping together several questions in one email is a good strategy so you don't wear your network down with a question-of-the-day.

Get a proposal together. If you're legitimately pulling together a team of consultants to submit a proposal for a consulting assignment, your subcontractors will tell you what they typically charge. You're now familiar with the going rates of your colleagues, some of whom may have skills similar to yours. Price yourself a little higher if you're the person managing them in this project.

Ask consultants. Ask professional consultants what the going rate is in your field. Saying "I don't have a clue what to charge" will bring out the mentoring side of many people. Professional associations of independent consultants, such as the Institute of Management Consultants, can provide additional information.

- **Define Your Pricing System**
  Consultants are paid in various ways—hourly, per diem, by project, or according to perceived value. Each method has some legitimacy, depending on the image you wish to set and the goals you wish to achieve.

Pricing Your Consulting Work

Payment Type	Definition	Pros	Cons
Hourly	Hourly work is paid one hour at a time. You track your work and bill the client. The number of hours per week and the number of weeks may be set, or the work may be ongoing.	This method looks less expensive and more controllable to clients. The client may be more likely to commit to you. This work is usually open-ended (or is this a con?). Specific outcomes and a termination date typically are not defined, so the work may go on for a while. You can end this work quickly if a better offer comes through.	This work is not relationship oriented. Clients think twice before picking up the phone to discuss issues. There is some paperwork involved in keeping track of your time. Commuting and planning or design time are often not billable. You need to keep your rates high to maintain your image. The company can end this work abruptly. The only way to make more money is to work more hours.
Per Diem	Per diem work is paid one day at a time. It works well for brief, clearly defined commitments, such as evaluating client needs, running seminars, or doing training workshops. This method can be used for work that is complex and long term but irregular, such as valuing acquisitions or consulting throughout a project rollout.	The net for one day should be higher than for hourly work. Companies are usually comfortable with per diem arrangements. They don't have to overcommit.	Commuting and planning or design time are often not billable. You may complete a short assignment and find that the client forgets about you. You are 100 percent on duty during the days for which you are hired, so keeping a job campaign going simultaneously becomes challenging. The only way to make more money is to work more hours and days.

Pricing Your Consulting Work, cont.

Payment Type	Definition	Pros	Cons
Project	A project is a well-defined piece of work. It has a beginning and an end, with agreed-upon outcomes. Pricing is typically based on projections of estimated time involved and estimated costs—including subcontractors, materials, and operations (not travel)—then a desired percentage of profit is added. Make sure up front who's making the travel arrangements and how it will be reimbursed if you're responsible.	This method works well with a temp-to-perm relationship. You have a strong relationship with the client during the project. The client and others in the organization can call you whenever they choose for no additional charge. You control when and where you spend your time. You can spend more or less time on a project, as needed. You can carry on your job marketing campaign at the same time. The only billing paperwork is your invoice and reimbursable expenses.	A project can take longer and cost more than you estimated. Your success is easily evaluated. Did you reach the desired outcomes within the estimated time frame? Did you stay within your budget? You may need to submit a report with outcomes and recommendations.
Value	Value is based on the return on the client's investment. What is the problem, and what needs to be done? How much is the client currently losing because of the problem? How much can you save the client and how quickly? You quote a reasonable percentage beneath the savings to the company and well over your expenses.	This work has the highest income potential. You develop a strong ongoing relationship with the client and others in the organization. You're a partner. The client and others in the organization can call you whenever they choose, for no additional charge. This builds trust and the relationship. You control when and where you spend your time. You can spend more or less time on a project, as needed. The only billing paperwork is your invoice and reimbursable expenses.	You will need more initial time with the client to assess issues related to the project and estimate related costs. Redundancy is easy to price; poor morale is not. You need to be sure they are committed to working with you before quoting prices. Your success is easily evaluated. Did you reach the desired outcomes within the estimated time frame? Did you stay within your budget? You may need to submit a report with outcomes and recommendations.

Although value pricing is the holy grail for professional consultants because of its margins, flexibility, and relationships, other methods of pricing may suit you better given that consulting is not your long-term goal. You may prefer pricing a three-month assignment as a project, which you hope will springboard you into a company you want to work for. Or you may bill hourly if you're a novice at a skill you need and want to develop it while consulting.

HOMEWORK

Pricing Yourself

1. What areas of expertise could you offer as a consultant?

2. What type of pricing would work best for you—hourly, per diem, project, or value?

3. What are three other consultants in your field charging?

4. What range of fees would make sense for you?

- **Hold off on Quoting Rates**
  Remember the rule when negotiating salaries, "whoever mentions numbers first loses"? Well, you don't want to rush into quoting consulting fees too early, either. Although in this case you may be the one to reveal figures first, since you're bound to know what you charge as a consultant (right?), doing it too soon has two disadvantages. You probably haven't gathered enough information to accurately estimate the time and complexity of the work, and it makes you appear to be a commodity. If someone is comparing consulting rates over the phone or in a first meeting, you don't have to play their game. In his book *Million Dollar Consulting* (McGraw-Hill, 2009), Alan Weiss, the guru for many professional consultants, recommends saying, "'I can answer that when I learn some more and have time to consider how we might help you,' in response to, 'How much?' But once you say, 'We charge $1,500 a day, plus expenses,' you've had it. From that point your fee can only decline and your margins erode." Wait until the relationship is solid and you know the scope of the

work before you quote your fee, especially with project or value-based consulting. You could end up losing money and looking less expert otherwise. "Will I lose the opportunity if I don't quote them a price right away?" Ideally, you will be the only one talking to the company about the consulting work. With no competition there shouldn't be any risk of losing the work if you hold off on naming your fees for project or value-based work. It's tougher to duck a discussion about hourly or per diem charges, but try to wait until a second meeting. When you do declare your rates, remember the rule from the salary section about what to do if you're the first one to break the ice: *Always follow up with a question so you can get their immediate feedback.* "Are we in the same ballpark?" or "The rate I'm quoting you of $80,000 for the project will be a fraction of what you save within the first year after eliminating at least two redundant salaries and streamlining your processes. You'll then be set up to continue and improve upon these savings over the long term. Does that make sense to you?" Notice how you focused on results, their side of the Marketing Circle. You have a great advantage if you meet face-to-face with your potential client (and anyone else who might be interested) to go over your proposal and pricing. Waiting for a response to a written proposal (that the client is reading by herself, comparing with others, and fainting if the numbers sound high) is risky. You can continue the financial discussion more easily if you're sitting in front of her.

- **Subtract Value If You Lower Your Price**
  If you get less, give less. Negotiating experts agree that if you're asked to lower your prices and you want to keep talking, you should definitely reduce what you give as well. Do not eliminate the main components of what will make your consulting successful, but consider cutting some training, research, or report writing that is not critical in return for the lower cost. Drawing again from Alan Weiss, "The client has the choice as to how much value justifies what investment, but should never have the choice of benefiting through your sacrificing your margins. This is not collaboration. This is a transfer of wealth from you to the client." Giving up something for nothing also erodes your image. You don't want to be the cheapest consultant in town. It's fair to stand firm at some point. One option at this point is to part ways politely, being glad that this person is not your full-time boss. Another option I use is to refer them to a colleague

who does hourly work and he, in turn, refers me potential clients who want more of a senior-level, comprehensive service than he offers—a win-win.

- **Save Time for Your Job Search**

  This is critical! When you come to the end of your consulting work or project, what are you going to do next? Hopefully, you're becoming indispensable while consulting because you're spotting problems that need to be solved on a full-time basis. If you immerse yourself solely in the present project, however, you'll be "running off a cliff" when the project is over. The need to develop new business even when you're in a peak crunch period with your current clients is a hard-learned lesson. Remember Wile E. Coyote, the cartoon character, chasing the roadrunner off a cliff, with his legs still going ninety miles a minute when he finds himself over the abyss? When you look down and see that your leads have dried up and your network has disappeared, you can anticipate a crash. Protecting time for your job search is a negotiating point. Just don't articulate it as such. Your scheduling needs are on your side of the Marketing Circle, so you bring them up only to imply that there is competition for you. "I appreciate the compliment of your wanting me to be here full-time during the project, Sheila, but that wouldn't be the most cost- or time-efficient way to structure its implementation. We should talk about an employment arrangement if that is the goal. You'll be able to reach me on my cell phone if you have questions, but a lot of this can be done much more reasonably off-site. You'll be seeing me multiple times each week, and this project will come in on time and on budget, just as we've planned." There is no guarantee that a consulting assignment will turn into a job, so be wary of putting all of your eggs in the full-time assignment basket. A lesser commitment, say ten to fifteen hours a week with your favorite firm, is ideal. Approach it from their point of view. "The practices we set up are more likely to become habit if I train an operations manager who then supervises the day-to-day integration. He'll establish his authority faster if I'm not there watching him constantly." Subtle, aren't you? What you said is correct; you just wriggled out of being on-site every day and made a proposal that was in their best interest all at the same time. Do you see marketing for mutual benefit in practice?

- **Get the Agreement in Writing**

  If a proposal isn't already in place, take the initiative. You're the consultant, so you have a standard letter of agreement that you use (right?). You can get started sooner, and you can make sure the letter says exactly what you want it to if you write it yourself. It should start with a description of the company's problem, the scope of your project, the methods you would use, and your anticipated outcomes, timing, and cost. Don't make it too long; two pages is plenty for an independent consultant. Its primary purpose is to clarify the process for both of you.

Now you have a method for setting both your consulting rates and your compensation as an employee. You can provide an employer (or a client, when you're consulting) with a breadth of choices. There's more than one outcome to the negotiating process that could satisfy you both. If you look at the different ways that you could package yourself, and the different ways that an employer could hire you, you clearly have multiple ways to reach an agreement. How can they say no?

THE BOTTOM LINE

So here's a riddle for you. What's the difference between negotiating with a car salesman or a real estate broker and negotiating with your new boss, at least for as long as you're working for her? Do you know the answer already? You can't walk away from your boss. With the way you've negotiated your compensation, however, you won't need to. You actually built your relationship when you demonstrated your ability to act professionally, calmly, with humor, and with an awareness of both parties' needs. You prepare ahead of time, you know what's going on in the marketplace, you listen, and you solve problems. You're going to be a pleasure to work with.

CONCLUSION
You Don't Have One

Does not having a conclusion to your career (until you're ready for it, of course) sound like good news or bad news? If you love your work, it should be good news, and now you know how to create work you love. The goal is to enjoy your work and be thoroughly engaged with it for as long as you choose to be. More than 80 percent of baby boomers (those born between 1946 and 1964) want to continue working in some form, according to Robin Talbert, president of the AARP Foundation. And it's not just the boomers; the satisfaction and meaning that can come from our work attract all of us.

If not having a *planned* conclusion to work sounds like bad news, you have some company. During the economic downturn of 2008–2009, thousands of workers were "pushed into retirement as a result of a weak labor market" as well as stock market losses. The number of older workers grew at a faster rate than overall numbers according to the www.wsj.com article "For Older Workers, a Reluctant Retirement," by Evans and Needleman. Let me turn bad news into good news, though. As Rahm Emanuel, Barack Obama's chief of staff, famously said, "Never let a serious crisis go to waste . . . it's an opportunity to do things you couldn't do before." It's an opportunity to change your attitude instead of getting discouraged, to create jobs instead of chasing openings, to look for problems and trends that will create work instead of waiting for highly competitive ads to be posted, to help others, and to be the leader for change. You can do this. With the New Job Security under your belt, you can help yourself as well as others think about work differently. If you want to turn bad news into good for a group of people, see the link at the end of the book under the bio.

MAKING YOUR REPUTATION, NOT JUST LETTING IT HAPPEN

"I didn't realize that I could consciously manage my reputation," a sales director told me after a Harvard Business School seminar. It's not that hard, and it has a big payback. This is not about bragging or boasting. It's about letting others know how you can help them and about staying tuned into external business forces. You have a reputation whether you want one or not. You might as well make it work for you. If you'd like to assess your current reputation before working to enhance it, ask a colleague or two above you, below you, and laterally about how you're perceived, and let them know that you're willing to return the favor. They may be interested in setting up some informal feedback loops so you can help each other grow.

There are many ways to become and remain a star that are consistent with your values and personality. A scientist will present her research at professional gatherings and publish in her industry's journals. Though this is seen as a professional responsibility, promoting the advancement of science for all, it also builds the scientist's reputation and that of her company. Choose methods that work for you. If you base your choices on helping others, you create win-wins along the way.

There are five main avenues for developing your reputation described below. Combining all five of these brings you the most powerful results.

- Executing your job well. Hey, if you're on probation because you're busy with your social networks instead of your work, what's that going to do for your reputation? Delivery is job one.

- Connecting with external groups such as professional and industry associations. Your external reputation is not only instrumental in case you ever want to make changes in your work, but it also builds your reputation internally. Being a leader of a professional group accomplishes multiple goals. Even in retirement, Norm was on the board of and president of two actuarial societies and taught math at a local school. He was doing what he enjoyed and giving back at the same time. His reputation as a civic leader grew even though he wasn't seeking it. People at his company where he used to work full-time but now served as an advisor heard about these professional and civic commitments, and his internal reputation was further enhanced.

- Writing and publishing. It's easier to write now, isn't it? People are actually making an income, not to mention building a reputation, using their blogs alone, and there are multiple other ways to write. Kate Brooks, director of Liberal Arts Career Services at the University of Texas at Austin, says, "Writing is vital for career development in many fields. Getting your name out there in a positive way can lead to consulting jobs, speaking engagements, etc., that may or may not have anything to do with your primary job. In this economy, it never hurts to develop a side profile that can lead to other opportunities if something happens in your primary job." She's talking the New Job Security talk.

- Speaking and teaching. Do either or both. Both should be motivated by a desire to educate or talk about your mission rather than the desire to sell. There are always small groups, including nonprofits, that are looking for content for meetings, not to mention learning needs within your own company, so come up with three engaging subjects that you would present and start talking about the topics (*not* selling) to pique people's curiosity. (You don't need to come up with all of the content before you have the gig!) Teaching any age from elementary to executive education, as well as internally at your company, forces you into learning *well* the changes in your profession . . . a side benefit to an important educational mission.

- Networking (internally and externally) by helping others. You already know about this one, right?

Reputations are built and changed by behaviors, not by wishes. As you accomplish your goals in the homework, add more. "I don't have time!" you say. Go back to Iris's story in Strategy #3: Stop Looking for Jobs. She gave away the 20 percent of her job that wasn't as interesting to her to someone who found it developmental. Reputation-building behaviors become habit forming because you're helping and sharing with others in the process. Marketing for mutual benefit pays off.

Develop Your Reputation: Become a Star

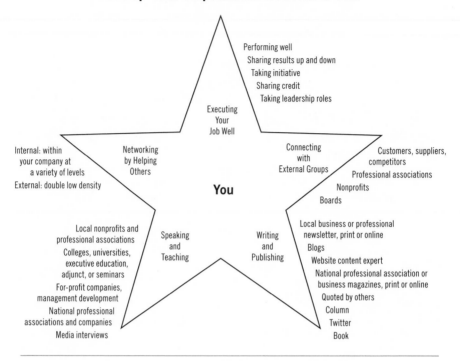

Performing well
Sharing results up and down
Taking initiative
Sharing credit
Taking leadership roles

Executing Your Job Well

Connecting with External Groups

Customers, suppliers, competitors
Professional associations
Nonprofits
Boards

Networking by Helping Others

Internal: within your company at a variety of levels
External: double low density

You

Local nonprofits and professional associations
Colleges, universities, executive education, adjunct, or seminars
For-profit companies, management development
National professional associations and companies
Media interviews

Speaking and Teaching

Writing and Publishing

Local business or professional newsletter, print or online
Blogs
Website content expert
National professional association or business magazines, print or online
Quoted by others
Column
Twitter
Book

HOMEWORK

Become a Star

What three minor activities will you start in the next couple of months that will help you become more visible?

LEVERAGING YOUR TRACK RECORD FROM NOW INTO RETIREMENT

Consciously managing your reputation not only pays off when you're working full-time, but it also pays off when you decide to slow down. Notice that I didn't say "stop," because my bet is that you won't want to stop working completely for a long time. Think of your career as a hike up and down a comfortably sized mountain rather than a dive off a springboard. A dive off a springboard requires a disciplined approach and focus, which is admirable, but after a rapid peak and some acrobatics, it's over in a flash (or splash). People don't really want that for retirement. Even if you suddenly have an enormous amount of money from an economic boom, which seems to happen at least once every decade, early retirement isn't all it's cracked up to be. I frequently get calls from people who have amassed the assets they need to retire (regardless of age), play golf for two years, and then start going stir-crazy. You have a good brain or you wouldn't be where you are today. There are only so many golf strokes the brain can analyze before it wants some new stimulation. If you live to be ninety years old, do you really want twenty to forty years of "retirement"? You and your spouse might kill each other first. Demographics have changed. You're going to live longer, be more active, and have blood flowing through less-clogged arteries than your grandparents did. In other words, you have a longer career to plan for than the traditional, hang-it-all-up-at-sixty-five norm. You have a variety of skills you can "unbundle" as you hike down the hill. During an active retirement, you can concentrate on the work that you enjoy the most. The operative word I use when doing preretirement coaching is "taper." What skills do you enjoy using that you would like to "taper" out on? Use your career management skills to identify target markets that would consume these skills. Your well-established reputation will pay off in spades. The challenge, however, is that you *can't wait until you're ready to change your lifestyle to develop your reputation.* Waiting until you're sixty-four to develop a reputation as an expert in logistics management so you can start consulting in that field when you're sixty-five is closing the barn door after the cows are out: it's too little, too late. Start thinking about where your passions and pleasures are now, when you can work on building your reputation around them, and develop the relationships you'll need to taper off your work when you choose to do so.

Tim combined his values with his work skills to find a meaningful segue into an active retirement.

Tim was still physically and mentally young at fifty-four when his company was acquired by a larger instrumentation company. His expertise was in sales and marketing. He had traveled the world not only managing the sales and distribution of products, but actually improving the quality of life in third-world countries on multiple occasions with his company's water filtration processes and systems. In addition to "doing good" in his professional life, Tim was active on the board of a well-known hospital and on the vestry of his church. After the acquisition, it was time for Tim to move on. He could have gone after a similar job, and had a résumé toward that end if something irresistible should surface. With a strong values orientation, however, he wanted to explore mentally engaging, values-driven work that would also give him more flexibility in his schedule. Income wasn't as much of a concern as it was when his children were younger. Now, his quality of life was increasingly important. Tim focused on the types of nonprofits that were of the greatest interest to him: the environment and conservation. Focus pays off, just as it does in full-time job searches. Most functions in the for-profit world are easily transferable to the nonprofit arena, as long as you take it upon yourself to find the right vocabulary. Tim's skills in sales and marketing transferred into fund raising and business development. He used these skills as an entry point. His goal was to combine his skills (sales and marketing), his knowledge (developing people and operations and closing deals), and his values (giving to others, conserving and protecting the environment). Although his work experience was with for-profit firms, he had spent significant amounts of his personal time supporting nonprofit operations. He wove these threads into his résumé to show his transferability and to acquire the flexible lifestyle he wanted. Tim repackaged his expertise, changed his vocabulary, and focused on the new market and its issues, which lowered the resistance of several targeted nonprofits. (Just because you're ready for them doesn't mean that they're ready for you.) Strategy, planning, and repackaging paid off, as always. He is now on various boards of his choice, writing strategic plans for several organizations, and building marketing programs for groups that truly need them. Some of these jobs are volunteer and some are paid. Not one of these were traditional job openings. He created them all by unearthing needs in conversations and developing relationships. He's making a difference. He has the type of job security and flexibility that he wants because he knew how to create a new job rather than waiting for the right opening to develop. Tim's having fun.

Did you see how Tim took the initiative in his planning (Strategy #1: Send Clear Signals) and shaped his outcome as a result? In the process, he needed to help other people (gave away some of his marketing and fundraising expertise) to obtain his goal (a more value-driven position), which is Strategy #2: Market for Mutual Benefit. He stopped looking for job openings (Strategy #3: Stop Looking for Jobs) because what he liked doing—strategy and marketing—didn't exist as full-time jobs in cash-strapped nonprofits. His networking (Strategy #4: Build Sustainable Networks) led to the meetings that led to the work that he wanted. Without clever negotiating (Strategy #5: Negotiate in Round Rooms), all his efforts would have been satisfying, but pro bono. Once he proved himself, compensation in different forms followed.

AGE DISCRIMINATION? NO WAY!

Tim is in his sixties now and still going strong, doing work that he loves with boards and nonprofits. He's turning work away. In no way is he concerned with age discrimination. The way he has set up his work, it's a non-issue. A lawyer in my audience at the Harvard Law School reunion was seventy-eight and planning his next career. How cool. Your mind-set determines everything.

I *know* that there is age discrimination out there, just like there is discrimination based on race, gender, weight, disability, ethnicity, religion, and multiple other variables that make each of us different from everyone else, including what schools we went to. Let me share with you my contrarian viewpoint, however. I often see age discrimination used as a cover for not finding work when the *real* reasons may be more uncomfortable: I don't know how to look for work wisely, my skills are out of date, I haven't paid attention to the status of my industry while I've been working. It's sort of like complaining, "I didn't do well on the test because I didn't study." You can correct the condition.

Can you get younger? No. Does an employer care if you're younger? Most of the time, no. In fact, being young can be a liability, depending on the job. Here's what many blunt employers would say:

1. Show me your track record of profitability.

2. Show me that you know what's happening with my company and my industry, and that you have a vision of how you're going to make me profitable going forward.

3. Show me that you stay up to date with technology and use it as part of your life.

That isn't age discrimination; it's running a successful business. And you can address all of these concerns using the strategies you've learned in this book. The first can be addressed with the market research and résumé format described in Strategy #1: Send Clear Signals; the second you can deliver on using the skills described in this book; and the third comes from a willingness to play with new toys. If you're telling yourself, "I'm too old to learn X," who's discriminating against you first? Many "toys" are the right price (free) at libraries, and instruction is often available. One-Stop Career Centers, government training programs, and adult education centers will offer reasonably priced instruction, as will many thirteen-year-olds. (Hey, you don't discriminate against younger bosses, do you?) Manufacturers make the BlackBerry, iPhone, and other smart phones as easy as they can for you to learn. They want you to keep coming back for more. Learning now, when you're not under pressure, is an ideal time. You may end up being cooler than your boss. Start something yourself—*be* the boss—and you'll have even more options.

FLEXIBLE WORK OPTIONS

There's a growing interest in being able to work flexibly that I'm researching now. Whether you're one of the brilliant young women I work with who are reentering the job market after having stayed home with children, a recently cashed-out investor or top executive at an acquired company, or an executive retiring from full-time active duty, you want to keep the brain stimulated and to contribute under *your* conditions. There are several paths to follow to create the choices that you'd like.

The path of least resistance is to stop looking for jobs. You already have the secret to creating flexible work. Given that a help wanted ad reading, "Meaningful part-time work available at your convenience in your field; pays well" is not going to appear, how else do you get what you want? If you're analyzing trends and needs, packaging your communications to respond to your markets, and then connecting to decision makers, as we've talked about, you're going to be beating everyone else to the punch. You're not talking about "jobs"; you're talking about problems to be solved and business results. Those can result in work that is flexible as long as you're talking in your market's terms, not your needs. Once you and a company agree on the business need to be addressed and the approach, the stage is set. "You can get this done without the fixed overhead of a full-time person," or "What if I get together three best-in-class people to write the different sections of the report? I'll take the compensation piece, then get Dan Brown to do . . ." You get the drift. You're marketing for mutual benefit as you're creating flexible work.

Regardless of your age or why you're leaving the full-time workforce, achieving satisfying flexible work starts with defining it. What do you enjoy doing that the marketplace values? For ideas, think back to the "master of two" areas of expertise that you've identified already, and use your trend analysis skills to predict where work will be developing. Craft an Elevator Story around it so you can start talking about your interests. Check out the more than forty companies on the AARP's National Employment Team for companies that think flexibly in their hiring practices. Deborah Russell, their director of workforce issues, established the Best Employers for Workers Over 50 awards. The winners are progressive companies that may well be near you and already have a mind-set about employee engagement that will benefit you regardless of age. Whether it's changing locations with the same employer (Robin Talbert reports that some companies allow their employees to move from north to south during the winter) or consulting back into the company you're leaving, you can create multiple choices. Former presidents of the United States open up law practices, build houses for nonprofits, and work with relief organizations to help with disaster recovery. What would you like to do?

HOMEWORK

Deconstructing Your Skills

What three skills would you consider focusing on if you were going to create flexible work?

What steps could you start on today that would help you build your reputation and relationships in these areas?

Try out your ideas. "I want to be considered an expert in lean manufacturing within my company and within the industry of semiconductor manufacturing." "I want to be known for setting up great human resource functions for small companies when they reach a critical mass and need to develop their own HR systems." Marc Freedman has great nonprofit examples in *Encore* (PublicAffairs, 2008). If you test your ideas now, you'll have time to find the ones that prove most interesting before leaving full-time employment. You have a lot to look forward to.

YOU'VE GOT THE NEW JOB SECURITY

Congratulations! You know how to send clear signals (Strategy #1), determine your value, define your skills clearly to others in their terms, and enjoy yourself in the process. You know how to market for mutual benefit (Strategy #2), identifying the hot buttons of your target groups and then getting your needs met by meeting theirs. When you stopped looking for jobs (Strategy #3), it hopefully raised a whole range of options for you. You can find problems and package yourself as the solution in ways that you choose. You already knew that building sustainable networks (Strategy #4) should be a priority, though it's been easy to put off until now. Now that you have a structure that makes your time investment more manageable, you can sustain and grow both your network and yourself. Knowing how to negotiate in round rooms (Strategy #5) isn't to be reserved solely for compensation discussions when entering a new company. You know how to do your negotiating homework, be creative, and present the outcomes that you want in terms that motivate the listener to agree, whether it's your employer or your teenager. You have the 5 best new strategies under your belt. You're on a roll.

Keep the momentum going. As you continue to practice the 5 strategies, you will build your reputation and manage your career successfully for as long as you choose. Instead of waiting for others, you will now make things happen for yourself. Your hands are on the steering wheel.

Practicing these strategies puts the New Job Security where it belongs: in your hands. By building minor daily practices in each of the five areas, you make major things happen. What will you do today to start this process? Would you like to find out where contracts have been awarded recently? Would you like to set up a database for managing your contacts? How about joining a committee of a professional association or talking to someone who is working in an industry that might be of interest to you? The choices are endless and often are a lot of fun. The point is to plunge in. The next time someone asks you how your work or your job search is going, smile. You know where you're headed and you have the means to get there. You have the New Job Security.

ABOUT THE AUTHOR

© 2008 Ron Pownall

Pam Lassiter is principal of Lassiter Consulting, a firm that provides career management services to companies and individuals worldwide. As a consultant in career management for more than thirty years, Lassiter works with companies and mid-career professionals that are managing career transitions. She designs programs, seminars, and coaching sessions for companies that are outplacing or retaining key employees. Her internal career development work enables professionals to grow within their current companies, improving corporate productivity and profitability. Her work with companies and individuals that are facing transition focuses on directing searches of senior-level executives toward timely, satisfying conclusions, whether it's the next job or retirement with flexible work.

Lassiter makes appearances on regional and national television and radio, and as a keynote speaker for professional groups and national conferences. She has received multiple awards and recognition from professional associations. Her articles on career management appear in human resource and business publications including *Fast Company, Fortune, Financial Times, Bloomberg Radio, Financial News Network,* and *CFO.* With an undergraduate degree from the University of Texas in English and Spanish, a master's degree from Boston University in psychological counseling, and graduate coursework in career development and business management, Pam lives in Boston, Massachusetts.

If you'd like to help others through career transition using the principles in this book, email pam@thenewjobsecurity.com, putting "Good News Group" in the subject line.

INDEX